Offender Profiling

Wiley Series in

The Psychology of Crime, Policing and Law

Series Editors

Graham Davies
University of Leicester, UK

and

Clive R. Hollin
University of Birmingham, UK

Offender Profiling
Theory, Research and Practice

Edited by

Janet L. Jackson

*Netherlands Institute for the Study of Criminality and Law
Enforcement, Leiden, The Netherlands*

Debra A. Bekerian

MRC Applied Psychology Unit, Cambridge, UK

JOHN WILEY & SONS

Chichester • New York • Weinheim • Brisbane • Singapore • Toronto

Other Wiley Editorial Offices

John Wiley & Sons, Inc., 605 Third Avenue,
New York, NY 10158–0012, USA

WILEY-VCH Verlag GmbH,
Pappelallee 3, D-69469
Weinheim, Germany

Jacaranda Wiley Ltd, 33 Park Road, Milton,
Queensland 4064, Australia

John Wiley & Sons (Asia) Pte Ltd, 2 Clementi Loop   02–01,
Jin Xing Distripark, Singapore 129809

John Wiley & Sons (Canada) Ltd, 22 Worcester Road,
Rexdale, Ontario M9W IL1, Canada

Library of Congress Cataloging-in-Publication Data

Offender profiling : theory, research and practice / [edited by] Janet
L. Jackson, Debra A. Bekerian.
   p.   cm. — (Wiley series in psychology of crime, policing, and law)
Includes bibliographical references (p.   ) and index.
ISBN 0-471-97564-8 — ISBN 0-471-97565-6 (pbk.)
   1. Criminal behaviour, Prediction of. 2. Criminal investigation—
-Psychological aspects. 3. Criminal behaviour—Research—
-Methodology. 4. Criminal methods—Research—Methodology.
I. Jackson, Janet L. II. Bekerian, Debra Anne. III. Series.
HV6080.045 1997
364.3—dc21   97-17402
                                                                            CIP

British Library Cataloguing in Publication Data

A catalogue record for this book is available from the British Library

ISBN 0–471–97564–8 (cloth)
ISBN 0–471–97565–6 (paper)

Typeset in 10/12pt Century Schoolbook by Saxon Graphics Ltd, Derby
Printed and bound in Great Britain by Bookcraft (Bath) Ltd, Midsomer Norton,

Contents

List of Contributors

Richard J. Badcock has worked as a Consultant Forensic Psychiatrist at the Regional Secure Unit in Wakefield, West Yorkshire, since 1984. In recent years, he has become more involved in working with the police during a variety of investigations. He also has a particular interest in the psychology of stalking for both victims and offenders.

Dr R.J. Badcock, Newton Lodge, Regional Centre for Forensic Psychiatry, Ouchthorpe Lane, Wakefield WF1 3SP, UK.

Debra A. Bekerian is the principal author of many academic papers on eyewitness memory, autobiographical memory, and the effects of trauma on memory. She has collaborated extensively with statutory agencies involved in child protection, particularly on interview techniques for victims of violent or sexual crimes. She has recently moved from the MRC Applied Psychology Unit to the Department of Psychology, University of East London.

Dr D.A. Bekerian, Department of Psychology, University of East London, Romford Road, London E15 4LZ, UK.

Julian C.W. Boon is a Chartered Forensic Psychologist and a lecturer at the University of Leicester, where he teaches personality and abnormal psychology. He also lectures on psychological profiling to graduate students on the Psychology Department's MSc course on Forensic Psychology and to police personnel, both in the UK and abroad. His research interests include the psychology of interrogations and testimony, and the psychology of love and destruction, with particular reference to criminal conduct.

Dr J. Boon, Department of Psychology, University of Leicester, Leicester LE1 7RH, UK.

Gary Copson has been a London Metropolitan Police detective since 1982 and is now a Detective Chief Inspector. He spent four years on a scholarship project researching the operational value of offender profiling. He then returned to operational policing in 1996. He has published

several reports and articles on the subject and is an associate lecturer in the Department of Applied Psychology at the University of Leicester.
Detective Chief Inspector G. Copson, Metropolitan Police, New Scotland Yard, Broadway, London SW1H OBG, UK.

Anne Davies is head of the Crime Analysis Unit at the Directorate of Intelligence, Metropolitan Police, London. Before joining the Unit, she worked for many years at the Metropolitan Police Forensic Science Laboratory, where she established a DNA database. She has been a member of the ACPO Crime Sub-Committee on Offender Profiling since 1988. Her research work includes offender profiling and behavioural and geographic patterns of serial rapists.
Ms A. Davies B.Sc., The Directorate of Intelligence, Metropolitan Police Service, New Scotland Yard, London SW1H OBG, UK.

Paul van den Eshof studied psychology and law at the University of Amsterdam. Since 1988, he has worked at the National Criminal Intelligence Division of the National Police Agency of The Netherlands. He has published articles on murder and manslaughter, shootings, bank robbery, rape and offender profiling. Since 1989 he has been involved in the development of behavioural investigative analysis in the Netherlands.
Mr P. van den Eshof M.Sc., M.A., National Criminal Intelligence Division, National Police Agency, Postbus 3016, 2700 KX Zoetermeer, The Netherlands.

David P. Farrington is Professor of Psychological Criminology at Cambridge University and President of the European Association of Psychology and Law. He has been President of the British Society of Criminology and Chair of the Division of Criminological and Legal Psychology of the British Psychological Society. His main research interest is in the development of offending and antisocial behaviour from childhood and adulthood, and he has published 15 books and nearly 190 papers on psychological and criminological topics.
Professor D. P. Farrington, Institute of Criminology, University of Cambridge, 7 West Road, Cambridge CB3 9DT, UK.

Gisli H. Gudjonsson is a Reader in Forensic Psychology at the Institute of Psychiatry, University of London, and is also Head of Forensic Psychology Services at the Maudsley Hospital. He has acted as an expert witness in many hundreds of criminal cases, both for the defence and the Crown Prosecution Service. He is also regularly consulted by police services in major cases. He has publshed numerous arti-

cles on forensic psychology and is also author of *The Psychology of Interrogations, Confessions and Testimony (Wiley, 1992)*.
Dr G. Gudjonsson, Department of Psychology, Institute of Psychiatry, de Crespigny Park, Denmark Hill, London SE5 8AF, UK.

John C. House has been a member of the Royal Newfoundland Constabulary in Canada for sixteen years. He is presently the Sergeant in charge of the CID's Criminal Behaviour Analysis Unit, where he provides various 'offender profiling'-related services to investigators. He has an MSc in Investigative Psychology from the University of Surrey, UK and is currently engaged in his PhD studies.
Sgt J. House, Royal Newfoundland Constabulary, PO Box 7247, St John's, Newfoundland A1E 3Y4, Canada.

Janet L. Jackson is a cognitive psychologist who worked for many years as senior lecturer at the Department of Experimental Psychology at the University of Groningen in the Netherlands. Since 1992, she is a principal researcher and Deputy Director at the Netherlands Institute for the Study of Criminality and Law Enforcement (NISCALE) in Leiden. Her current research interests include police interviewing skills, perceptions of credibility of witnesses, false allegations of rape, the processes of offender profiling, and criminal planning and decision making.
Dr J.L. Jackson, NISCALE, PO Box 792, 2300 AT Leiden, The Netherlands.

Esther E. de Kleuver studied social psychology at the Free University of Amsterdam. Since 1991, she has been carrying out crime analyses at the National Criminal Intelligence Division of the National Police Agency of The Netherlands. She has several publications in the field of stranger rape and geographic analyses.
Ms E.E. de Kleuver M.Sc., National Criminal Intelligence Division, National Police Agency, Postbus 3016, 2700 KX Zoetermeer, The Netherlands.

Sandra Lambert is Senior Intelligence Analyst in Hampshire Constabulary. She has been employed by the Police Foundation and by the Cambridge University Institute of Criminology as a researcher on projects directed by Professor Farrington. She has also worked as a Criminal Intelligence Analyst for the Metropolitan Police and as a Research Officer in the Home Office Police Research Group.
Dr S. Lambert, Crime Analysis Unit, Hampshire Constabulary, West Hill, Winchester, Hampshire SO22 5DB, UK.

Dick Oldfield has had 12 years of research experience with a variety of policing issues at the Home Office in London. He has worked in information technology groups focusing on the research and development of systems to support the investigation of crime and the criminal intelligence process, including the UK's major crime system HOLMES. In the Police Research Group (PRG), he has led research in offender profiling and crime pattern analysis. He is currently director of the PRG's Serious Crime Research Programme, run in collaboration with the National Crime Faculty.

Mr D. Oldfield, Police Research Group B.Sc., Home Office, 50 Queen Anne's Gate, London SW1H 9AT, UK.

D. Kim Rossmo is the Detective Inspector in charge of the Vancouver Police Department's Geographic Profiling Section. Over the course of his 19-year policing career, he has worked assignments in organized crime intelligence, emergency response, patrol, crime prevention, and community liaison. He holds a PhD in criminology and has researched and published in the areas of policing, offender profiling and environmental criminology. He is an Adjunct Professor at Simon Fraser University and a member of the editorial board for the international journal *Homicide Studies*.

Detective Inspector D.K. Rossmo PhD, Geographic Profiling Section, Vancouver Police Department, 312 Main Street, Vancouver, BC, Canada V6A 2T2.

John A. Stevens has served for 32 years in the Police Service. He was a detective in the Metropolitan Police and flying squads heading murder enquiries and later served as Assistant Chief Constable of Hampshire and Deputy Chief Constable of Cambridgeshire. In 1991, he became Chief Constable of Northumbria Police and Chairman of the ACPO Crime Committee Sub-Committee on Behavioural Science and Investigative Support. He became Her Majesty's Inspector of Constabulary in September 1996.

Mr J.A. Stevens, HMIC, Block B2, The Westbrook Centre, Milton Road, Cambridge CB4 1YG, UK.

Series Preface

The Wiley Series on the Psychology of Crime Policing and the Law publishes concise and integrative reviews on important emerging areas of contemporary research. The purpose of the series is not merely to present research findings in a clear and readable form, but also to bring out their implications for both practice and policy. In this way it is hoped that the series will not only be useful to psychologists but also to all those concerned with crime detection and prevention, policing and the judicial process.

Offender Profiling can claim to be the first full-length critical treatment of one of the most controversial innovations in criminal detection today. The public perception of the profiler fuelled no doubt by public portrayals in television series like *Cracker* and films such as *The Silence of the Lambs*, is of the brilliant loner, the gifted psychologist, whose unique insights into the criminal mind lead the police unerringly to the most likely suspect. There is a wealth of anecdote which seems to support this view. One thinks of the fascinating case of the American psychiatrist James Brussel, who pinpointed the 'mad bomber of New York' after a decade of fruitless police work, or the insights of David Canter into the likely background of 'the railway rapist', which brought an end to the criminal career of John Duffy and introduced profiling to the British police in 1986. However, as this book makes clear, every individual triumph can be balanced with another investigative disaster, where police resources have been wasted pursuing a mythical fugitive who, it subsequently emerges, bears little or no resemblance to the true perpetrator. Profiling is an area full of potent myth but where scientific fact has, until now, been noticeable by its absence.

The current book aims to redress this deficiency by bringing together contributors from the UK, mainland Europe and North America to pool their experience and knowledge of offender profiling. Some espouse a clinical approach to profiling, based on the application of existing theories of personality and psychopathy. Others believe that the only way forward is through the objective analysis of offence records: using past crimes to predict future offending. Some authors are working profilers

who provide a frank description of their methods. Others are consumers: senior police officers who must decide what weight to attach to
the always well-meant but sometimes conflicting advice offered to them.
Others again are researchers, who must attempt to tease out the facts
from the claims in an area where opinion is rife but where facts are in
short supply.

The editors, Janet Jackson and Debra Bekerian, are well placed to
preside over a cool overview of an often overheated field. Both are experienced and internationally known researchers in the field of forensic
psychology, whose background and training equips them well to provide
an even-handed and objective overview. They have been fortunate in
being able to recruit, as authors, leading authorities in the field whose
views and findings have often until now been confined to the pages of
confidential reports and official documents. As the editors note, a great
deal of time and effort has gone into bringing this book to fruition, but
a generation of police officers, criminologists and psychologists will be in
their debt.

GRAHAM DAVIES
University of Leicester

Preface

A large proportion of violent contact crimes occur between people who know each other: a drink with a mate in a bar that escalates to a punch-up and a stabbing, a man who beats up his wife, child sexual and/or physical abuse that occurs within the family circle. In such cases, the perpetrator is easily identified. There are other cases, however, where ties between the victim and assailant are absent: victims of serial rapists and child murderers often appear to have been selected in an arbitrary, random fashion. Fortunately, such incidents occur less frequently than the former. When they do occur, however, they cause a great deal of fear and unrest, not only locally but often nationally. They also result in large-scale, costly police investigations which frequently require sifting through masses of tips without having any clear leads. It is therefore not surprising that the police have been open to assistance from other professionals such as offender profilers. But who are offender profilers and what do they do?

Over the last few years, offender profiling has received a large amount of media attention not only in productions such as *Cracker* and *The Silence of the Lambs*, but also in response to its use in real-life crimes such as the brutal and unprovoked murder of Rachel Nickell. The general public may therefore think they know the answers to the questions posed.

Unfortunately, scientific literature exploring the premises underlying offender profiling and an evaluation of its worth have been a very poor second to the media hype. Although some such literature exists, the quantity is small and is to be found in many disparate journals and reports that are not always easy to find. The main aim of this book is to help remedy this situation. Professionals from different fields, and therefore with different expertise, have collaborated to ensure a broad overview of the important issues related to offender profiling. Theories underlying offender profiling and police reactions to the use of the approach in practice are discussed. Given that this reaction is broadly positive, issues relating to choice, timing and development of different approaches are considered. The general need for research in the area is specified, and examples of how researchers have responded to this need are given.

Although we both felt there was a great need for a book of this sort, the decision to become its Editors was made somewhat reluctantly: we know how busy profilers are! However, Graham Davies, the Series Editor, and Michael Coombs of John Wiley & Sons, were fairly persuasive. In retrospect, now that all the hard work and cajoling are behind us, we are glad we were persuaded. We have enjoyed working together and steering the book to fruition.

We would like to thank all the people who helped us to achieve the end product. At NISCALE, the project was encouraged from the beginning by the Director, John Michon. Rieny Albers, Robert de Vette, Henk van der Vegte, Semir el Fakih and Hans Salfischberger worked hard and long to ensure that we caught the boat to Dover, even although the ink was still wet. Jacqueline Harper of the APU was a wonderful go-between, coping with numerous telephone calls and manning the Fax machine for what must have seemed like hours at a time.

Our last two-day editorial get-together was at the Police Research Group at the Home Office in London. We would like to thank Gloria Laycock and her colleagues for allowing us to be guests in the department, Dick Oldfield for letting us take over his office and for looking after us so well, and Anne Davies of the Metropolitan police for lending us a computer complete with WordPerfect.

Finally, we would like to thank our partners for their encouragement and for putting up, yet again, with the strains and stresses involved in completing such a project; also the London Jacksons, who found their mother a 'logistic nightmare' but who, nevertheless, made the final lap a lot of fun as well as a culinary success.

CHAPTER 1

Does Offender Profiling Have a Role to Play?

Janet L. Jackson & Debra A. Bekerian

'Criminal profiling will never take the place of a thorough and well-planned investigation, nor will it ever eliminate the seasoned, highly trained and skilled detectives — but it has provided another weapon in the arsenal of those who must deal with violent crime.' (H. Paul Jeffers, 1991)

THE PROBLEM

Fortunately, stranger violent contact crimes such as sexual murder, child abduction or (serial) rape are low incidence crimes. Nevertheless, when they occur, they are inevitably accompanied by two phenomena. First, apart from the violence and tragedy inherent in the crimes themselves, the publicity surrounding them provokes high levels of fear and tension in the community at large. For an example, one has only to think of the press and media coverage of the Dutroux case, not only in Belgium but more generally throughout Europe and beyond. The increased public anxiety generates heavy pressures on police and prosecutors and demands significant resources from them. Second, most murders and rapes are solved because there is a connection between the perpetrator and the victim. When serious sexual crimes occur outwith the relational sphere, the investigation may involve sifting through hundreds of suspects and thousands of tips (see Stevens, Chapter 5 of the present Volume; Rossmo, Chapter 9 of the present Volume for examples of the magnitude of such information). Consequently, police (who may never have had any previous experience of leading this type of enquiry) are likely to suffer from problems of information overload. Their lack of experience may also prevent them from being able to sift out the important from the more peripheral. Of perhaps even greater importance, however, is their lack of referential material. They are not able to compare the present case with ones they have personally dealt with in the past. No matter how gruesome or bizarre a crime may be, the number of motives that underlie the crime and the method of carrying it out (the *modus operandi*) are fairly restricted. Therefore, there are always patterns to be recognized and, in turn, these can be compared to patterns in other cases (see Ressler & Schactman, 1992; van den Eshof, Jackson & Nierop, 1997). Considered in this way, neither a crime nor an offender is completely unique.

If one does not have the necessary experience to recognize more unusual patterns of criminal behaviour, however, to where, or whom, does one turn and when should such an approach be made? Exploring such issues is an important theme of this book. More specifically, the ability of offender profiling and profilers to help interpret patterns of behaviour will be examined in some depth. First, however, it is necessary to define what we mean by terms such as *offender profiling* and *profilers*.

WHAT IS PROFILE ANALYSIS?

Specific profile analysis (or offender profiling, psychological profiling, criminal profiling and criminal personality profiling, which are all terms that have been used interchangeably to describe the same technique) has been defined by many different authors over the years using different terminologies. However, the underlying concept on which these definitions are based remains the same. Behaviour is exhibited at a crime, or a series of similar crimes, and studying this behaviour allows inferences to be made about the likely offender. For example, Douglas, Ressler, Burgess & Hartman (1986, p. 405) have defined profile analysis as the identification of 'the major personality and behavioral characteristics of an individual based upon an analysis of the crimes he or she has committed'. The definition of offender profiling adopted by TREVI* in 1992 describes it as 'attempting to produce a description of the perpetrator(s) of a criminal offence on the basis of analysis of characteristics of the incident'. Copson (1995) suggests that offender profiling can be defined as an approach to police investigations whereby an attempt is

---

* TREVI is a European initiative in which police representatives of the member states discuss practical police cooperation in many areas.

made to deduce a description of an unknown offender based on evaluating minute details of the crime scene, the victim, and other available evidence.

Whatever the exact definition adopted, a profile is assumed to involve the construction of a behavioural composite — a social and psychological assessment (see Rossmo, 1996). A profile is based on the premise that the proper interpretation of crime scene evidence can indicate the personality type of the individual(s) who committed the offence. It is assumed that certain personality types exhibit similar behavioural patterns and that knowledge of these patterns can assist in the investigation of the crime and the assessment of potential suspects. As will become clear in the subsequent chapters of the book, profiling can be based on clinical experience, research and statistical analyses of offender databases.

There is reasonable consensus about the role played by profilers. Profilers assist in investigations of violent sexual crime by addressing three questions:

1   What happened at the crime scene?
2   What type of person is most likely to have done this?
3   What are the most likely personality characteristics of such an individual?

However, the answers that are offered are *not* solutions. Offender profiles do not solve crimes. Instead, as will be argued throughout this book, profiles should be viewed as simply one more tool that can be extremely useful in guiding strategy development, supporting information management, and improving case understanding. That this specific role for profiling has, in the past, not always been the one anticipated owes much to its historical development.

A BRIEF HISTORICAL OVERVIEW

The first widely acknowledged application of psychological profiling in the criminal investigation process can be traced to the almost magical description in 1956 of New York City's 'Mad Bomber', George Metsky, by a psychiatrist, Dr James A. Brussel (described in Brussel's book *Casebook of a Criminal Psychiatrist*, 1968). From a psychoanalytic interpretation of the crime scenes and his study of the bomber's letters, Brussel made several predictions, including the fact that the bomber was a heavy, middle-aged man, single and living with a brother or sister (he was actually living with two sisters) and would be wearing a double-breasted suit neatly buttoned up when he was found. Though the bombings continued for a number of years after Brussel gave his description to the police, when Metsky was finally apprehended, as a result of good detective work, he fitted the description perfectly, right down to the details of his attire.

In spite of the impact of this feat, it was not until the late 1970s that the possibilities of psychological profiling for investigative purposes were explored in a more systematic fashion. This innovative work, employing principles of behavioural science in the investigation of serious contact crimes, was instigated in the USA by the FBI Behavioral Science Unit (now called the Investigative Support Unit) at their Academy in Quantico, Virginia. FBI agents had become increasingly aware that the new developments taking place in the forensic laboratory were offering new dimensions in criminal investigations, but that the evidence they were producing was still limited in one respect. Forensic information might indeed clinch a case, but this evidence was often only of value when there was a suspect or someone already in custody. Only in a small number of cases (e.g. when a hair is found that indicates the race of the perpetrator) could forensic evidence offer advice in relation to the *sort of person* the police should go out and look for. For the same type of reasons as those presented in the opening paragraphs, it was recognized that a more specific type of advice was needed and that it presented behavioural scientists with an important role to play. This role was obviously not to provide the name, address and phone number of the guilty person but was to provide the police with a psychological profile of the personality of the perpetrator that could then be used to direct the investigative search. In other words, it would be an educated attempt, based on behavioural analysis, to provide law enforcement agencies with detailed information about the probable personal characteristics of an unknown individual who has committed a violent crime (Geberth, 1981).

The initial approach adopted by the FBI Behavioral Science Unit was based on in-depth interviews with a restricted number ($N=36$) of convicted sexually-oriented serial murderers, plus the extensive collective experience that members of the Unit had had in the field of serious sexual crime and homicide. It is an investigative technique which seeks to identify objectively the major personality and behavioural characteristics of serious offenders, based on an analysis of the crimes he/she has committed. Although obviously an oversimplification, the basic blueprint for the FBI approach involves considering the available aspects of the crime scenes; the nature of attacks; forensic evidence; and information related to the victim: then classifying the offender and, finally, referring to the appropriate predictive characteristics. Results from such investigations are incorporated in a framework which basically classifies murderers according to whether they are 'organized' (which implies that murderers plan their crimes, display control at scene of crime, leave few or no clues, and that the victim is a targeted stranger), or 'disorganized' (which implies that murders are not planned and crime scenes show evidence of haphazard behaviour), or a mixture of the two. Somewhat later, a series of interviews with 41 convicted serial rapists led to the adoption of a model of four rapist typologies — power assurance, power assertive, anger retaliatory, and anger excitation (see description in Hazelwood & Burgess, 1995). These initial groupings of murderers and rapists eventually led to the development of the *Crime Classification Manual* (Ressler, Douglas, Burgess & Burgess, 1992). This is a classification system for the type of crimes in which the behaviour of the perpetrator plays an important role.

This FBI approach has developed over the years into a systematic process that follows a sequence of widely accepted stages. These are:

- *Stage 1:* data assimilation — involves the collection of all available information from as many sources as possible (e.g. police reports, autopsy reports, photographs of crime scene).
- *Stage 2:* crime classification — attempts to classify the type of crime on the basis of the data collected.
- Stage 3: crime reconstruction — attempts to reconstruct the crime and to generate hypotheses about the behaviour of victims, sequence of crime or *modus operandi*.
- *Stage 4:* profile generation — the generation of a profile including hypotheses about demographic and physical characteristics, behavioural habits and personality dynamics of the perpetrator.

As stage 4 tends to imply, the profiles generated in this manner often show a uniformity in that they tend to follow a standard format, presenting information such as: (1) demographic information such as age range, race, degree of occupational skills, marital and socioeconomic status; (2) educational level and estimates of intellectual functioning; (3) legal and arrest history; (4) military background; (5) family characteristics; (6) habits and social interests; (7) evidence in relation to crime scene; (8) age and type of vehicle; (9) personality characteristics including possible forms of psychopathology; and (10) suggested interview techniques.

Offences most suitable for profiling involve those where the suspects' behaviour at the crime scene reveal important details about themselves. Arson and sexually motivated crimes where the criminal has demonstrated some form of psychopathy seem to offer the best chance of useful information being disclosed. Examples of appropriate instances where profiling is most effective include crime scenes revealing evidence of sadistic torture, ritualistic behaviour, evisceration, posturing of the body, staging, or acting out of fantasy. According to the FBI view, cases involving mere destruction of property, assault or murder during the commission of a robbery are generally unsuitable for profiling since the personality of the criminal is frequently not revealed in such crime scenes. Likewise, drug-induced crimes lend themselves poorly to profiling because the true personality of the perpetrator is often altered (McCann, 1992). Not all types of crime are therefore suitable for offender profiling.

Many criticisms have been leveled at the FBI approach, particularly in relation to the relatively insignificant size of the original research populations on which the method is based, the utility of the dichotomous organized/disorganized classification and the rape typologies, and the paucity of available publications about the developments and efficacy of their methods. In particular, the programme has been censured for lacking 'programmatic validity and reliability research and for lacking a proper theoretical basis' (Rossmo, 1996, pp. 71–72). In spite of this, not only has investigative support, research and training in behavioural analysis continued unabated in the USA since 1978 but many, if not all, of the psychological profiling units in other countries (such as Canada, the UK and the Netherlands) have been modelled to a large extent on the FBI approach.

In Britain, the term 'offender profile' gradually became more well known both to police forces and the general public during the 1980s. This came about partly as a result of the huge publicity that attended the successful application of profiling techniques to a number of high-profile cases (e.g. the John Duffy case; see Canter, 1994). The reported successes led to increased requests for profiling services. Canter suggests that the popularity of profiling can also, in part, be traced back to the original coining of the term 'offender profiling' by the FBI. He argues that its use created the impression of 'a package, a system that was sitting waiting to be employed rather than the mixture of craft, experience and intellectual energy that they themselves (the FBI) admit is at the core of their actions' (p. 10). This misguided impression amongst investigating officers may in part be responsible for the somewhat negative judgements given by them in a recent evaluation study of British officers' satisfaction with the advice given by independent profilers (see Copson, 1995).

For offender profiling to realize its potential, two things must happen. First, profilers must understand better the requirements and needs of police investigation. This requires that scientific and investigative methodologies are concerned with issues of validity and reliability in the context of real investigations (see Oldfield, 1995). Second, investigators must understand better the nature and use of profiles. This will require the investigator to have some understanding of the theory and research behind offender profiling techniques.

This book combines expertise in all areas of offender profiling, from theory to practice to research. Chapter 2 by Badcock, introduces the relationship between behaviour and personality, and provides illustrations of how offence behaviour can be linked to the lifestyle and personal needs of the offender. Boon (Chapter 3) provides specific examples of the applications of theories of personality to cases of extortion. Gudjonsson & Copson (Chapter 4) first describe the general role that experts can play in forensic investigations, before focusing more specifically on offender profiling. Stevens (Chapter 5) offers the perspective of a detective, by providing a clear description of the investigative procedures, highlighting the skills already in the detective's repertoire. Oldfield (Chapter 6) discusses the areas in which offender profiling might be most useful, specifically in low-incidence crimes where the detective is likely to have gaps in knowledge, and provides examples of research that is currently being conducted. Jackson, van den Eshof & de Kleuver (Chapter 7) complement Oldfield's chapter by providing similar information about research being carried out in the Netherlands. Chapters 8–11 all focus on recent research findings, specifically Farrington & Lambert (Chapter 8) on burglary and violent crimes; Rossmo (Chapter 9) on geographical profiling; House (Chapter 10) on recent cross-cultural studies of rape; and Davies (Chapter 11) on analyses of databases collected on rape. The final chapter (Bekerian & Jackson, Chapter 12) considers critical issues that are likely to be important for the development of offender profiling.

CHAPTER 2

Developmental and Clinical Issues in Relation to Offending in the Individual

Richard J. Badcock

'The appetite doth grow by that on which it feeds' (*Macbeth*)

'One comes to be of just such stuff as that on which the mind is set' (*The Upanishads*)

INTRODUCTION

In this chapter the term 'developmental issues' will refer to those thought and behaviour patterns associated with offending which develop in response to the intrinsic personal needs and life experiences of an offender. Not all offences contain a clear link between an offender's development and the offence, although in others the link appears straightforward. For some offenders, however, developmental issues give rise to complex and persistent behaviour patterns in which deviant means are routinely employed in order to satisfy personal psychological needs.

The term 'clinical issues' will refer to those patterns associated with offending which occur as a result of recognizable mental illness or mental disorder in the offender. An example of this would be violent behaviour arising from an offender's need to deal with the internal experience of delusions or with the effects of confusion created by mental disorder.

The relationships between the nature and content of offences and the lifestyles and personal needs of offenders are generally not well researched. However, thinking about these issues in selected offences will often yield useful clues to the precise motivation of an offence. This chapter concentrates on issues relevant to a range of violent and coercive offences, since developmental and clinical issues are often highlighted in such cases. The boundary between developmental and clinical issues is not always clear-cut and the chapter may contain oversimplifications in the pursuit of establishing certain important points.

DEVELOPMENTAL ISSUES

Where developmental issues are great enough and begin early enough they can change the entire concept of what is 'normal' for an individual. Everyone tends to assume that what they are used to must be normal and some people grow up with what most others would consider abnormal ideas of the meaning of normality. People who have been seriously abused from an early age, for example, can grow up believing that abuse is the basis of normal relationships. They may have great difficulties in relating to others in ways that do not include abuse and some of them will become abusers themselves.

Some people do not possess the language skills to give expression to their developmental difficulties. Nevertheless, they still have the experience of the difficulties themselves and the tension heightened by being unable to articulate them can give rise to situations in which acts of destruction or violence provide a substitute outlet. Similarly, some offenders find themselves in situations where they have vocabulary and thought capacity but, nevertheless, cannot give expression to their experiences because strong internal emotional conflicts render them effectively speechless. It is important to understand that the emotional conflicts themselves may involve intrinsically insoluble dilemmas — such as the position of a person who is dependent on a parent for care but who also believes that parent to be hostile towards him/her. Acts of destructive violence may then provide a channel for repressed rage and frustration. To the offender, these acts provide a necessary means of reducing internal tension when the problem cannot be resolved.

Some offenders consciously pursue abnormal means in order to satisfy personal needs which, in themselves, may be quite normal. In these situations, elements of secrecy and manipulated control often appear to be important. It is as if the offender can only satisfy his/her needs if he/she can do so in a disguised and hidden way. Sexual offences provide some good examples of this type of relationship between an offence and the developmental needs of the offender.

Three patterns of offence-related behaviours which generally spring from developmental issues are those that involve the expression of *control*, *power* and *fantasy*. In real life these behaviours often overlap but it is helpful to consider them separately, since the psychological background to each may be different. They can all be seen as arising from a serious difficulty for the offender in developing and maintaining normal personal relationships. In particular, they reflect a failure to tolerate or accept a sense of personal vulnerability.

Normal relationships are associated with a mutuality and reciprocity in the interactions between those involved and this necessarily means that a person remains vulnerable to the reactions of others. In normal life, this vulnerability is made manageable by a sense of trust in the other person or a sense of agreed and negotiated conditions for the relationship. For a number of people, this state of maturity in style of relating is never reached. Perhaps as a result of experiencing important abusive, exploitative or denigratory relationships during development, there is a failure to establish a stable sense of personal identity, integrity and self-directness. Often this is coupled with a failure to understand the needs of others in relationships and the problems tend to become self-perpetuating. In such circumstances various forms of controllingness or fantasizing can substitute for the satisfaction more normally obtained by emotionally warm and reciprocal relationships. These activities can then, in themselves, create a need for further behaviour. Since it is necessary to manipulate and control another person in order to have the offender's desire for personal satisfaction fulfilled, by its very nature, this behaviour can result in offences.

Two normal developmental processes that are important to understand at this stage are those of *jealousy* and *envy*. Since significant offending patterns can be directly related to failures in developmental processes, it is important to understand the circumstances in which jealousy and envy develop and the ways in which they normally become modified by other developmental processes and experiences.

Jealousy

Jealousy is a state of suspicion that one will be displaced by a rival. It generates resentful or vindictive behaviour towards the person who is the object of the jealousy. At the same time, it makes demands for exclusive loyalty in relationships. During normal development, correcting experiences and suitable conditions of upbringing allow jealousy to be grown out of and reduced to a more manageable internal state. In normal adult life, jealousy that is modified and coped with contributes to such things as a sense of ambition or a sense of competitive rivalry. If a jealous temperament persists, however, it leads to demanding, controlling and vindictive behaviour in personal relationships.

Though its roots lie in early childhood, jealousy does not seem to develop until the child already has a capacity to love and form relationships. From the age of about 15 months onwards, children are confronted by the realization that they do not have exclusive rights to the other important people in their lives — particularly mother. For example, the birth of a younger sibling will confront the child with the fact that somebody else also wants the mother and that he/she does not have exclusive rights of possession. The child is then in a position where he/she can 'want' without any guarantee that they can always 'have'. The source of jealousy is, therefore, a direct threat to the child's relationship with his/her mother or, alternatively, a threat to a possession (such as a toy), which can symbolize the same relationship.

Many of the early jealousies centre on feeding, the ownership of toys and demands for the exclusivity of parents' time. As the child grows older, however, the jealousies can become more complex and expand to include other relationships. During the experience of jealousy it is as if the jealous child both loves and hates his/her parents simultaneously. This feeling is itself overwhelmingly painful and disturbing and the child will seek to rid him/herself of it. In the beginning, this may involve strong expressions of anger, such as screaming, messing, spoiling or destroying. In time, and sometimes quite quickly, this behaviour becomes modified.

It is important to understand the factors that can help a child grow out of this jealous state, since it is their absence that directly shapes later abnormal behaviour:

1   The child finds by experience that his[1] parents survive his hatred of them and continue to love, care for and protect him. In this way, he learns that it is relatively 'safe' to hate. In turn, this makes it easier to reach a point where only a fraction of his anger needs to be directly expressed and more can be modified and dealt with in some less disturbing way. Conversely, if he does not learn this, then he may never come to terms with the potential destructive force of his anger and hatred. He becomes frightened of expressing it at all and when it is converted into behaviour, the behaviour tends to be explosive.
2   The child develops a capacity for imagination. He can then learn to use imagination as a process for expressing feeling and, through his imagination, emotion can be expressed without having to take direct physical action. This reduction of an immediate need to act in

---

[1] For simplicity, in the rest of the chapter a masculine version will be used unless the discussion centres on females specifically.

the face of strong emotion helps the child to feel safer with the actual experience of jealousy.

3 As the child grows he can, through the use of imagination, develop a capacity to live a little of his own life through the experiences of others. In play situations, for example, he can pretend to be other people. This allows him to develop and enrich his own life to such an extent that the mechanism of jealousy is less readily stirred into action.

4 In normal development, the experience of jealousy is more than adequately balanced by other satisfying and satisfactory physical and emotional experiences. The child gradually accumulates the sense that not only is he loved, but he is loved in excess of what he generally needs. In turn, this helps to foster a state in which he himself can spare love for others. The need for jealousy is thus reduced.

The following case study, which describes a relationship involving stalking, shows how a failure to process jealousy in early life can lead to offending in adult life.

Case Study. A 35 year-old single woman voluntarily entered a relationship with a 46 year-old man. She was attracted by his attentive and affectionate attitude towards her and because he made her feel that he needed her. Within a short time, however, she felt that he was becoming increasingly controlling and demanding towards her. He required constant proof of her loyalty and devotion to him, which she was required to demonstrate by making a series of personal sacrifices in her normal routines. At the same time, he started to denigrate her personal skills and abilities and at times seemed to go out of his way to humiliate or upset her. It became evident that, even though he claimed he was popular, he had no other close relationships. Moreover, he was unable to sustain normal relationships with members of his own family without the support or intervention of third parties. A pattern also developed of her being expected to accept the full consequences, particularly adverse ones, of any decisions that he had made. She found that she was not allowed to discuss issues in her own right. Conversations largely became a matter of him shouting at her and, when she tried to discuss their problems, his response was to say that it was her fault that he was constantly under pressure. Further, he accused her of constantly trying to manufacture something to make him feel guilty.

She terminated the relationship but, after a short time, became the recipient of a series of experiences, which included vandalism to her car, oil being sprayed on her drive, getting silent phone calls, graffiti referring to her which was prominently and publicly displayed locally, and a number of anonymous postings — including chocolates, a bunch of flowers and shotgun cartridges. Phone calls, letters and postcards made it clear that her ex-partner was responsible for these activities. Sometimes he expressed a wish to restart their relationship and often, if he met her, he would act as if nothing untoward had occurred.

Envy

The state of envy is one of a sensation of discontent that is aroused by thinking about the achievements, personal qualities or possessions of another person. The sensation becomes the desire to have the things which the other person possesses. Although there may be a sense of grudging admiration for the fact that the other person has what the envying person wants, there is a destructive desire in envy which can be very powerful and which separates it from, for example, jealousy. Envy which is coped with, and to some extent resolved, can contribute in adult life to a desire to strive for equality and fairness, thereby avoiding the risk of envious attacks by others. However, if it survives into adult life in a more pathological form, it leads to states of mind where the envious person feels trampled down by other people at every opportunity and to a state in which he feels profoundly isolated, lonely and 'unalive'.

In developmental terms, it is useful to think about envy in association with jealousy. Although they are different states, the circumstances that give rise to the one will also tend to give rise to the other. For example, the child who becomes jealous towards a younger sibling because it is also making demands on the mother is, at the same time, also likely to feel envious because the younger child, rather than he, possesses the mother's attention at various times. The same circumstances that allow a child to grow out of the excesses of jealousy also allow it to moderate the experience of envy and so render the emotion more manageable and less disruptive in adult life. The experience of seeing his parents survive the envious attacks made on them and still continuing to care for him, the active use of imagination to substitute for direct action, and the cumulative effect of a wider range of experiences and feeling secure in the knowledge that one is loved, all help a child to negotiate the traumas of envy as they do for those of jealousy.

If unmodified envy persists into adulthood, however, the life of the envious person is bleak. Envy produces avoided and socially barren relationships, since, although the envier may want what other people have, he would prefer not to associate with them. The more intense the envious experience, the more the person involved thinks obsessionally about the envied object and finds himself thrown back on himself in self-pity. The envier does not want to be recognized as envious by others and, despite the desire for the things possessed by the envied person, is not principally interested in the transfer of the other's possessions to himself but would rather see the envied person dispossessed, humiliated, hurt or destroyed.

The next case study directly illustrates the working of envy.

Case Study. A 44 year-old man with a history of unsuccessful relationships was introduced to a female pen-friend whilst he was serving a prison sentence. They married a few months later and while he was still in custody. On his release, he went to live with his new wife but, after a few months, she reported that he had threatened to kill her and he moved out to a hostel. Over subsequent years he maintained their relationship by daily telephone calls (up to 40 a day) and they would periodically meet and spend brief periods of time together. He was described as being very clean in his personal habits but periodically would also demonstrate insecure dramatic and attention-seeking behaviours, such as deliberate self-harm. His wife noticed that when she questioned any of his movements and actions he always had a plausible reason ready to hand, even when it was subsequently obvious that he must have been lying. He was used to giving deceptive answers about his personal life and keeping his real thoughts and feelings hidden.

On one occasion he learned, through his telephone calls, that she was going out for the evening with some female friends. He appeared angry over the telephone and later rang the venue that his wife and friends had gone to and complained about her to the staff. On the same day he went drinking himself and picked up an 18 year-old female prostitute. They returned to her home where he strangled her to death — taking a long period of time over the strangulation. After she was dead he stripped her body and laid it out ritually. He inserted an object in her vagina and burned her pubic hair. When subsequently interviewed his main concern was for the preservation of the relationship between himself and his wife. In this case, therefore, the victim can be seen as a displaced object for the envy primarily directed at his wife.

Control-related Issues

Control, expressed in offences and related to developmental issues, is normally directed at one of two things. Either it is necessary for the victim's actions to be directed and controlled so that the offender can act out and develop a *fantasy*, or the experience of being in control of another person is itself directly satisfying and empowering to the offender. The former can be seen as either an over-reliance on, or an under-functioning of, the power of imagination to help an offender maintain his sense of status quo. The latter can either be related to *obsessive personality traits* in the offender or to *sadomasochistic* strivings. The purpose of the control is to reduce the offender's internal sense of anxiety or to boost his sense of self and identity.

We have seen how controlling offence behaviour can arise from the acting out of developmentally unresolved problems of jealousy and envy. Later in the chapter, some of the relationships between sexual fantasies and sadomasochistic needs and control will be considered. At this point, we will consider the development and impact of control-related character traits.

A *trait* is a distinguishing feature in a person's character or habit. Each individual has many traits and those few that are used more extensively than others contribute to the individual's *personality*. In psychoanalytic theory, traits are thought of as arising from developmental issues. A recognizable cluster of traits are recognized as being associated with difficulties in managing the experiences of anger and fear during early life. These are all associated with an emphasis on *control* of different aspects of experience in adult life. They are generally thought of as *obsessional traits* because they reflect a state of personal rigidity and inflexibility. In turn, this embodies a fear of anything that is not certain and predictable and with which the individual therefore feels uncomfortable.

When they are present in a modified form, some such traits are seen as normal and even desirable. Qualities of *orderliness, punctuality* and *cleanliness*, for example, are ones which most people would want. When they become part of an obsessive personality structure, however, these qualities appear to have been taken to excess, so that they have a rather empty, arid and sterile air to them. They become converted into forms of pedantry and rigid dogmatism in which the individual can only establish very controlling and limited relationships with those around him.

Other character traits which are associated with this process include parsimony and stubbornness. *Parsimony* is a state in which excessive carefulness about giving things to others amounts to meanness, whilst at the same time, the individuals indulge themselves freely. *Stubbornness* is a state in which an individual will rigidly resist any imposition of change to ensure not having to cope with any results of change. Stubbornness has another value for the individual in that, simply through preserving the sensation of being immovable, an inner experience of impotence can be converted into one of omnipotence.

People with a fully established obsessive personality disorder do not commonly become offenders. Indeed, they are often noted for their law-abiding nature and desire to find a place within the hierarchy of a work organization. However, the presence of one or more such character traits is a common finding amongst offenders who may, for example, commit sexual homicides or display marked sadomasochistic behaviour. The following case study is that of an individual with an obsessional personality and is included to illustrate the mechanism by which violence can occur when the coping effectiveness of such personality traits become threatened and break down.

Case Study. A 45 year-old man with a long history of being rigid, inflexible and pedantically precise in his personal attitudes became involved in a boundary dispute with his neighbours. The dispute dragged on and eventually his wife, who believed that he was becoming bogged down in the dispute and that the health of everyone in the family was suffering as a result, disposed of documentation relating to it. His response was to feel that he had lost control of the situation completely and that his wife, on whom he depended, had turned against him. He felt powerless to act without the support of his wife and she found it impossible to talk about the situation with him because of his rigid and narrow opinions. He stabbed her to death. This was his first and only experience of personal physical violence.

The precipitating factor for the attack was the breakdown in effectiveness of his character traits of orderliness and stubbornness. The killing expressed an over-reaction in a person who was normally over-controlled and under heavy pressure. It is not unusual to find that over-controlled people react excessively when they reach the point at which they act at all.

There is one further aspect of obsessionality to consider here and that is the way in which *obsession* and *narcissistic preoccupation* can interact and lead to offending. An *obsession* is a thought or emotion which dominates the mind. It appears to be beyond the control of the will of the person experiencing it. Obsession leads to a desire for control in order to possess. A state of expectant preoccupation by the individual with himself leads him to ignore others or regard them only as things to be possessed by and incorporated into himself. In its advanced form, destruction of the object may be seen as the best way of possessing it for ever in the form that the individual wants.

By becoming obsessed in this way, and allowing it to take this form, the individual can expand his sense of his own world by attempted identification with another and become temporarily released from an awareness of his own state of personal distress and difficulty. By becoming totally focused on a narrow subject of his own choice, the individual can enhance his sense of personal mastery — increasing his effective level of intelligence or giving him a sense of direction and purpose. The obsessive focus provides a stimulus to act and overcome a sense of inner emptiness and inertia. The following case study helps to illustrate the value that a fanatical and narcissistically focused obsession can have for the individual involved.

Case Study. A 21 year-old single man, intelligent but with poor social skills, adopted the habit of stalking teenage boys — often when they were in groups with their peers. As part of this process he would sometimes deliberately place himself at risk of humiliation. For example, he would remain outside the boys' schools waiting for them, even though he knew he would be jeered at by the other children. He never tried to assault the boys he was stalking but did find that he had to change his pattern of contact with them in order to keep achieving a state of personal satisfaction.

He felt that in risking humiliation he was 'daring' himself. This raised his levels of personal anxiety but also made him feel more alive and energetic. Once he could feel 'alive' in this way, he could enhance and develop the experience by telling himself that he no longer cared about the consequences of what he was doing. This feeling then created a sense of omnipotence which, in its turn, was accompanied by a huge sense of relief from personal anxiety.

This experience of relief from anxiety was very similar to the benefits that he had previously hoped for when he tried to find a more normal social relationship. However, his experience of trying to establish real relationships had always ended in failure. From his point of view, the advantage of his stalking relationships was that once the process started he felt that he did not risk any real rebuff or deprivation since no one could take his feelings away from him. However, he did find that in order to restore or maintain this state of satisfaction, he had to do more than simply follow the boys. For example, he would throw stones at the boys' houses or at public transport in which they were travelling.

Power-related Issues

The commonest expression of power-driven behaviour in offences is threatened or enacted physical or sexual violence. It is helpful here to distinguish between instrumental and expressive categories of violence (see also Jackson, van den Eshof & De Kleuver, 1997, Chapter 7 of the present Volume). *Instrumental violence* is that which is used as an 'instrument' to pursue some other purpose. For example, threat of violence during the course of a robbery might occur in order to make the process of robbery easier and reduce the personal risk to the offender. The main focus of interest is the robbery, and violence is simply a tool to make the robbery easier. In the case of *expressive violence*, however, the violence itself is the focus of interest for the offender. It fulfils a need in the offender and has a personal rather than a practical function. Clinically it is often found that the use of expressive violence is also related to feelings of sexual excitement or arousal and, at the same time, to feelings of personal self-validation and to a sense of personal identity. There are, therefore, situations in which the elements of power-based violent behaviour, sexual arousal and the preservation of a sense of personal identity coexist in the same actions.

It is helpful to consider the classification of rape as a means of understanding the relationships between power, anger, sexual violence and developmental needs. The classification system illustrated here is empirically derived from American experience and uses a categorization approach which utilizes a mixture of offence style and inferred motivation as its basis. This hybrid style presents real difficulties in developing the concepts incorporated in the classification. Nevertheless, the system contains real information and each of the typologies suggested is regularly encountered in investigative practice (cf. House, 1997, Chapter 10 of the present volume; Davies, 1997, Chapter 11 of the present Volume).

Classification of Rapes

One group of rapists are described as being inadequate, quiet and passive. They tend to be under-achievers, have few friends and are more likely to be doing unskilled jobs. The purpose of the rape is often primarily to resolve self-doubts by reassuring the offender about his masculinity. For this reason such rapists are described as *power-reassurance rapists*. Their preparations for the rape can be quite elaborate and they often have extensive fantasy systems in relation to the rape. Indeed, one of the main purposes of this type of rape is to gather experiences during the offence which can be used later to enhance or improve the quality of subsequent masturbatory fantasies. Although they tend to approach their victims with a combination of surprise and force, the level of force tends to be the minimum necessary for the control of the victim. Because they will sometimes attempt to engage their victim in conversation during the attack, they are sometimes referred to as 'polite' rapists.

A second group of rapists are more socially organized and are notable for their self-centredness and the importance they attach to a having a 'macho' image. As rapists they have a feeling of entitlement to sex as an expression of their male domination and superiority. Because of this preoccupation with self-image and body and power consciousness they are described as *power-assertion rapists*. An important post-rape feature of this group is that they tend to feel that the rape only counts if other men know about it. They are therefore highly likely to boast about their activities in their own social circle.

Another group of rapists have disturbed domestic lives. Although they may be married, their marriage contains an imbalance of power in favour of their partners. Their rapes are often an attempt to punish or degrade women and to get even with them by using sex as a weapon for what they see as injustices done against them. For this reason, they are described as *anger-retaliatory rapists*. The style of these rapes includes greater use of profanity, degrading sexual behaviour and physical violence before, during and after the sexual assault than is found in the other types.

The most thought-out and premeditated of all the rape types is one where the principal purpose of the attack is to inflict emotional and physical pain on the victim. The sexual activity as such is not the main concern and the assaults tend to be ritualistic in technique, with either a great deal of experimental sex, or little sexual activity at all. Instead, the satisfaction for the offender comes from telling the victim, in detail, in advance, what he is planning to do and in making use of prolonged assaults or assaults with a high violence content. These attacks are essentially sadistic in nature and are described as *anger-excitation rapes*. Such rapists are often sexually impotent under normal circumstances and can only have a successful sexual experience through the use of control and power-based violence.

Sadomasochistic Urges

The development of *sadomasochistic behaviour* is one of the areas in which strong direct links can be found between personal development and later offending behaviour. The nature of the behaviours required by sadomasochistic urges necessitates the treatment of other people in such a way that offences are automatically generated.

Sadism and *masochism* are related emotional drives in which the forces of sex and power become mixed together. There is a natural human need for satisfactory experiences of both sex and being somebody. When sadism and machochism are active, both erotic satisfaction and the satisfaction of personal empowerment become closely associated with the production of pain. In the case of sadism, this satisfaction comes from inflicting pain on another person, whereas in masochism it comes from having pain inflicted on the individual himself. In both sets of actions, the purpose of the pain is to facilitate a feeling of control and mastery in the individual. In the case of sadistic behaviour, this comes from seeing other people powerless and experiencing pain or humiliation as a result of one's own actions. In the case of masochistic behaviour, the sense of mastery comes from the satisfaction of being able to rise above and control (and therefore be superior to) the pain being inflicted on the individual.

Both behaviours require the individual to live his life satisfactorily only through the control and degradation of other people. Sadistic actions mean that the individual can turn another person into an extension of himself. Masochistic acts enable him to lose his own identity in that of a superior force and thereby turn himself into an extension of something or someone else. Either way, the desire to completely control another human being becomes the central focus of the sadomasochist's life.

The power desired by a sadomasochist is specifically that of power over other people. Initially, the tension created by the sadomasochist's actions can make him feel alive and both individual and creative. As the pathology progresses, however, sadomasochistic behaviours serve only to increase and perpetuate themselves.

For the sadomasochist, the idea of intimacy with other people produces a strong sense of threat. In contrast, the idea of being in complete control produces a feeling of security. Isolation from other people may be desired at times but cannot be completely achieved: sadomasochists require another person to manipulate, otherwise personal satisfaction cannot be obtained. The sadomasochist therefore develops relationships with other people in which control substitutes for intimacy. The requirement for control of the relationship creates a need for visible, tangible and repeatable proof that he has complete power. It is this that makes it necessary to use pain, cruelty, and humiliating and degrading behaviour towards his victims. Forcing victims to undergo these experiences reassures him that he has complete power and mastery. Without such reassurance, the sadomasochist feels impotent, unalive and powerless.

The following case study illustrates the enactment of sadomasochistic behaviour during the course of an offence.

Case Study. A 28 year-old single man with a history of being physically and sexually abused met a 21 year-old single girl. They cohabited for a period of several weeks although the relationship remained superficial. One day he asked her for sex. She refused. He had the thought, 'What's a life anyway' and went and got a hammer with which he hit her about the head and shoulders some 26 times. He attempted vaginal intercourse with the body but was unsuccessful. However, he did ejaculate when he attempted anal intercourse. He then searched the body for faeces with the intention of consuming them. After completing his activities he felt calm and more settled in himself. He telephoned the police and told them what he had done and where he was. Because of a misunderstanding over the address, the officers initially went to an adjacent location. The man remained where he was until he was arrested. During subsequent interviews he was contemptuous of the police for having initially gone to the wrong address.

A useful way to look at the relationships between power-based actions, sexual behaviour and offence-related behaviour is to think of both power-based and sexually-based behaviour as providing *alternative routes to personal fulfilment* — with the possibility of the one converting into the other if a 'blockage' occurs in the desired activity. Power-based behaviours offer a feeling of excitation (through control of the victim) and a sense of mastery (through the use of violence) and, with the completion of the behaviour, result in feelings of purged tension. Similarly, sexually-based behaviour offers the stimulus of desire (from sexual arousal), with a sense of physical and emotional pleasure (through the sexual activity itself) and, as a result of ejaculation or climax, leads to feelings of relaxation.

There is a difference in the emotional tone of the two sets of behaviours but both offer a means of self-expression. They can substitute for each other if there are particular developmental restrictions, or if circumstances mean that the preferred activity cannot be followed through to its desired conclusion. For example, an action which starts out as sexual behaviour may not result in ejaculation because there is a state of impotence in the individual. The nature of the behaviour, however, can switch from being sexually-based to being power-based and, through the use of violence, can lead to a state of purged tension which effectively compensates for the sexual block. Similarly, control and violence may be required to overcome a deficiency in an individual's ability to become sexually aroused and may therefore be used to enable him to achieve sexual satisfaction and ejaculation. An offence that appears power-based can therefore be used to achieve a sexual end. Similarly, an offence that appears to be sexual can be used to achieve personal empowerment.

The following case studies illustrate two examples of alternative fulfilment.

Case Study. A 24 year-old single man was arrested after snatching a shoulder-bag from a young female student waiting at a railway station. He ran at her without saying anything, pushed her against the wall, snatched her bag and ran away. Subsequent discussion showed that he had been taking large quantities of drugs and that these had made him impotent. He wanted to feel sexually aroused but had trouble in achieving this. After he had snatched the student's bag he took it away to a quiet corner and masturbated over it. He then discarded the bag.

Although there was no overt sexual component to the offending behaviour, the offence was primarily motivated by a sexual need. The limited physical aggression displayed during the offence enabled him to overcome his feeling of sexual impotence. Once he felt 'energized' in this way, he was able to bring about the result he wanted – in this case, successful masturbation.

Case Study. A 28 year-old single man with a history of estrangement in his family came to believe that any woman to whom he was attracted would somehow try to 'invade' him and destroy him as a person. It was significant that he had been largely brought up by a parent on whom he was dependent but with whom he had a hostile relationship. Whilst walking in the street he saw a teenage girl who attracted him. He immediately had an image of her as some kind of monster that might want to attack him and take him over. He ran at her and attacked her — attempting to rape her.

During subsequent discussions, he was insistent that the sexual attack was mainly to degrade and humiliate the girl. He believed that if he could achieve this then she would have no real power or control over him. The perceived threat to himself as a result of finding her attractive would have been neutralized. There was no intent to seek sexual satisfaction.

Fantasy-related Issues

Fantasy is a mental process of private imagining, daydreaming or fancying. The individual fantasizes about what he would like, but cannot have, and imagines how much better and more effective he would be if he were playing the part of someone else. Imaginative activity begins very early in childhood. The process of imagination becomes one of the important methods of overcoming developmental difficulties or limiting their impact so that the individual can continue to grow mentally.

Fantasies can relate to offending behaviour in at least two ways. In some cases the offence arises as a result of the individual's desire to convert a frustrated, fantasized wish into real-life activity and real-life experience. In other situations, the offence behaviour may be required to obtain further real-life experiences which can, in turn, be used as a basis for further satisfactory fantasizing. For people who find the experience of reality unsatisfactory, their 'real' life may be lived out in fantasy.

The relationship between fantasizing and offending behaviour can be conveniently illustrated through a study of the paraphilias. These are not, of course, the only cases where fantasy-related issues play an important part in offending and other examples are contained throughout the chapter. However, they do provide a convenient focus for thinking about fantasy-related issues.

Paraphilias

Paraphilias are sexually motivated behaviours which do not lead a particular individual to the normal sexual goal of genital sexual intercourse, but to a different type of activity which leads to sexual satisfaction. The activities often have a high symbolic content and the fantasy element involved in carrying out the paraphilia is of major importance. Without it there would be no sense of sexual or personal satisfaction and no sense of sexual or personal potency.

Some sets of paraphilias involve remote or non-intimate contact with a target. For example, some individuals find that they are sexually impotent unless they have in their possession, or are wearing, an item of female clothing, underclothing or some other object such as a shoe. The objects all have sexual associations for the individual and may either become the object of sexual desire in themselves or be necessary for the individual to have satisfaction through normal sexual activity. This behaviour is known as *fetishism*. Other individuals become sexually aroused by viewing sexual activity between other people from a distance. It is not simply a case of becoming vicariously sexually stimulated like 'Peeping Tom', but the viewing may be the only circumstance in which the individual feels it is safe to be sexually stimulated. This activity is known as *voyeurism*. For others, the sense of satisfaction comes from glancing contact by rubbing up against the clothed bodies of other people. This can happen in a variety of social settings and sometimes the individual will unobtrusively 'tag' his contact with semen or paint as part of the sexually arousing stimulus. This is the state of *frotteurism*. All these activities involve remote or non-intimate contact with the target.

There is a further set of paraphilias, however, in which forceful intimate intrusion into the target becomes a necessary part of the behaviour. It becomes natural to speak of the targets as 'victims' in these situations, since they are increasingly controlled and violated. The use of domination, forced submission, bondage and imposition of discipline is the basis of the practice of *sadomasochism*. For some individuals, sexual satisfaction is arrived at through the actions of stabbing, cutting or slicing. This state is known as *picquerism*. Beyond these activities there are ritualized sexual killings (*sexual homicides*) and satisfaction arising from sexual activity with dead objects (*necrophilia*). Necrophilic activity can represent ultimate control, but also a preoccupation with what makes living people work and what the 'rules' of life are. The ultimate paraphilia is sexual satisfaction associated with the eating of body parts (*cannibalism*).

This list of paraphilic behaviours is ranked in terms of increasing levels of control of the victim and increasing expressions of eroticized power and aggression. One of the interesting findings, when considering offences related to the more violent paraphilias, is that there is sometimes evidence of other paraphilic behaviours from lower down the ranking order included in the same crime activity. Some, but by no means all, paraphilic offenders show signs of development through progressive paraphilic activities with increasing levels of eroticized aggression.

Case Study. A 51 year-old woman, living alone, was attacked in her own home. After gaining entry and control, her attacker forced her to put on a pair of women's shoes that he had brought with him as preparation for rape. Near the climax of the rape he stabbed her several times in the back at about the point of ejaculation. Before leaving the house he went through her shoe cupboard and took a pair of her shoes with him.

The shoes were fetishistic objects and her attacker needed them to be physically present so that he could achieve successful sexual arousal. Stabbing her at the moment of ejaculation was an act of picquerism.

Case Study. A 38 year-old man attacked an elderly woman in her own home. He was married but had a low status at home and in his social relationships. His initial intent was rape but because of the physical infirmity of the victim this was not possible. He punched, strangled and stabbed her. After she was dead he laid her unclothed body on the floor. He stabbed her through the eyes and cut off her nose. He opened up her body cavities and examined her internal organs. He cut and dissected out part of her intestines. He cut off parts of her breasts. Before completing his activities, he inserted a foreign body into her abdominal cavity from below.

Although the initial intent was an anger-retaliatory style of rape, the offence developed into a sexual homicide with necrophilic elaboration.

CLINICAL ISSUES

The percentage of all offenders who are mentally ill is small. Figures in the region of 1% are quoted for this group. Studies of remand prisoner populations, who are a more selected group of offenders, suggest that up to 25% of those studied can be identified as being mentally ill or disordered (although this figure includes those with drug- and alcohol-related problems). How this statistic relates to the offences for which the prisoners are remanded is not known.

Most studies of people with a psychiatric diagnosis do not show huge differences between their rates of offending and that of the general population. Nevertheless, some types of mental disorder can result in offending behaviour. Even though the actual numbers may be quite small, the cases can be notable for their high profile or unusual nature. By contrast, there is also a natural inclination to assume that a particularly bizarre or revolting offence must arise from mental disorder, although in reality this is far from being the case.

The mental disorders most commonly associated with offending are *the psychoses, sociopathic personality disorder* and *drug/alcohol addictions*.

Psychoses are serious illnesses of the mind that may lead to obvious insanity. They involve disturbances in the ability to accurately perceive, judge and interpret events that are both external and internal to the person concerned. The illness can affect the whole of the personality: the patterns of behaviour and response by which people are normally recognized as particular individuals may be completely altered. It is characteristic of these illnesses that the person involved does not understand what is happening to him. As the disease progresses, awareness of the nature of external reality tends to become increasingly distorted or lost.

The two commonest psychoses relevant to the present discussion are *schizophrenia* and *manic depressive psychosis*.

In *schizophrenia,* there is a disruption of the normal synchronicity between various mental functions such as thinking, feeling and acting. In effect, these activities become disconnected from each other and change independently of each other, making life confusing, unpredictable and frightening for both patients and those around them. Some of the most basic functions of personality become disrupted, such as the patients' sense of individuality, uniqueness and sense of self-direction. The abnormal experiences that can accompany this illness can include *hallucinations* (hearing or seeing something that is not actually present in external reality, but is identified as if it were) and *delusions* (the firm holding of beliefs which are intrinsically irrational or illogical in the context of the person's normal experiences and beliefs). The illness affects the ability to understand cause-and-effect relationships between events and can lead to *passivity experiences,* in which the person feels that his thoughts, feelings or even behaviour is being dictated and determined by some agency other than himself.

In *manic depressive psychosis*, there are periods of either mental *elation, exultation* and *over-activity* or periods of major *depression* in which various morbid beliefs and delusions may be present. There is also a general slowing of mental and physical activities. The episodes of illness tend to resolve, particularly with treatment, but may then recur in either a periodic or an unforeseen way.

Personality disorders represent consistently anomalous ways of behaving or reacting that are not a product of mental illness or other disorders and are so consistent as to be incorporated into the person's recognizable personality structure. *Sociopathic personality disorder* (also known as *psychopathic personality disorder*) describes a particular personality type in which the main characteristics are persistently impulsive judgements, an inability to learn from personal experience, a primitive sense of conscience and a particular quality of self-centredness. These traits can lead to persistent behaviour which is recognizable as either seriously irresponsible or abnormally aggressive in comparison to the population as a whole.

Abuse of alcohol and drugs creates states of both mental and physical *dependence.* Mental distortions and symptoms are related to either withdrawal or to intoxication states connected with the substance of abuse. There are also major difficulties which become associated with the addict's *lifestyle.* These relate to changed behaviour necessary to ensure a continuing supply of the addictive substance and also to a process of neglect of self and ordinary activities that results from addiction. Typically, drugs or alcohol are initially used to suppress personal anxieties or facilitate social acceptance by groups who are similarly using the substance. It is much harder to change the lifestyle associated with alcohol and drug taking than it is to treat the immediate physical and mental symptoms of addiction.

General Issues in Violence and Mental Illness

Sex Differences

There is a general preponderance of male offenders in crimes of violence in the general population (approximately five male offenders to every one female offender). This also applies to mentally abnormal offenders, although the correlation with adolescence and young adulthood is perhaps less sharp than in the general population. However, where women who kill are concerned, there is a very much greater chance that the homicide will be recognized as containing abnormal features. Women are less likely to be involved in a 'normal' killing than an 'abnormal' one. In addition, approximately two-thirds of women (as opposed to one-third of men) who are convicted of homicide are legally found to be suffering from diminished responsibility at the time of trial.

Nature of Illness

Amongst mentally abnormal offenders as a whole there is thought to be no greater or lesser tendency towards violence than amongst the general population. However, within the group of mentally abnormal violent offenders, more people are diagnosed as suffering from schizophrenic illness than would be expected from the distribution of this illness in the population. In a recent confidential enquiry into homicides and suicides by mentally ill people, schizophrenia was the most common single diagnosis (27%).

Type of Violence

The level of violence in offences committed by the mentally abnormal is generally minor. It also tends to be relatively disorganized and determined by the situation in which the person finds himself. It is related to the degree of threat which he perceives in his immediate environment. Although there is a common anxiety that the mentally abnormal will be more likely to commit bizarre sexual crimes than other offenders, a major study of crimes of violence by mentally abnormal offenders in the Federal German Republic showed that less than 10% of the offences committed by male mentally abnormal offenders (and none of the offences committed by female mentally abnormal offenders) had evidence of sexual activity associated with the crime.

Duration of Illness

The duration of illness is relevant and although some offences are committed in the early stages of illness, this is relatively uncommon. Most violent acts by the mentally abnormal are related to long-standing rather than acute illness. The offenders are, therefore, frequently already known to the psychiatric and social services.

Choice of Victim

This can be shaped by the presence of mental illness. The victims of violence by people with a diagnosis of schizophrenia or manic depressive illness are much more likely to be members of the offender's own family or immediate social circle than would be the case for violent offenders as a whole. Where other people become victims of schizophrenic violence it is often as a result of the victim intervening in some official capacity, as the following case illustrates.

Case Study. During the development of a schizophrenic illness, a 42 year-old single man adopted a vagrant lifestyle. He was constantly plagued by hearing other people's voices talking inside his head and saying bad things about him. On one occasion he was found sleeping rough in the doorway of a local church. His case was reported to the police and an officer came to investigate and asked him to move on.

The man did not appear to respond to the officer's request — which was repeated. The officer then touched the man. His response was to produce a pair of scissors from his trouser pocket and stab the officer in the arm and the leg. He said nothing at the time but later examination showed that he believed the officer to be responsible for some of the hallucinations that he was experiencing.

Multifactorial Considerations

Although it is possible to link offences to one or more effects of mental illness it should be borne in mind that episodes of violence are generally multifactorial. Therefore, the presence of mental illness does not mean that other personal issues become unimportant. This can be illustrated by the following case.

Case Study. A 35 year-old married mother of three children revealed during the course of a depressive illness that she had smothered her youngest child as an infant. The death had been ascribed to natural causes. She felt it was necessary to smother the child to prevent it becoming a victim of sexual abuse at the hands of her own father — as she had done — and suffering the same abusive fate as herself.

During subsequent periods when symptoms and signs suggestive of major depression reappeared, they were always accompanied by a return of this delusional belief that she had to do away with her children because she believed they were being abused. There was, therefore, a clear link between the presence of mental illness (depression) and the risk of violent behaviour towards her children — a risk that was not present when she was not depressed.

Working further with her, however, revealed that during the period when her own father had abused her, she had become dependent on this relationship. As a result, she could not avoid intense feelings of jealousy towards her own children in case they took over her place in this relationship. These feelings of jealousy were relevant to the motivation behind smothering her child but were not, in themselves, a product of mental illness. The jealousy was only allowed disguised expression during the periods of depressive illness and at other times was kept firmly repressed. Therefore, although there was a close correlation between the presence of mental illness and direct risk to her children this did not, in itself, explain all the relevant issues at work.

Processes Associated with Risk of Violence in Psychotic Illnesses

Delusions, Hallucinations and Distorted Thinking

In one-third to one-half of cases where someone with a diagnosis of schizophrenia has acted violently, it is possible to definitely, or probably, relate that action to a delusional experience. Similarly, although it is unusual for the resultant act to be one of violence, up to one-half of patients suffering from schizophrenic delusions report that they have at some stage acted them out. Delusional beliefs are also rather more common in schizophrenic offenders who commit acts of violence than in other schizophrenic patients who are not offenders — even though delusional beliefs are a common feature of the illness for offender and non-offender alike.

In general, it is well-developed, well-structured systematic sets of delusional beliefs rather than undifferentiated or poorly structured delusional ideas that are more likely to be associated with violent acts. The more organized and developed the delusional beliefs, the more likely they are to be incorporated in the individual's pattern of coping with the effects of illness. The patient then uses these delusional beliefs to help make sense of his experiences and tends to interpret other things happening to him in the 'light' of them.

From this perspective, the delusions become important ideas around which the individual organizes both his relationships with others and his coping strategies. When the delusions become an important part of his way of coping, threat to the integrity of the delusions, as well as threat created by the nature of the delusions themselves, can both give rise to violence. As is illustrated in the following case, sometimes both processes can be at work simultaneously.

Case Study. The mental health of a 43 year-old single man began to deteriorate during the period he was serving a life sentence for murder. Even before this event he was inclined to be impulsive in his judgements and paranoid in his attitudes. He began to hear people whispering about him. The voices seemed to come from outside his cell door, although whenever he checked, there was never anybody there. The experiences continued and he formed the belief that they were part of a plot by the prison to drive him mad. He therefore determined to protect himself and found that becoming explosively violent was a good way of making himself feel more energetic. It also temporarily reduced his delusional belief that people were trying to drive him insane. Accordingly, on a number of occasions, he launched unforeseen attacks on those around him. At about the same time, a relative of his murder victim made contact with him in real life with a view to becoming reconciled about the tragedy. As a result, his condition further deteriorated. He found that whilst he could become 'successfully' paranoid to combat the thought that he was being deliberately driven mad, he could not use the same mechanism with the relative. He felt that the relative represented a different kind of threat to his method of coping and the resulting tension intensified his symptoms of illness. This, in turn, led to further acts of violence as he tried to hold on to paranoid ways of coping as being the ones by which he could most consistently make sense of the world as he understood it.

When we examine the relationship between the content of delusional beliefs and the risk of violence, we find that delusions of being poisoned and delusions about infidelity by a partner are both more common than would be expected. There is also an association between delusions of poisoning and delusions of jealousy and sexual confusion, although this association may simply illustrate the transforming power of delusions in situations where the offender believes that there is an emotional tie between himself and the victim. This situation is common. Although the relationship may itself be delusional, the victim's inconsequential gestures or remarks provide 'proof' of threat to the offender. He has then to assert himself in self-defence or revenge. The existence of a delusional relationship between offender and victim is even more important in patients suffering from manic depressive psychosis than it is in offenders suffering from schizophrenia (up to two-thirds of such cases compared to one-third of schizophrenics).

Other Psychotic Processes

Some patients with psychotic illnesses report periodic feelings of acute tension, anxiety and confusion. These feelings are not related to other symptoms of illness, although they sometimes also report *passivity phenomena*. Sometimes, unexplained and overwhelming emotions of anger or depression also sweep over them. This sensation of *psychotic confusion* is very disorientating and provokes unpleasant feelings of intense anxiety. Sometimes it is associated with acts of violence, either as a result of feeling panic or as an attempt to overcome the problem and restore a feeling of calm.

One of the unusual features of these acts is the sense of relief and calm that can follow — sometimes leading to the impression that the offender has dissociated himself from his actions. The following cases help to illustrate these points.

Case Study. A 29 year-old man was arrested after setting a series of fires. The fires all occurred near the premises of a well-known chain of newsagents and it was assumed that he had a grudge against them. Nothing unusual about him was noted and he was tried and sentenced. Whilst in prison he began to have a series of acute crises in which he appeared acutely anxious and reported multiple bizarre physical sensations — such as feelings of heat and cold running all around his body. The episodes were intense but short-lived. Further questioning revealed that he had, for a number of years, had the belief that alien forces had landed on Earth and had taken over his mind. Sometimes the aliens would 'make' him think or feel things but mostly they spoke to him inside his mind in a derogatory way.

Occasionally they would instruct him to carry out acts of destruction — such as setting fires. Although he was able to resist these instructions for most of the time, there were occasional episodes, similar to the unusual anxiety experienced in prison, in which he felt he would be destroyed if he did not act. He targeted the particular newsagents' chain because he believed they had some association with the alien forces. After he had set each fire he had an immediate sense of calm, later followed by feelings of guilt.

Case Study. A 27 year-old single man with a history of both schizophrenic illness and taking illicit drugs was admitted to a hostel for rehabilitation. One of the other residents was an elderly lady with whom he appeared to get on well. Although he was generally a cheerful soul, he found the pressures of ordinary living difficult to contend with. However, he was still resisting the temptation to resort to taking drugs to relieve the tension. One day he experienced an acute feeling of tension, confusion and anxiety. Without any preamble he went to the elderly lady and began to attack her. He attempted to strangle her. He got a knife and stabbed her. When the knife broke he went in search of a further one and continued the attack. He kicked her and punched her about the head and body. The attack was intense but terminated as abruptly as it had begun. He thought he had killed her and reported a sense of immediate lifting of tension and a feeling of calm, after which he went in search of someone to tell them what had happened.

Violence Occurring as Act of 'Symbolic Suicide'

Where this occurs in the context of mental illness, it is very much more likely to be associated with manic depressive psychosis than with schizophrenia. The general risk of violent behaviour by patients with manic depressive psychosis is much greater towards themselves than it is towards others (a 1 in 6 risk compared to a less than 1 in 1500 risk). However, when it does occur, the killing of close family members in what amounts to an act of extended suicide is common. A part of the offender that he wishes to destroy in himself is projected onto other members of the family, or he feels that killing the family is the only way of making sure that they do not have to undergo further trauma, stigma or humiliation. A substantial proportion of such people then kill themselves.

Since delusional beliefs amongst depressed patients are very common, but acts of violence are uncommon, it follows that other factors may also be operating. Where these can be identified, they are usually found in pre-existing conflict in the family relationships or in unusual dynamics in the relationships, such as one partner habitually making all the decisions.

Case Study. An apparently happily married middle-aged expatriate Indian man who was firmly at the head of his family became depressed about himself and his future. He believed that his outlook was hopeless but, as head of the family, did not want to communicate despair to the rest of the family. He told them that they were all going away on holiday — although he refused to discuss the destination. The family packed and prepared accordingly, putting on their best clothes. He got the car ready and filled up the petrol tank for the journey.

Beginning with his wife, he then took his family, one by one, and, under the guise of inoculating them for the journey, he injected each with a rapidly acting, fatal chemical compound. As they died he laid them out in an attitude of restful repose. Finally he injected himself. The bodies of the entire family were found the following day.

The sequence of events was pieced together from relatives' accounts and crime scene information. In retrospect, it was clear that the actions had been planned in detail for some time. Enquiries failed to reveal any evidence of preceding mental abnormality other than depression in the man involved.

Influence of Illness on Victim Selection

Where violence results in death, the victims of psychotically ill people are much more likely to be members of their own family than not. Despite widespread public concern, homicidal attacks by psychotically ill patients on strangers are comparatively very uncommon. Of homicidal assaults made by people with schizophrenia, about one-fifth are against spouse or cohabitee, one-fifth against parents or siblings and one-fifth against friends or acquaintances. The remaining two-fifths are roughly equally distributed between their children, people in authority and strangers. Matricide, although uncommon, is very strongly associated with the offender being schizophrenic, and the commonest background to this is said to be a hostile yet dependent relationship towards a possessive mother by a sexually indeterminate or homosexual son.

Nearly all homicidal attacks made by people with a diagnosis of depression are launched either towards their spouse or partner, or towards their children. Although there is the same excess of attacks within the family and social network as shown by people with schizophrenia, the choice of victims is much more restricted, with children being the commonest target and spouses the next most common.

Processes Associated with Violence in Personality Disorder

Impulsivity and Dissociation

Impulsivity tends to be associated with other attributes such as a need for instant gratification, difficulty in maintaining foresight and a greater than average degree of self-centredness.

The impulsivity-driven person causes trouble by avoiding painful and disruptive feelings and memories through a process of converting states of inner tension into immediate *acted-out* behaviour. The behaviour offers an alternative to the psychological process of remembering, confronting and experiencing distress (usually anxiety). The acted-out behaviour commonly has a destructive and therefore sometimes criminal element to it.

> *Case Study.* A 25 year-old single man with a long history of psychopathic personality disorder (accentuated after a head injury) resorted to regular misuse of drugs to alleviate tension. His drugs were supplied by a youth in the neighbourhood — whom he felt began to regard him with contempt and open ridicule. He felt trapped but did not want to think about his problems directly. Whilst he was brooding on this, a company employee called at his house to read a meter. He knew the man had arrived in a van and asked him for it so that he

could visit a relative some distance away and talk to her. When the employee refused, he struck him about the head with a spanner and took the van. He drove to his relative and reported what he had done. He knew that what he had done was wrong, but felt he had no choice in the matter — he had acted opportunistically to escape from his state of inner tension.

A similar process of converting inner tension into disturbed behaviour, but from which conscious recollection is then fully cut off, is the process of *dissociation* found in some people with an hysterical personality structure. This is a different process from *lying*, where the behaviour is consciously manipulated. The dissociative process can lead to complex and sustained behaviour — sometimes accompanied by demands that the case be investigated. By removing a state of tension and conflict from the person, dissociation can leave the individual apparently well-integrated, organized and energetic.

Case Study. A 36 year-old woman, separated from her family, reported that she had been raped in her own home by someone who had previously stalked her. The alleged rape had occurred over a period of time and resulted in damage to the contents of her home. A detailed examination of the crime scene led to serious doubts as to whether the damage done could have occurred in the way she reported. Attempts to reconstruct the damage strongly indicated that different behaviours to those reported would have been required and there was a strong possibility that the crime scene had been staged. Further investigation failed to substantiate her account, but did reveal that she had reported a similar incident in the past and had suffered hysterical symptoms over a number of years. The basis for this behaviour was the sexual abuse she had undergone as a child. The staged rape represented dissociative behaviour designed to accommodate, without directly addressing, relationship difficulties in her current life.

Dependency

Feelings of dependency on other people are part of normal life. In abnormal personality development, some people become consumed by feeling insignificant in their own right, and feel that they can only have a sense of themselves that is of any worth through selected special attachments to other people. Once they have chosen someone with whom to have such a relationship, they feel they cannot survive without that person being continuously present. Their own identity can then become bound up in maintaining the special attachment or of taking care of other people in some special way.

Any threat to the relationship, either real or imagined, can lead not only to high levels of anxiety but also to impulsive jealousy and destructive violence. The violence can have as its object either reassertion of control of the relationship or its destruction in an act of envy, or its destruction in a way which then preserves the relationship in a preferred form for ever.

Case Study. The bodies of a middle-aged woman and her male cohabitee were found at her house by friends. Both victims had been stabbed a number of times. Careful examination of the crime scene suggested that the male cohabitee had been attacked first and despatched, as it were, to get him out of the way. The main focus of the assault then concentrated on the woman, who had been repeatedly stabbed with several weapons and possibly in several locations. Enquiry into her background revealed that prior to taking up with her cohabitee she had established a relationship with a younger man who could be intense in nature but who was socially isolated. He took an intense and possessive attitude towards the relationship that he had with the female victim and which was all the more important to him because he had few other relationships. After she broke off their relationship he felt bereft and unable to function. The homicidal attacks were prompted both by his jealousy towards her and feelings arising from the frustration of his previous state of dependency on her.

Under- and Over-controlled Hostility

Learning to express anger and self-assertiveness in an appropriate way is an important part of development. However, it is also a very difficult task and both under-controlled and over-controlled assaultative personalities can be identified. Under-controlled offenders have weak inhibitions against the use of aggression. They respond readily with aggression to low levels of provocation or arousal, although the aggression itself also tends to be short-lived and relatively low-level unless other factors complicate the picture (such as the victim's response to being attacked). People with a personality trait of this type are often also identified as showing psychopathic disorder.

By contrast, someone with an over-controlled personality trait has high inhibitions against the use of violence. Their acts of violence are characterized by being infrequent, but, when they occur, are intense, extreme and often excessive to the provoking situation. A common pattern is for such a person to enter into an over-involved relationship with another person and then seek to placate him/her during difficulties in the relationship, repressing feelings of anger and frustration in the process. The repressed feelings may sometimes appear indirectly as symptoms of anxiety, depression or hypochondriasis, but the main mental effort goes into maintaining excessive control of the person's thoughts and feelings about the relationship and himself. Further stresses, which may be trivial in themselves, then act as a last straw and unleash intense and excessive violence. The actions are often so intense that the subsequent recollection of them is quite hazy and, since such people are normally regarded as mild-mannered and conventional, the violence may be described as being 'out of character'. However, it is in fact very much part of the character structure which they possess.

Case Study. A 28 year-old single man of quiet and apparently settled disposition, apart from some symptoms of anxiety, formed an intense relationship with a female student. He wanted to push the relationship along with an intensity that she found controlling and disquieting.

After a series of quarrels in which he did not act unduly aggressively, she wanted to end the relationship. He pleaded with her with what he hoped was rational argument and bent over backwards, as he saw it, to avoid pointing out her shortcomings. She eventually agreed to a final meeting — at which time he attacked her with a totally unexpected ferocity and intensity, including stabbing her with shards of glass from a window that broke during their fight. His subsequent recollection of the attack remained apparently genuinely hazy and indistinct.

Paranoid Projection and Displacement

Projection is a form of coping in which an insoluble personal dilemma is broken into parts and part of the conflict (usually the hostile or damaging part) is then identified and located in someone else by 'projecting it into them'. The process is essentially unconscious, although the person involved may be partially aware that something of the sort is taking place. *Paranoid thoughts* are ones which are felt to be attacking or destructive towards oneself. The purpose of paranoid projection is to remove an attacking, destructive conflict from within oneself and relocate it in someone else. Apart from anything else, it means that a problem which one cannot solve oneself can then be safely attacked in another. To make the matter more complicated, however, there can often be the added anxiety that the projected paranoia may be put back into oneself by the other person. A certain degree of defensive action against the projected paranoia coming home to roost must therefore be undertaken.

Investing someone else with part of your personal characteristics in this way makes him/her a more powerful figure. This can increase the possibility of attacking the recipient of the paranoia in order to keep it at bay. This risk is greatly increased by disinhibiting influences such as drugs, alcohol or other mental disturbance.

Displacement is also a form of self-protection by ridding oneself of part of an internal conflict — but in this case the conflict is 'displaced' onto somebody who is considered to be of lesser importance. The classical example is of frustrations at work resulting in a display of petulance towards the family pet on returning home.

The aim of displacement is again to make an apparently insoluble personal problem more controllable by limiting the amount of anxiety or conscious thought that one has to give to the issue. There is, however, an increased risk of violent behaviour — along the lines of 'acting out' as described earlier.

Processes Associated with Violence in Drug and Alcohol Misuse

Probably the commonest process is the use of instrumental violence and aggression to extort money or goods in order to buy further drugs or alcohol — as in a lot of street crime and property offences. They can also sometimes be used to supply 'dutch courage' to someone who has already planned to either commit a specific offence or place himself in a position of general risk for offending. There is a tendency to stop looking for other levels of explanation once the involvement of drugs or alcohol in an offence has become clear. It is frequently felt that there is a self-evident relationship between drugs, alcohol and violence, and increased disinhibition or misinterpretation of social situations as a result of substance misuse is likely to be the mechanism at work.

It is true that about 50% of people who commit homicide and about 50% of victims of homicide have been drinking during the period leading up to the killing. What is not so clear, however, is the nature of the relationship between the taking of the alcohol and the subsequent violence. In contrast, it does seem clear that the behavioural effects of the alcohol partly depend on pre-existing mood and mental state and partly on the social environment in which the alcohol is taken.

Pathological Intoxication

Although a link between alcohol and violence is well known, a small number of homicides carried out under the influence of alcohol impress observers as being the result of some process additional to that of ordinary drunkenness. The level of violence shown in the attack may be disproportionately great for the amount of alcohol consumed. The attack may also show an intensity and furore which may be outside the person's normal character and may not be explicable in terms of personality-based over-controlled hostility. The nature of the event makes these homicides difficult to investigate. There is a suggestion, however, that they are associated with a process of hypoglycaemia (low blood sugar) resulting from the sudden ingestion of a relatively marked amount of alcohol. This, in turn, leads to specific stimulation of the limbic system of the brain which may then result in an act of violence.

Case Study. A 16 year-old boy of industrious and stable character went out with friends to celebrate favourable examination results. He was not experienced in drinking but drank a moderate quantity of alcohol. This was sufficient to produce intoxication, although he was not considered to be greatly drunk. He became separated from his party and wandered around town on his own in a slightly disorientated state. He then ran at, sexually assaulted and savagely killed a young woman who was just finishing work for the evening. She was a complete stranger to him. He acknowledged his involvement in the attack but had amnesia for much of the event.

Detailed investigation suggested that he had some symptoms associated with hypoglycaemia shortly before the attack. These had followed consumption of alcohol. The reconstruction was conjectural but the killing appeared to be associated with 'pathological' rather than 'ordinary' intoxication.

Psychotic Type Processes

A substantial proportion of regular heavy drinkers experience psychotic-type symptoms at one time or another. In addition, drugs such as amphetamines, heroin and cannabis in prolonged heavy usage can produce most of the symptoms of schizophrenia. In these circumstances the drug user is susceptible to the same processes that may result in violence in psychotically ill patients.

Case Study. A 19 year-old single man was a regular heavy user of intravenous heroin. He had a brother who was also an addict and they often took their drugs together. During one such shared drug-taking episode, he believed himself to be under attack from animals and acted to defend himself. When the effects of the drugs had worn off, he discovered his brother's body lying near him. He had attacked, kicked and strangled him whilst suffering hallucinations as a result of the drug taking. He had a recollection of attacking threatening beasts, but no recollection of assaulting his brother.

Altered Impulsivity Associated with Chronic Use

There is a relationship between repeated offending and habitual drunkenness, although the offences tend to be of the public disorder type and, where there is violence, it tends to be disorganized, reactive and sporadic.

CONCLUSION

Behavioural details from crime scenes, reconstructed crime activity and witness accounts can offer an additional perspective to forensic information gathered by traditional investigative methods. This behavioural information can often provide insights into the thinking patterns and personal habits of offenders that extend beyond the limits of the offence itself. The offender's focus of interest, the type of relationship that he makes with the victim, the criteria by which he chooses the circumstances of the offence, the amount of planning he engages in and the risks he is willing to run, all help to build up a picture of the offender's mental world. This, in turn, can provide useful insights into his likely motivations, his personal needs, his lifestyle and his past history. The professional who considers these issues is more likely to understand the contexts within which the offender commits the offence. This broad, contextual information can help generate, or support, particular lines of enquiry during investigations. This type of information can be particularly useful, for instance, where linked series of offences are being investigated, where the victim may be a stranger to the offender, or where an offence seems bizarre and inexplicable.

Clinical investigative analysis, as an adjunct to investigation, is still in its infancy. Nevertheless, even in its present form, it can add a different type of understanding to a case. In turn, this somewhat more unusual perspective to a case can be of great assistance to investigators. The purpose of this chapter has been to illustrate, through case examples, how developmental and clinical influences can shape and form offending behaviour. It is hoped that an awareness of the role of such influences in certain offences will allow enquiry teams to make more informed decisions about the type of cases which would gain most from consultations with forensic psychologists and psychiatrists.

SUGGESTED FURTHER READING

The Anatomy of Human Destructiveness by Erich Fromm, published by Penguin, Harmondsworth (originally in 1973). This book offers an excellent introduction to informed discussion about human violence, including the relationship between cruelty, sexual need and power.

Sexual Homicide: Patterns and Motives by R. Ressler, A. Burgess & J. Douglas, published by Lexington Books, New York, 1988. The book is based on a study of 36 convicted serial murderers. Discusses concepts not covered in this chapter, including those related to 'organized' and 'disorganized' sexual offences.

Practical Aspects of Rape Investigation 2nd edn by R. Hazelwood & A.W. Burgess, published by CRC Press, Boca Raton, FL, 1995. The rape classification developed by Groth, Prentky and Knight, illustrated in this chapter, is fully described in this book.

Crimes of Violence by Mentally Abnormal Offenders: A Psychiatric and Epidemiological Study in the Federal German Republic, by H. Hafner & W. Boker, published in translation by Cambridge University Press, 1982. The book is based on a study of all the 533 men and women in the Federal German Republic who were detained in hospital as being mentally abnormal after committing homicide or serious violence between 1955 and 1964.

Seminars in Practical Forensic Psychiatry, edited by D. Chiswick and R. Cope, published by Royal College of Psychiatrists, London, 1995. There are two chapters on the relationship between crime and mental disorder as well as a chapter on the topic of dangerousness.

Homicide — A Psychiatric Perspective, by C. Malmquist, published by American Psychiatric Press Inc, Washington, DC, 1996. This is based on one psychiatrist's professional experience of examining over 500 people who have committed homicide.

CHAPTER 3

The Contribution of Personality Theories to Psychological Profiling

Julian C.W. Boon

INTRODUCTION

This chapter discusses the ways in which personality theories can be applied to the psychological profiling of criminal offenders and their behaviour. It begins with a brief outline of what personality theories are and what they attempt to achieve in the context of psychology. Thereafter, the focus will shift to presenting one possible explanation of personality theoretics as a whole, with particular reference being placed on the wide-ranging ideas which have been advanced over the years. To clarify how these theories can be applied to operational profiling, a number of case studies (from which any identifying features have been removed) will be presented. Every attempt has been made to minimize the use of jargon and to avoid discussion of scientific and epistemological issues of psychological profiling (for a more in-depth discussion of this topic, see Boon, 1995, in press).

PERSONALITY THEORIES — THEIR NATURE AND THEIR AIMS

The term 'personality' has bedevilled straightforward definition. However, most theorists would agree that there has been a recognition of something understood to be personality for centuries — indeed, since the time of Hippocrates (4–3 BC). Kernel, consensual elements of descriptions of personality are (a) relatively enduring characteristics of individuals over time and space, (b) characteristics which in their entirety are unique to the individual, and (c) the characteristics concerned being reflected in individuals' thought patterns, attitudes and behaviour. Personality theories and their contingent research attempt, to varying degrees, to advance an account of these issues in terms of their causative factors. Different theories come from different basic orientations and provide alternative, though not necessarily mutually exclusive, explanations of personality. Before moving on to provide an account of the process of applying personality theoretics to operational, psychological profiling, it is first necessary to expand on this point and explain how such co-existence of theories is not only possible but desirable.

Readers unfamiliar with science and psychology may be surprised to learn that psychologists have advanced literally scores of different theories in their attempts to provide scientific accounts of human personality. It may also be puzzling to the reader to understand why no single theory has emerged from the myriad of those available as being the 'correct' one for understanding personality. Before being able to apply personality theory to psychological profiling, it is essential to understand how it is that so many different theories can continue to co-exist and why none of them can be considered in black and white terms as being 'right' or 'wrong' in explaining different aspects of personality.

The first point is that while there are many different theories, there are markedly fewer general orientations or frameworks from which they have been generated. Specifying an exact number of parent frameworks is difficult since it depends to some extent on the classificational criteria adopted, but most personality theories could be subsumed under five of them (though some theorists work with still more — see, for example, Reber, 1985). One possible anatomy of personality theoretics is described in Table 3.1. It presents five parent frameworks and gives examples of the theories generated from them. While an exposition of these different theories is beyond the scope of this chapter, there are a number of accessible introductory texts on the subject available for interested readers (e.g. Feshbach, Weiner & Bohart, 1996, Pervin, 1989, Schultz & Schultz, 1994).

It should be noted that the selection of these examples is intended to give a flavour of the diversity of theory that exists and is very far from being an exhaustive representation of the total available. In addition, it should be noted that some theories are hybrid in nature and do not readily fit into any one category. However, each parent framework represents a general orientation or perspective for understanding human personality. For example, learning theories tend to emphasize the importance of the environment in the formation and shaping of personality, while trait theories place emphasis on the importance of individual differences in people's physical make-up as being key factors in

Table 3.1 Generative frameworks — examples of specific theories.

Psychanalytic/ dynamic	Learning theory	Dispositional/ trait theory	Humanist/ cognitive	Alternative/ Eastern
Freud	Skinner	Allport	Maslow	Zen-Buddhism
Jung	Tolman	Murray	Rogers	Szasz
Adler	Dollard & Miller	Cattel	Kelly	Sartre
Horney	Bandura	Eysenck	May	Marx
Fromm	Rotter	McCrae & Costa		

determining personality. In contrast, existential/humanist and cognitive theories place most emphases on the role of phenomenological experience, individuals' abilities to make their own decisions, and free will. Different again are theories generated from a psychoanalytic perspective — the emphasis tending towards the integration of psychological forces, subceived (unconscious) motivation, and developmental influences. In addition, there are alternative theories of man which not everyone would class as being 'personality theories' *per se*, but which in certain circumstances (e.g. political terrorism, interacting with cults, etc.) can be invaluable tools for helping to understand the behavioural and thought patterns of offenders.

In view of the sheer diversity and range of the respective frameworks, it is clear that each is going to possess varying scope for providing an explanation of any given set of data. In essence, each profiling case is unique, presenting different details and patterns and thus making different demands and raising different questions. Accordingly, the task of the psychological profiler employing personality theoretics is to identify which framework and specific theory (or theories) will be most helpful in providing insight in the case concerned.

OVERVIEW OF THE PROCESS OF OPERATIONAL PSYCHOLOGICAL PROFILING AND THE USE OF PERSONALITY THEORY AND RESEARCH

The process of adopting and applying personality theories from a clinical perspective proceeds in the way outlined in Table 3.2. The process begins with the collation of as rich a data set as is possible, attempting to draw together everything relating to the crime(s), the victim(s), the crime scene(s), and the circumstances — each laid out in minute detail. From this basis, salient issues relating to the crime are identified and specified on a series of levels which are dependent on the unique details of the case and the questions raised by it. Usually one of the first tasks is to identify the crime type at a fundamental level and then move on to

Table 3.2. The psychological profiling process utilizing personality theories.

Collation of case details		Identification of salient issues/points		Framework/ theory selection		Application to unique case data
	→		→		→	
						↓
						Development of individual profile

be more specific about its character. For example, a given case may clearly appear to be one of murder but its specific characteristics, e.g. nature of weapons used, nature and extent of injuries, evidence of amount of time taken, etc., would each have to be specified.

With such preliminary conclusions in mind, the process can then move on to assess and weigh the case details and the contingent psychological concerns raised within the context of the identified crime type(s). In this way, the aim is to progressively refine the understanding of what has taken — or in some cases is currently taking — place. Having performed such analyses, the psychologist applying personality theory has then to address the dual tasks of (a) selecting which framework is best equipped to provide an insight into the crime(s), and (b) identifying which theory or cluster of theories and their associated research are likely to be of most use in accurately meeting the operational needs of the investigation.

Before moving on to illustrate this process with some case examples, it should be made clear that there is no suggestion being made that personality theories alone can in any sense 'solve' intractable cases. Rather they are seen as assisting in providing coherence and guidance in the process of prioritizing and evaluating the large quantities of case details, and in deepening insight into the nature of both the case and the offender(s).

PERSONALITY THEORIES — CASE ILLUSTRATIONS OF THE SELECTION AND APPLICATION PROCESS

In order to provide both breadth and depth to the illustrations, the case examples were chosen to highlight the contribution of different personality theories to a common core crime type, namely cases of extortion. The three cases discussed all come from Europe and have had all details of persons and places removed so as to prevent identification of the actual cases concerned. They have also been presented in a manner that will prevent any future staging or 'copycatting' by offenders reading the chapter. As will be apparent from the above, the process of operational profiling requires a very significant amount of professional time — at least 40 hours has been cited as a base rate (see Gudjonsson & Copson, 1997, Chapter 4 of the present Volume; Jackson, van den Eshof & de Kleuver, 1997, Chapter 7 of the present Volume) and not uncommonly can involve the noting and assessment of several hundreds of details. Given such high volumes of information, for the present purposes it is necessary to condense the description of the respective cases into the following sub-sections:

1   Initial summaries.
2   The rationale for the framework and theory selection.
3   The contingent implications for the development of a psychological profile.

In addition, each case will be accompanied by a table articulating 10 of the salient case details, some of the contingent inferences drawn in selecting the most helpful theory, and finally, some of the conclusions that were produced as a result of applying the particular theory. In this way it is hoped that, in spite of the loss of detail, the profiling process can still be effectively illustrated.

Extortion Case 1

Abstract

The head offices of more than 250 top companies around Europe were in receipt of terrorist threats in relation to menacing extortion demands. The many communications which were sent via untraceable faxes and letters to the senior company figures and various government and media organizations were very distinctive in nature. They purported to be sent from a self-styled 'Peoples' Court of Justice'. The group claimed to be a powerful, continentally-based paramilitary organization that had successfully infiltrated the target companies. The mission of the 'Court' was to make big business repay ill-gotten profits and the communications claimed that extreme retribution would be exacted were the demands not to be met on time, and in full. The nature of the communications was overtly superior in tone (both intellectually and morally), unquestioningly self-righteous and uncompromising. In addition, their content was heavily laced with references to the retribution that would be inflicted on behalf of the oppressed and dispossessed of the world, the inferiority (mental and social) of the figures being attacked, and the omnipotence of the perpetrators' organization. The extortion demands required the companies to make large and secret donations to illegal, fringe causes and paramilitary political organizations of political contra-persuasion. The substantive threats had not been carried out at the time of soliciting assistance from forensic psychology but there had been 'punitive reminders'. These informed the companies that, as a result of their non-compliance with the previous demands, their donations would now be raised X-fold. What might otherwise have been dismissed as a relatively harmless prank was elevated in terms of operational significance when the companies involved received vicious poison attacks.

The targeted companies together with the police investigating the case were searching for answers to three questions:

1   Would the substantive threats be carried out?
2   How many offenders were involved?
3   Were there any clues available in the communications that could lead to the development of psychological profile(s)?

Having gathered as much of the data relating to the case as possible, the key psychological issues which emerged as worthy of focus concerned: the quality and structure of the terrorist plan; the political, moral and intellectual stance of the perpetrator(s); and the nature of their 'self–other' orientation. Analyses of the plan suggested it to be over-ambitious, naive in conception relative to the elaborateness of its design and, in terms of thoroughness, not commensurate with the self-acclaimed experience and power of its perpetrator(s). The portrayal of invincibility and exclusive, intellectual and moral superiority revealed by the perpetrator(s) was interpreted as being rooted in the need for status enhancement. This would reflect: (a) feelings of disgruntlement with their position in life; (b) an unconscious denial of personal responsibility for having that position; (c) the likely belief that others had thwarted their progress. It was also concluded that, in addition to distorting their own self-image through self-aggrandisement, the perpetrator(s) also held inverse, negative, distorted perceptions of others.

Rationale for Framework and Theory Selection

A consideration of these main elements suggested that, in view of the evidence of the generality of the misperception of reality, a psychodynamic framework would be most likely to generate a theory that would be most germane to the case. With the theoretical orientation established, a further evaluation of the core issues such as superiority, inferiority and goal frustration suggested that Adlerian theory (Adler, 1925) and the research developed by this school over the subsequent decades would be the most effective for offering further insight into the case, the perpetrator(s), the underlying motivation, the thought processes involved, and the contingent behaviour.

Adlerian theory would hold that each individual sets healthy and/or unhealthy goals throughout his/her life and that these goals, unhealthy or otherwise, would reflect life experiences and life concerns as they appear in any given individual's perceptual field. Healthy goals are seen as those that are potentially attainable but carry a bona fide degree of risk of failure, and thus of potential damage to the ego. By contrast, unhealthy goal setting is characterized by individuals choosing to aim either too low, thus ensuring complete certainty of success, or too high, thus ensuring the near complete certainty of failure. In either event, the ego is seen as unrealistically protecting itself by ensuring the outcome of a set goal with success or *a priori* justifiable failure. It is important to state, too, that Adlerian theory would hold that unhealthy goal setting and the reasons for it are, at best, on the periphery of awareness of the afflicted individual and may even be completely unconscious.

The Application of the Theory

The first step in applying the theory is to instantiate the case details previously identified as being salient to the putative psychological orientation of the offender. In this instance, the latter was thought to be that the perpetrator(s) had large-scale subceived (pre-conscious) concerns with issues of inferiority, with the contingent psychological tension being dealt with by unhealthy goal setting. The theory would suggest that this would be characterized by: (a) the minimization, denial and spoiling of the achievements of others — the specific targets would represent those persons of companies whom the perpetrator(s) perceive as thwarting their particular life concerns and goals; (b) over-statement and self-elevation in the portrayal of self-worth — in this particular case, the recurrent themes of annoyance at senior management figures obtaining recognition in terms of status, adulation and money suggested that the perpetrator(s) worked as employees of a large company which they felt did not recognize their worth. In addition, the championing of causes of the dispossessed not only provides a focal vehicle for the justification of their actions in terms of some form of crusade, but also allows us to gain insight into their personal concerns in goal setting and life perception.

As well as the general stance of the perpetrator(s) in the communication, there were also clues in terms of the nature of the would-be beneficiaries. These were all anti-establishment and, with one exception, contradictory in their political aims. From psychoanalytic theory, it would be predicted that the selection of the major contradictory organizations was made to: (a) cause maximum disruption to the establishment by, in effect, promoting civil unrest; (b) pave the way for the perpetrator(s) to take over by operating a divide and rule policy and, most importantly; (c) to feed the ego(s) of the perpetrator(s) by affirming that they were active at an international level. The atypical beneficiary — an obscure, extreme animal rights group which was comparatively parochial and not directly contrary to the aims of the other causes selected — was of special interest. The theory would predict that this was the one that was of particular relevance to the life and goals of the perpetrator(s). Taking the prevailing themes of animal rights, big business, oppression, company infiltration and reflecting these back on to the theoretical predictions regarding the life concerns of the perpetrator(s), a picture of the perpetrator(s) lifestyle emerges. This is depicted in Figure 3.1.

With regard to the police question as to whether the terrorist threats were coming from one person acting alone or from more than one offender (as claimed), the theory would predict the former, while common sense would predict the latter. Specifically, the sheer scale of the number of communications and the number of companies receiving threats militated against there being only one offender. However, during timed trials conducted to test whether one lone person could have sent the communications, it emerged that given sufficient commitment to the task it would be possible to achieve. The theory would not only predict that this perpetrator was highly committed to pursuing the plan, but also that he/she would be likely to be acting alone anyway. The rationale for this prediction was that the sheer scale and centrality of the attempts to compensate for inferiority would mean a corresponding reluctance either to trust any other individual to be part of the illusory inner circle, or to share information with them relating to the much cherished master plan. On the other hand, the theory would be consistent with the involvement of subordinates assisting at a purely menial level (e.g. posting letters). Such individuals would neither represent a threat to the perpetrator nor be regarded as any more than an unquestioning foot-soldier in the 'organization'.

From the ten salient case details (SCDs) included in Figure 3.1, it can be seen that applying a psychoanalytic theory provided a number of important suppositions:

1   Six lead to the suggestion that the perpetrator was amateur.
2   Eight suggest he was acting alone.
3   Seven propose that he would not carry out the full threats against the companies but would instead increase the demands and carry

POLICE QUESTIONS: a. Is this carried out by a bona fide terrorist group or amateur(s)?
b. Is there one or are there more perpetrators?
c. Will they carry out threats if non-cooperation policy adopted?
d. Any clues as to personal history?
e. Any information as to location?

CASE APPRAISAL		IDENTIFICATION OF FRAMEWORK/THEORY		APPLICATION OF THEORY TO CASE	
Salient case details (SCDs)	Preliminary Inferences	Framework	Theory	Suggested answers to police questions	Additional information suggested by theory
1. Very large-scale campaign	Over-ambitious and some naivety			a – Amateur c – No, but will give reminding gestures d – Yes	Non-social loner in character Regarded as strange/weird by peers
2. Communications and plan flawed in terms of inconsistencies	Thought disorder and/or distortion			a – Amateur b – One c – As above d – Yes e – Yes	Living with parents or alone Not in a sexual relationship
3. Professed omnipotence of perpetrating organization	Issues of inferiority relevant	P S Y C H O A N A L Y T I C	A D L E R I A N	a – Amateur b – One c – As above d – Yes	Above average intelligence Considers self very much above
4. Intense concern with secrecy	Issues of personal insecurity relevant			b – One d – Yes	average intelligence and that is not recognized by others
5. Intense concern and complete confidence in moral self-righteousness	Evidence of reality distortion			b – One c – As above d – Yes	In low-level manual or clerical job Underachiever
6. Frequency of statement of own high IQ	As for SCDs 2, 4 and 5			a – Amateur b – One d – Yes	Works for large company connected with animals and
7. Frequency of denigration of others who have succeeded	As for SCDs 3, 4 and 5			b – One c – Yes d – Yes	industry Late teens/early twenties
8. Vicious reminder attacks (cf: overall plan)	As for SCD2, plus evidence that crusade is for self not others			a – Amateur b – One c – As above d – Yes	Into fantasy games, especially solitary computer types (cf: interactive games
9. Quasi-altruistic stance re: 'oppressed'	As for SCD8			a – Amateur b – One c – As for c's above d – Yes e – Yes	like 'Dungeons & Dragons') Will neither deny nor confirm involvement if apprehended
10. Intense concern with the meting out of justice	As for SCD8, plus perpetrator(s) have sense of injustice against selves			d – Yes e – Yes	

Figure 3.1. Case 1 — Terrorist extortion.

out smaller-scale attacks in attempts to bolster his self-perception of power.

4   All ten provided clues as to his personal history and lifestyle.

5   Two gave indications as to where he may work.

Extortion Case 2

Abstract

A large European supermarket chain was in receipt of demands for cash from an anonymous source. Initially, senior personnel were informed by the perpetrators that the food products of a major super-market chain would be contaminated if (a) their demand for a sum equivalent to £25 000 in used notes was not made in full, and (b) if the instructed means of delivery were not complied with to the exact detail. In addition, the targeted supermarket group was informed that only one person was to be involved in handing over the money and that any police involvement was absolutely forbidden. The perpetrators also claimed to have sufficient man-power and technical expertise to effect any counter-surveillance measures necessary to foil police or security staff interference. As is usual in such cases, the directions involved fol-lowing a chain of complicated instructions before the final drop was to be made. All the perpetrators revealed by way of description of the final point in the instructional chain was that it was unique in nature, and once used could not be used again. This point was clearly made in order to underline the 'one-off' nature of the plan and the victim's contingent invulnerability to further demands.

From the analyses of the SCDs, it was concluded that the plan, its coherence together with its realizability, reflected the fact that the offenders were both high in intelligence and not subject to distortions in the perception of reality. It was also clear that immense care had been taken to implement the plan and that the perpetrators showed a high level of impermeability to any attempts made by the authorities to put pressure on them. The perpetrators neither surrendered control during the communications nor permitted any deviation from their plan. They were the ones who set and enforced the agenda for action. This agenda was supported by a system of communication that was both technically advanced and all but untraceable. In terms of the content of the com-munications, at no point did the perpetrators give any reason for their demands nor did they overtly volunteer any information about them-selves. The communications were businesslike and there was a marked absence of any affective tone such as anger, anxiousness or desperation.

As the extortion progressed, the perpetrators claimed to have evi-dence that the police had become involved (which was true) and that any further deviation from the specified orders would result in a cessation of contact and the implementation of the threatened campaign of contamination.

Rationale for Framework and Theory Selection

Among the key points which determined the choice of the framework to be adopted for this case were: (a) the clarity of the planning; (b) the meticulousness of the execution of the plan; (c) the near-complete absence of affective tone; and (d) the strong focus on actions pertaining to personal gain without the need for justification. Collectively, the absence of human concerns such as motivation, self-expression and affect suggested that the use of a learning theory would be the most appropriate way of understanding the offenders' behaviour. Furthermore, the complex yet not over-ambitious nature of the plan (cf. Case 1), its coherence in structure, and its very careful design, which incorporated sophisticated counter-measures to surveillance attempts, made it clear that a cognitive level of explanation should also be considered. The account which was judged to be most suitable for this particular case was a cognitive–social learning theory, such as that proposed by Albert Bandura.

In Bandura's (1962, 1976, 1989) theory, the behaviour of the individual is understood in terms of 'reciprocal determinism'. Specifically, the individual is seen as operating amid three interlocking and interactive factors, namely behaviour, person and environment. The person is not envisaged as an executive control agent but rather as a 'self-system' capable of understanding the surrounding environment and reacting and shaping behaviour on the basis of past learning, current perceptions and future expectations. In addition, the theory lays particular emphasis on the importance of a particular type of learning, namely that of modelling or learning by watching and imitating others. In this way, people vicariously educate their self-systems and shape their behaviour towards positive stimuli and away from negative stimuli.

Although readers may find the term and concept of *reciprocal determinism* jargonistic and/or difficult, in order to properly follow why the theory was selected for Case 2, it is very important to have a clear understanding of the fundamental tenets, such as the interlocking factors, modelling processes and contingent effects on shaping behaviour. Perhaps the best way to help illustrate this is to take an everyday example of television viewing discussed by Bandura:

'... personal preferences influence when and which programs, from among the available alternatives, individuals choose to watch on television. Although the potential televised environment is identical for all viewers the actual televised environment that impinges on given individuals depends on what they select to watch. Through their viewing behaviour, they partly shape the nature of the future televised environment. Because production costs and commercial requirements also determine what people are shown, the options provided in the televised environment partly shape the viewers' preferences. Here all three factors – viewer preferences, viewing behaviour, and televised offerings – reciprocally affect each other' (Bandura, 1978, p. 346).

For the purposes of understanding the relevance of the theory to Case 2, the crucial points to grasp are that the same stimuli can have different effects on different individuals and that the behaviour is seen as being shaped by both the environment (as personally or vicariously experienced), and the person's own history of reactions, preferences, etc.

The Application of the Theory

In applying the cognitive–learning theory to Case 2, the first step was to specify the known behavioural variables of the reciprocal determinism model and attempt to work outwards to infer characteristics of the environmental and person variables. In terms of the offenders' behaviour it is clear that they: (a) are prepared to engage in a very serious crime; (b) show clear signs of forensic awareness; (c) have the mental ability to prepare and enact a viable and coherent plan; (d) do not show signs of affective engagement; and (e) have no or little fear even when they believe the police to be actively involved. Among the environmental variables which are likely to facilitate such behavioural characteristics can be included an upbringing in which criminal activity is the norm, a current association with the criminal fraternity and, in the case in question, specialist knowledge of both the content and operation of the businesses involved. In terms of the implied person variables, the primary suggestions from the model are that the offenders have local knowledge, are of high intelligence and have a criminal record (see Figure 3.2).

Apart from these primary indicators, the theory also offers other suggestions. For example, in relation to the behavioural variables of forensic awareness, lack of fear of the police, and the viability of the plan, it is likely that to achieve success more than one offender is probably involved. Furthermore, the first two variables suggest a high likelihood of criminal antecedents although, in view of the forensic awareness variable, not necessarily in crimes of extortion: collectively, the behavioural variables do not indicate that the offenders believe it likely that they would be considered as suspects. The offenders' claim that this was a 'one-off' offence, using a method that could only be used once, was therefore considered to be valid. It seemed likely that a unique opportu-

POLICE QUESTIONS: a. Is this carried out by experienced criminal(s) or amateur(s)?
b. Is there one or are there more perpetrators?
c. Will they carry out threats if non-cooperation policy adopted?
d. Any clues as to personal history?
e. Any information as to location?

CASE APPRAISAL		IDENTIFICATION OF FRAMEWORK/THEORY		APPLICATION OF THEORY TO CASE	
Salient case details (SCDs)	Preliminary inferences	Framework	Theory	Suggested answers to police questions	Additional information suggested by theory
1. Feasible fundamental demands	Non-thought disordered or distorted	LEARNING THEORIES	COGNITIVE LEARNING THEORY	a – Criminal d – Yes e – Yes	Will adopt position of exteme caution
2. Untraceable and technically sophisticated means of communication	Sophisticated and forensically aware			a – Criminal d – Yes e – Yes	Will be likely to seek dummy runs to learn opposition tactics
3. Meticulous novel and near foolproof plan	Intelligent and careful construction			a – Criminal b – Plural c – Yes d – Yes e – Yes	Will have gained novel idea for eluding detection from another case
4. High level of clarity in instructions	As for SCDs 1 and 3			e – Yes	Will have specialist knowledge of location either through work or having lived nearby
5. Highly vulnerable target	As for SCDs 1, 2 and 3			a – Criminal b – Plural d – Yes e – Yes	Will have been raised in criminal community
6. Highly professional overtly anti-criminal conduit	Very high confidence and low fear levels			a – Criminal b – Plural c – Yes d – Yes	Will carry out threats in non-cooperation
7. No personal information volunteered	–		(e.g. BANDURA)	a – Criminal b – Plural d – Yes	Will have history of robbery, fraud and acquisitive offences
8. Absence of affective tone	–			a – Criminal b – Plural d – Yes	If apprehended will not comment on any aspect relating to offences
9. No rationale for attack supplied	–			a – Criminal b – Plural d – Yes	
10. No 'reminder threats'	–			a – Criminal b – Yes d – Yes	

Figure 3.2. Case 2 — Extortion attempt against supermarket chain.

nity had presented itself to them. This in turn suggests local knowledge, particularly in relation to the perceived level of risk analysis. For example, if the local police were not in a position, *in the perpetrators' view*, to forecast the means that would be used to collect and make off with the cash, then that knowledge must be very specialized indeed. Secondly, if, again *in the perpetrators' view,* the plan is foolproof, they could be expected to carry out their contamination threats and to renew their demands at some later date, probably increasing their value.

The theory also suggests other ways of learning through observation and modelling. For instance, it is possible that the plan was adapted from another case. The reason for this hypothesis is that the behavioural variables are clearly indicative of a need for certainty in outcome and thus of reliance on a previous example of a successful crime. In addition, the offenders are more likely than not to carry out several dry runs to check the feasibility of their plans and to consider the possible counter-surveillance techniques that could be used against them.

Although only a brief overview of the case has been given, it should provide some insight into the way an appropriately adopted theory can be applied to case details, as well as how it can be used to develop answers to police questions and allow statements about the offenders, and their past, present and future behaviour to be inferred. In this case, the application of a learning theory to the ten SCDs detailed in Figure 3.2 accurately provided:

1 Nine suggestions that the offenders were hardened criminals.
2 Seven indicators that a team was operating.
3 Two suggestions that they would if necessary carry out their threats.
4 Nine sources of information which allowed inferences about their personal history to be made.
5 Three cues relating to their familiarity with the local venue selected as dropping off point.

Extortion case 3

Abstract

A provincial, medium-sized supermarket received a demand for £42 000 in cash from an individual claiming to be suffering from HIV and wishing to make provision for his family. As with Case 2, the threat was one of contaminating goods, although in this case the source would be a personally related contaminant of HIV-infected semen. The letters were hand-written and were addressed to the store manager. They contained large amounts of personal statements, together with expressions of regret for having to take such action but stated that they were the result of personal desperation, devastation and despair. Other communications came in the form of potentially traceable telephone calls. These gave the clear impression that the male caller was reading from a prepared script and was extremely anxious and nervous. However, when prompted, he would, albeit reluctantly, be prepared to make *ad hoc* decisions. The plan collapsed when the perpetrator aborted his extortion attempt at the collection phase. Unlike Cases 1 and 2, the perpetrator has not as yet been identified.

Rationale for Framework and Theory Selection

In this case the SCDs (see Figure 3.3) strongly suggested that there was a bona fide element to the perpetrator's claims about himself. He was under a great deal of stress and the behaviour he was demonstrating appeared to be out of character. The framework that was considered to be most appropriate for this case was that of an existential/humanist perspective. Such a framework is specifically geared to personal perspectives of the world and to the understanding of human qualities such as love, despair and anger. The particular theory thought to be the most appropriate was that of Carl Rogers (1961, 1963, 1980). This theory suggests that individuals require a free and undistorted awareness of the world, themselves and others. Failure to have such an awareness, the theory suggests, will result in anxiety and the distortion and denial of reality — all aspects which were resonant with the SCDs of the case. In addition, the theory suggests that complex and/or traumatic life events can force a wedge between self and reality which can lead to people experiencing distress and to thinking and behaving in ways which are at odds or out of character.

The Application of the Theory

Of the three cases presented, this one is probably the best match with people's perceptions of 'common-sense' reality. One of the reasons for this is that Rogerian theory, unlike the psychoanalytic or learning theories, holds that people as humans have the capacity for self-understanding.

The theory is able to suggest viable answers to the police questions in this case and also to predict characteristics of the offender (see Figure 3.3). For example, the theory would suggest that the anxiety apparent in the offender's behaviour was not simply the product of a life-stressor but also involved a mismatch between self as hitherto conceived of as a respectable citizen and self as a criminal. Furthermore, it would suggest that these feelings of anxiety would reach their peak when approaching

POLICE QUESTIONS: a. Amateur of experienced criminal?
                   b. Are one or more people involved?
                   c. Will the threat be carried out if thwarted
                   d. Will perpetrator have criminal history?
                   e. Will perpetrator live nearby?

CASE APPRAISAL		IDENTIFICATION OF FRAMEWORK/THEORY		APPLICATION OF THEORY TO CASE	
Salient case details (SCDs)	Preliminary Inferences	Framework	Theory	Suggested answers to police questions	Additional information suggested by theory
1. Modest specific sum of money demanded	For use to pay something in particular			a – Amateur b – One c – No d – No e – Yes	Knew target supermarket well Knew locality well through work and/or home
2. Difficult but potentially traceable communications	Would take risks	E X I S T E N T I A L	R O G E R I A N	a – Amateur d – No e – Yes	Hitherto respectable lifestyle
3. Forensic awareness but semi-meticulous planning	Stressed thinking (cf: disordered thinking)			a – Amateur c – No d – No e – Yes	Under pressing financial pressure not revealed to his family
4. Clear instructions but willingness to allow ad hoc arrangements	Stressed thinking and inexperience			a – Amateur b – One c – No d – No e – Yes	Would be highly likely not to go through with plan Would feel mixed guilty/desperate feelings towards actions
5. Medium vulnerable target	Others easier nearby			a – Amateur c – No	
6. Apologetic tone	Bona fide story			a – Amateur b – One c – No d – No e – Yes	Would be showing signs of sterss and absent-mindedness
7. Abundance of personal information	As for SCDs 2 and 6			a – Amateur b – One c – No d – No	Would be less socially orientated than usual Would admit offence readily if apprehended
8. Abundance of affective tone	As for SCDs 2, 3 and 6			a – Amateur b – One c – No d – No	Life stressor but possibly different from HIV e.g. redundancy
9. Abundance of rationale or extortion supplied	As for SCDs 1, 4 and 6			a – Amateur b – One c – No d – No	
10. Personally related contaminant	As for SCD 6			a – Amateur c – No d – No e – No	

Figure 3.3. Case 3 — Extortion attempt against single supermarket store.

the point of no return (i.e. in the collection phase of the plan). Given the already very high levels of anxiety displayed, this additional stress could well cause the offender to withdraw (cf. Case 2). The theory would further predict that the offender would be showing signs of rigidity in self-perception, be less outgoing than usual and tend to hold others responsible for his plight. There is also scope for the theory to encompass both the apparent intelligence of the offender and the high-risk plan that was being adopted — reflecting the symptoms of reality distortion and stressed thinking patterns. Since the theory will allow for the intelligence of the offender — and there is evidence of some forensic awareness even within this relatively high-risk plan — then it is entirely possible that the HIV information is a foil. It may have been advanced either to be congruent with the nature of the contamination and/or to divert police attention from another major life-stressor such as redundancy.

The SCDs showed an abundance of evidence of emotional disturbance, feelings of guilt and apology. Together with the anxiety evoked by being placed in an unfitting criminal mould, these features suggest that, if apprehended, the offender would readily admit to the offence. This is in contrast with what would be predicted by Adlerian theory for Case 1, where the offender would be unwilling to confirm or deny guilt, wishing neither to incriminate nor to relinquish his status of involvement with the offence, and cognitive–learning theory's prediction in Case 2 that the criminals' prior experience of similar situations would prevent any comments being made to any charge.

Although it has been argued that a Rogerian theory can help develop the SCDs for Case 3 in a coherent, accurate and potentially helpful way, unfortunately the perpetrator has not been found. Unlike the first two case examples, where many of the predictions were supported, the only one that could be confirmed for Case 3 was that the plan was aborted during the collection phase.

CONCLUSION

Careful selection among the available frameworks and theories of personality can help in the psychological profiling process by answering relevant police questions in ongoing investigations. However, nowhere is it suggested that personality theories alone can produce psychological profiles. Instead, the view that is adopted suggests that, in conjunction with existing research bases, personality theories can facilitate, and indeed have facilitated, the profile production process. In particular, the view expressed here is that each case data set is unique and must be treated as such when selecting and applying a particular theory or theories.

CHAPTER 4

The Role of the Expert in Criminal Investigation

Gisli H. Gudjonsson & Gary Copson

INTRODUCTION

'As the frontiers of knowledge, particularly scientific knowledge, have been pushed further and further out, the scope and development of expert evidence in the court has expanded dramatically' (Lord Taylor of Gosforth, 1994).

Lord Chief Justice Taylor's comment on the rapidly growing development of scientific knowledge and the increased scope of expert evidence is very pertinent to the growing role of experts in criminal investigations. The main objective of this chapter is to examine the extent that psychologists have a unique contribution to make in criminal investigations, particularly in relation to offender profiling; and how their specific contribution to profiling differs from that which they provide to criminal cases during the pre-trial, trial and sentencing phases of criminal proceedings.

An expert can be defined as a person who possesses an extensive skill or knowledge in a particular field. The role of the 'expert' in criminal investigations is to provide the police with a specialized skill or knowledge which is outside that of the ordinary police officer. Experts include those police officers who, having specialized in a particular area of police work, are themselves experts in a particular field, such as in the case of investigative interviewing or offender profiling.

In this chapter the focus will be on experts with specialized psychological knowledge which falls within the field of 'forensic psychology'. Haward (1981) defines forensic psychology as 'that branch of applied psychology which is concerned with the collection, examination and presentation of evidence for judicial purposes' (p. 21). The role of experts in criminal investigations falls within Haward's definition of forensic psychology. Their role in the investigative process may be instrumental in whether or not the case proceeds to court. On occasions they may be required to give evidence in court.

The contribution of psychologists to criminal investigations includes a number of different activities, such as advising the police about offender characteristics on the basis of the nature and circumstances of the offence, advising the police about interview strategy concerning a particular suspect, the memory enhancement of witnesses by such methods as hypnosis or the cognitive interview, and experts acting as an 'appropriate adult' in cases of mental disorder. Offender profiling is therefore only one of the contributions that experts make to criminal investigations.

This chapter is in two parts. The first part discusses the role of the expert within the broader framework of judicial proceedings and includes contributions to the investigative phase. The second focuses specifically on the role of the expert in cases of offender profiling.

THE ROLES OF THE PSYCHOLOGIST IN CRIMINAL CASES

There is limited information available about the role of English psychologists as experts in criminal cases. Some early experts believed that the role of the forensic psychologist had by far the greatest potential in relation to criminal investigations rather than in the courtroom (Connolly & McKellar, 1963; Cunningham, 1964). In contrast, an influential early forensic psychologist, Haward (1961), believed that psychologists had more to offer to the legal issues related to the pre-trial, trial and sentencing phases in the criminal courts. In his landmark book, *Forensic Psychology*, Haward (1981) describes the four roles that psychologists may fulfil when they assess cases in criminal proceedings. These are referred to by Haward as the *clinical, experimental, actuarial* and *advisory* roles. The specific role that psychologists fulfil will depend upon the issue they are asked to address.

The *clinical role* is most common and requires clinical training and experience. It overlaps considerably with the role fulfilled by forensic psychiatrists (Gudjonsson, 1984, 1985) and often involves the psychologist interviewing a client and carrying out psychometric testing (e.g. the administration of tests of intelligence, neuropsychological functioning, personality, mental state) and analysing behavioural data (Gudjonsson, 1985, 1994a; Haward, 1981). The nature of the assessment depends on the types of instruction from the referral agent and the type of problem being assessed. Informants are sometimes interviewed in order to obtain further information or corroboration.

In the *experimental role* psychologists either give evidence about general research findings (e.g. problems with eyewitness testimony) or carry out specific experiments that are relevant to the individual case. With regard to the latter, psychologists may perform a unique function which is typically outside the expertise of forensic psychiatrists. Human behaviour is studied by experimentation rather than by a clinical interview. The former requires the ability and knowledge to apply psychological principles and techniques to the individual case. This sometimes involves devising unique experiments relevant to the legal issues in the case (Gudjonsson & Sartory, 1983; Haward, 1981).

In the *actuarial role* the psychologist applies statistical probabilities to behavioural data. This role is also used by statisticians and other scientists when interpreting observational and behavioural data (Robertson & Vignaux, 1995). The types of probability and observational data sometimes analysed by psychologists are discussed by Haward (1981).

In the *advisory role* psychologists may advise counsel about what questions to ask when cross-examining psychologists who are testifying for the other side. Court reports are nowadays increasingly being reviewed by an expert for the opposing side who may have carefully studied the psychological report and carried out his/her own assessment of the defendant (Gudjonsson, 1996a).

The Contribution of Psychology to Court Proceedings

In the UK, criminal proceedings involve three distinct stages: *Pre-trial*, *trial* and *sentencing*. Each stage consists of different legal issues. It is important that forensic psychologists are familiar with the relevant legal concepts and issues relevant at each stage.

The defendant's fitness to plead and fitness to stand trial are sometimes raised at the pre-trial stage. This occurs when the defendant's physical or mental state at the time of the trial is likely to interfere with the due process of the law (i.e. the defendant may not have a fair trial if the case proceeds). The ability of the defendant to give adequate instructions to his/her lawyers, to understand the charge against him/her, to distinguish between a plea of guilty and not guilty, and to follow the proceedings in court are the main legal issues to be decided upon at the pre-trial stage. The fitness to plead and stand trial issues are generally only raised in serious cases in the UK because of their legal and clinical significance (Chiswick, 1990).

One of the main problems for forensic psychiatrists and psychologists is that the legal constructs of fitness criteria are defined and described unsatisfactorily in case law. This means that the expert may find it difficult to evaluate the defendant's vulnerabilities within the context of the legal criteria. As a result, the psychological or psychiatric evaluation is often going to be peripherally related to the legal criteria (Grisso, 1986).

In the UK, psychiatrists are mainly involved at the pre-trial stage of court proceedings. However, in recent years, psychologists are increasingly being instructed by defence lawyers to carry out a psychological assessment on these cases because it provides the court with an objective and standardized assessment of the defendant's functional deficits. This may involve an assessment of the defendant's intellectual and neuropsychological status, as well as an assessment of problems related to anxiety and depression (Gudjonsson, 1994a).

In English Law, a criminal offence consists of a number of different elements which fall into two main categories, referred to as *actus reus* and *mens rea*. The former consists of elements which are directly associated with the criminal act itself, whereas the latter generally focuses on the mental state of the defendant. During the *actus reus* stage the crown has to prove (a) that a criminal offence was committed, and (b) that the defendant committed it. *Mens rea* issues focus on the state of mind of the accused at the time of the alleged offence and its blameworthiness (e.g. whether the offence was committed either recklessly or intentionally).

The criteria for establishing *mens rea* are dependent upon the nature of the offence because each offence is defined separately in law and there are no standard criteria for defining *mens rea* across different offences. Some offences do not require an element of *mens rea* for the defendant to be convicted (i.e. they are offences of 'strict liability' and the crown only has to prove *actus reus*). In such cases, a mental condition relevant to *mens rea* can be used as mitigation at the sentencing stage.

Psychologists in the UK are often instructed to prepare court reports which are relevant to both *actus reus* and *mens rea* issues and their involvement in such cases is expanding (Gudjonsson, 1992, 1996a). The contribution of clinical psychologists to *mens rea* issues complements that of their psychiatrist colleagues (Gudjonsson, 1984). This includes issues relevant to 'abnormality of mind' and diminished responsibility in cases of homicide and the question of intent in cases of theft.

Sentencing takes place after the defendant has been found guilty of the offence. Various sentencing options are available, depending on the nature of the offence and the circumstances of the case. These include a financial penalty, probation, community service orders, and a prison sentence. In the case of minor offences, a fine is the most common sentence. In more serious cases the defendant may be sentenced to prison or given up to 240 hours of community service (i.e. given some tasks to do in the local community under close supervision).

Psychologists are commonly being asked to provide reports about factors which are relevant to mitigation and sentencing (Gudjonsson, 1996a). This may involve offering an opinion about treatment options and prognosis. The recommendation may involve offering treatment to persons convicted of sexual offences (Clare, 1993) and compulsive shoplifting (Gudjonsson, 1987).

Psychologists as Experts in the United Kingdom

Most forensic psychologists in the UK are in full-time employment. Accordingly, their private medico-legal work has to fit around their contractual duties. This is also a common problem for other experts, such as doctors (The Law Society, 1996).

There have been three surveys conducted for the British Psychological Society into 'psychological evidence in court' (Castell, 1966; Gudjonsson, 1985, 1996a). An important finding in the most recent survey was that 27% of the psychologists reported that they had been asked by the referral agent to alter their report in order to make it more favourable. Out of those, 56% reported that they had complied with such a request. On occasions this involved deleting unfavourable material or opinions from the report. Gudjonsson (1994b) has discussed the ethical and professional issues involved in producing compromised expert reports. Similarly, Lord Taylor (1994) argues that the two most important qualities of an expert witness are clarity and integrity.

The three British Psychological Society surveys do not provide any information about the role of psychologists in police investigations. The only study that provides detailed information about this role of the forensic psychologist is a recently published paper by Gudjonsson (1996b). Gudjonsson discusses 450 forensic cases he had worked on between 1980 and 1992. The majority ($N = 251$) of the cases involved cases of disputed confessions which had been referred either by the defence or the prosecution. As far as the investigative phase was concerned, Gudjonsson had worked on nine offender profiling cases, 12 cases where he advised the police on interview strategy, and in four cases Gudjonsson had acted as an 'appropriate adult' at police stations in accordance with the Police and Criminal Evidence Act (PACE) (Home Office, 1985) and its Codes of Practice (Home Office, 1991).

Poor Expert Evidence

No systematic research has been conducted into the quality of experts' reports and oral evidence in court. Gudjonsson (1993) argues that poor psychological evidence falls into two overlapping categories: (a) evidence which fails to inform, and (b) evidence which is either misleading or incorrect. On occasions, poor expert evidence may result in a miscarriage of justice. There are a number of reasons for poor expert evidence. As far as psychology is concerned, Gudjonsson (1993) lists the main reasons under the following headings:

1 Lack of knowledge, skill and experience.
2 Lack of preparation and thoroughness.
3 Inappropriate use of psychological tests or misinterpretation of results.
4 Eagerness to please the referral agent.

Criminal cases in the UK are referred to the expert by either the defence or prosecution rather than by the court. In respect to offender profiling, cases are almost always referred by the police. When instructed by one side, the expert may be feel under pressure to seek and report findings which are favourable to the instructing side. If the findings are not favourable, the expert may be asked to alter the report to make it more favourable. This is common practice when experts prepare reports for the defence and it can mislead the court (Gudjonsson, 1996a). Lord Taylor (1994) makes the point that some experts are far too eager to please the referral agent and they may as a result deliberately give a misleading opinion to the court, or to the police in cases of offender profiling.

INTRODUCTION TO OFFENDER PROFILING

It has often been convenient for the news and entertainment media to treat offender profiling as though it were a readily identifiable and homogeneous entity with scientific status. This is not the case; profiling is neither a readily identifiable nor a homogeneous entity, and its status is properly regarded as a professional sideline not amounting to a true science. This second part of this chapter will show why.

There is no universally accepted definition of offender profiling and, as pointed out by critics and advocates alike, until recently there had never been an independent research study of either the substance or the validity of offender profiling (Boon & Davies, 1993; Campbell, 1976; Grubin, 1995; Oleson, 1996). One project combines the largest and most comprehensive questionnaire survey of police users of profiling advice with what is as yet the only analysis of an eclectic collection of operational profiling advice (*Coals to Newcastle?* (*CTN*) project)[1]. The project

---

[1] The project is a joint London Metropolitan Police and Home Office venture conducted with the backing of the Association of Chief Police Officers (ACPO).

is published in two parts; Part 1 was released in November 1995 (Copson, 1995), while Part 2 is due for release early in 1998 (Copson & Holloway, in preparation). Some of the key elements of that project will be discussed here. We will compare the contribution of profiling with that of mainstream forensic psychology in contributing to the process of investigating serious crimes and trying those charged with them in the criminal courts. This discussion will embrace the following questions:

1   Who are the profilers?
2   What are their qualifications?
3   What do they actually do?
4   How do they do it?
5   Why do they do it?
6   How successful are they?

Definitions

As defined for the purposes of the *CTN* study, 'offender profiling' is a term of convenience. It is applied to a range of approaches to criminal investigation, in which the behaviour exhibited in a crime, or a series of similar crimes, is studied and inferences are drawn about the offender. The underlying principle is the inference of offender characteristics from offence characteristics, but there is almost no common basis for this process and different profilers each have their own idiosyncratic approach to cases.

An offender profiler, for the purposes of the study, is a person who offers advice to a police investigation team based on previously collected data on past crimes, or on relevant professional expertise, typically as a psychologist or psychiatrist. This may include people working inside as well as outside the police service, but only where they are acting as an appointed consultant to an investigation, rather than where they are operating some form of innovative intelligence system. The study is concerned, therefore, with reactive rather than proactive profiling, and with those who present themselves as having some kind of relevant expertise.

The Origins and Shape of the 'Coals to Newcastle?' Project

Although the development of offender profiling as a science could be pursued as an end in itself, the object for police has always been operational assistance in the investigation of serious crimes, especially, perhaps, those crimes committed on strangers in which traditional victim-focused approaches often do not lead to the identification of the offender. By the early 1990s it was quite apparent that, despite the accelerating process of developing new profiling systems and approaches, no-one had yet properly consulted police users to establish benefits and costs.

A major question posed by the *CTN* project was whether operational offender profiling advice tells the investigating officer only what he/she already knows. Little previous effort had been made to establish whether this is true, or even justified to any extent (but see the results of a Dutch survey; Jackson, van den Eshof & de Kleuver, Chapter 7 of the present Volume). A questionnaire survey was used to collect the judgements of the officers involved. This was in part to guarantee objectivity through impersonality. The questionnaire consisted of 29 questions, ranging from the officers' expectations, to their use of the advice they received, and the usefulness they found in it. The depth of information collected and the 184 instances covered make the project the most extensive survey of profiling to date.

The second part of the study, still active as this chapter is completed, analyses the profilers' written product and tests the accuracy of their predictions in solved cases. This exercise proved extremely laborious because of the difficulty of establishing a common coding format to accommodate a range of reports so diverse in nature as to hold little in common between each source and every other. It was necessary to be able to identify the focus of each element of advice, and to distinguish them on the basis of equivocality, e.g. whether a prediction was qualified as a probability or a possibility, or not qualified at all. It was also necessary to distinguish between elements of advice which were verifiable from standard police records, those which were only verifiable from particular records relating to the individual investigation, and those which — usually either because they amounted to some kind of value judgement or because they related to an event which would not necessarily be identifiable — could not be verified at all. These problems were eventually overcome, after a comprehensive inter-rater reliability exercise, by the adoption of a co-researcher and the development of very rigorous double checking and panel agreement procedures.

Who Are the Profilers?

To a great extent, profiling relies on the self-defining nature of expertise by potential profilers. Indeed, offender profilers generally consist of 'those who present themselves as having some kind of relevant expertise'. Profiling is not associated with the expertise of any one profession and the police have no way of recognizing the validity of profilers' claims of relevant expertise. Typically, any expert status is difficult to challenge or check.

There is no governing body specifically for the regulation of professional or ethical standards in offender profiling. The profiler may or may not be a registered or chartered member of a particular profession. Notwithstanding several postgraduate psychology courses which incorporate some study of it, there is no academic qualification for offender profiling, and there is very little academic literature which deals directly with either the principles or the validity of offender profiling. There is no official forum for learning and development of profiling skills, no mutual support network, and, apart from the *CTN* project, little evidence of any feedback by which profilers in Britain can be made aware of their strengths and weaknesses. There is a chief police officers' committee which 'accredits' profilers, but not on any scientific basis. Much profiling is still conducted by unaccredited 'experts', because police officers tend to approach profilers they know or with whom they have had experience in the past.

The *CTN* report shows that profilers are mainly psychologists and psychiatrists. Of 29 sources of profiling tested in the questionnaire survey, four were forensic psychiatrists, five were academic psychologists, four were clinical psychologists, six were forensic psychologists, three were therapists (unspecified), four were British police officers, one was a British police scientist, one was a British police data system, one was an American Law Enforcement agency. Twelve of the 29 sources were only used on one occasion. The data set was dominated by the work of two individuals, an academic psychologist and a clinical psychologist, who between them advised on 88 of the 184 instances featured in the study. Three of the four police officers, the police scientist, the police data system, and one of the academic psychologists each held their own British police data, collected and organized for the purposes of profiling. These came to be referred to, for the purposes of the project, as 'statistical profilers' while the rest, who held no such data, were referred to as 'clinical profilers' (see Farrington & Lambert, Chapter 8 of the present Volume, for a further discussion of this distinction).

What Are Profilers' Qualifications?

The psychologists and psychiatrists each hold qualifications appropriate for their own professional responsibilities, which is unlikely to incorporate any research experience directly related to profiling. Clinical psychology is the application of psychological knowledge, principles and techniques to the assessment and treatment of emotional and behavioural problems. Clinical psychologists with an interest in profiling also tend to be forensic psychologists, working in the overlap between criminal justice and mental health, within prisons or secure units. As such, they will draw expertise from their experience in interviewing convicted persons with a wide range of emotional and mental states, and sometimes with experience in working with their families, their victims and their victims' families. A psychiatrist is qualified as a doctor of medicine and has undergone a postgraduate training in psychiatry. Typically they concentrate on the diagnosis of mental disorder, drug therapy and psychotherapy. The police officers acting as profilers have typically progressed from post-graduate study of psychology, usually involving the assembly and development of a data-based profiling system which is then used as the basis of their profiling advice. While a few police officers have set themselves up as profilers, they operate mostly within the intelligence environment. They are therefore interventionary rather than reactive, applying their knowledge and skills to crime pattern or comparative case analysis. As such, they fall outside the *CTN* definition of profiling, and therefore outside the scope of the project.

What Do Profilers Actually Do?

There have been many articles and journalistic pieces discussing profiling and profilers. However, little is published about what profilers actually do and still less about how they actually do it.

There is a high degree of consistency in the material profilers ask for to consider a case. The basic ingredients are almost always the known facts of the case, witness statements, scene photographs and maps; autopsy photographs are usually also requested in murder cases. No instance was found in the *CTN* project of a profiler being refused requested material. Some profilers always visit the scene, and sometimes the incident room as well; others never do.

In most cases, profilers will offer a list of inferred characteristics of the unknown offender — what the news media call an offender profile. Many will go further, using these characteristics to form the basis of a range of observations, predictions and recommendations. These aspects of advice should be regarded as offender profiling just as much as the list of characteristics itself (cf. Jackson, van den Eshof & de Kleuver, Chapter 7 of the present Volume). During the 1990s, there has been a rapid increase in Britain in demand by detectives for profilers to offer them an understanding of the behaviour exhibited in a crime. There has also been an increase in demand for interview strategies, crime series linking, and witness evaluation. These five services are those most in demand from profilers in Britain, followed by text analysis in extortion cases.

Out of the 184 instances of profiling studied in the *CTN* project, 111 sets of advice were put into writing, while 73 were verbal reports only. Written reports are very time-consuming, especially where the profiler's involvement develops into an intimate liaison with the officer and they come to consider closely many aspects of the case. Nevertheless, there is a real danger for the profiler of being misunderstood, or even misrepresented, when only verbal reports are provided.

An analysis of the 111 written profile reports collected for the *CTN* project shows that there are very wide variations in substance, focus and style. The mean number of coded elements (or points) of advice per profile was 34, the range being between 9 and 96; the mean number of A4 pages was 7, with a range between 2 and 24 pages. Similarly, the focus of advice varied widely. The *CTN* data coding frame divided elements of advice into 10 fields:

1 Features of the offence.
2 Character of the offender.
3 Origins of the offender.
4 Present circumstances of the offender.
5 Criminality of the offender.
6 Geography of the offender.
7 Predicted future behaviour of the offender.
8 Interview strategy to be adopted.
9 Threat assessment.
10 Specific recommendations to police.

It was found that clinical profilers offer a markedly greater proportion of advice on character, which includes aspects of personality and demeanour, and on predictions of future behaviour. Statistical profilers offer a markedly greater proportion of advice on present circumstances, criminality and geography.

Degrees of expressed certainty varied widely, as did tendencies to give explanation, repetition and self-contradiction. One profiler explained the reasoning behind 48% of elements of advice offered and another explained only 7%. The overall mean was 16%. While one profiler offered 10% of elements of advice as possibilities, another offered 26%; while one offered 76% as positive (or unqualified) advice, another offered 45%. The aggregate means were 62% positive, 18% probable, 20% possible. This, of course, makes a difference. Interestingly, profilers have sometimes claimed to have accurately advised that an offender would be characterized in some certain way (i.e. positive advice) when, in reality, the advice given to the police was probabilitic, or speculative.

How Do Profilers Do what They Do?

Two approaches to profiling have been publicly defined: first, those of the US Federal Bureau of Investigation (FBI), in a series of books and articles emanating since the mid-1970s from their Behavioural Science

Unit (e.g. Douglas & Olshaker, 1995; Hazelwood & Burgess, 1987; Ressler, Burgess & Douglas, 1988; Ressler & Shachtman, 1992); second, those of British psychologists, e.g. David Canter has published articles on profiling since the mid-1980s and has also written a semi-autobiographical book (Canter, 1994); an autobiographical account of the profiling approach of Paul Britton has also been published recently (Britton, 1997).

The FBI books go into great detail on the thought processes involved in their own style of profiling, and many British profilers have used these models as the basis for developing their own style. There is a model depicted in Ressler, Burgess & Douglas (1988) which sets out all the major sources of profiling information and all the significant analytical considerations. This model is probably close to definitive in substance, in that there are few considerations which could be added to it.

Indeed, disagreements over approaches to profiling are more to do with the conceptual framework brought to bear on the process of analysis than with original thinking. The basic disagreement in British profiling is over the respective merits of statistical and clinical prediction. However, this is an argument which has never been properly expounded. Little insight has been offered into the process of statistical profiling and, until recently, no insight at all had been offered into the clinical profiling process. Recently a systematic approach to the process of clinical crime profiling was articulated in print (Copson et al., 1997). The model developed shows a series of steps depicting how clinical inference is developed and applied to offender profiling. A key feature in this model is the minute detail in which inferences are considered.

Why Do Profilers Do It?

Experts directly gain little financially from profiling: of 184 instances studied, only 28 involved the payment of a fee — varying from a few hundred to a few thousand pounds — and even expenses were only claimed on 19 occasions. There have been occasions where profilers have secured research grants on the basis of their association with police, but these have been quite rare. Most profilers who work outside the police service are essentially amateurs who can all too often find themselves, as one of them once notably complained in a private conversation, 'called in late, between the clairvoyant and the palmist, when the evidence is cold'.

It may be that profilers outside the police service offer their services for free out of a sense of public duty. Most are public servants of one kind or another, working in universities or in the National Health Service. For those involved in the mental health field, it may be that involvement in a police investigation allows an insight into their own profession which they would otherwise rarely, or even never, get from daily professional experience. It informs their professional judgement and sharpens their skills, and it gives them access to an exceptionally rich field of co-operative research.

How Successful Are Profilers?

If success in profiling were synonymous with accurate prediction, then profilers could claim much success. This is perhaps most simply illustrated by reference to accuracy ratios derived from the *CTN* content analysis exercise. The accuracy ratios are derived from solved cases by taking those elements of advice which are amenable to verification, and comparing them against the outcome of the case. This is not straightforward as, in aggregate across the 50 solved cases analysed, 46% of elements were not verifiable. This is because they were essentially value judgements of some kind — for instance, to do with personality or demeanour. These kinds of points are matters of perception. For example, an officer vindicating suggested personality traits means no more than that the profiler and the officer agree; it does not make the observation objectively or universally correct. There were many of these kinds of perceptual points of advice, and also many other kinds of 'unknowables'. Even amongst statistical profilers, whose advice purports to be generated directly from hard data in police files, there were 29% of 'unknowns'. They also generated 29% of 'unknowns' out of their theoretically verifiable points of advice, meaning that the facts required to designate the advice as being correct or incorrect were not readily available, either from criminal records or from standard investigation files.

After first removing those points of advice which are simply unverifiable and then those for which verifying facts were not readily available, only 33.9% of overall points remained open to testing for accuracy (22.1% for clinical profilers and 50.4% for statistical profilers). Although these limited proportions might appear to weaken the inferences which can be drawn from these data, they are, nonetheless, by far the most comprehensive data available in this field and offer a first insight into the accuracy of profilers' predictions.

The aggregate accuracy ratio was found to be 2.2: 1 (that is 2.2 points correct to each 1 incorrect). For clinical profilers it was 2.9: 1; for statistical profilers 1.8: 1. Amongst individual profilers it ranged from 1.5: 1 to 6.8: 1. There is a detailed discussion of various break-downs of these data in Copson & Holloway (in preparation); accuracy was found to vary between fields of prediction and according to equivocality. The greatest accuracy was delivered by clinical profilers expressing unqualified predictions. They were correct 79% of the time. So, even taking the very best result on offer, a detective must expect more than one-fifth of his advice to be misleading.

Prior to the *CTN* survey, there had been a few attempts to measure the value of profiling advice (Britton, 1992; Douglas, 1981; Goldblatt, 1992; Jackson, van Koppen & Herbrink, 1993). All used as a gauge the opinions of officers for whom the advice was formulated. Table 4.1 shows the effect of the advice on the police investigation based on the *CTN* project. The Table reveals the percentage of 184 responses answering 'Yes' or 'No' to the questions shown. In most instances, the advice was found to be operationally useful, but this positive view was dependent neither on its ability to assist in solving the case nor in opening new lines of enquiry, nor even, necessarily, in adding anything to the information supplied.

Table 4.2 shows that profiling advice very rarely leads to identification of an offender, being judged to happen in only five of the 184 cases. The officers most commonly valued advice which furthered their understanding or reassured them in their own judgement. It is inferred from this that the most important contribution of profiling, as it has been practised in this country to date, is its part in developing the investigating officer's thinking on the case (see Jackson, van den Eshof & de Kleuver, 1997, Chapter 7 of the present Volume). An 82.6% approval rate (see Table 4.2) seems a fair measure of success that is matched by the percentage of respondents (92.4%) who said they would either definitely (68.5%) or probably (23.9%) seek profiling advice again in similar circumstances.

How Do Profilers Differ from More Conventional Experts?

One major difference between profilers and other experts is that profilers are essentially self-proclaimed experts when acting in that role. Even those who are eminent in their own professional field — as a psychologist or psychiatrist — are stepping out onto a limb when they act as profilers. They are heterogeneous in their backgrounds, their qualifi-

Table 4.1. Effect of advice

Did the advice:	Yes (%)	No (%)
Assist in solving the case?	14.1	78.3
Open new lines of enquiry?	16.3	82.1
Add anything to information supplied?	53.8	38.6
Prove operationally useful?	82.6	17.4

Table 4.2. How was the advice operationally useful?

Aspects of usefulness	(N)	(%)
Led to identification of offender	5	2.7
Furthered understanding of case/offender	112	60.9
Expert opinion reassured own judgement	95	51.6
Offered structure for interviewing	10	5.4
Other	17	2.3*
Not useful	32	17.4

Total N = 184.
* This percentage is not consistent with the others in this table as the 17 instances of unspecified usefulness were from a possible total of 736, not 184.

cations and, especially, in their activities. They share no common professional discipline nor any code of ethics. They perform largely as part-time amateurs and their worth is difficult to evaluate. Even if any individual were truly brilliant at profiling, there has never been any scientific means of testing this. The *CTN* project cannot be regarded as much more than experimental, being based on relatively few instances for each key profiler.

Another major difference between profiles and other forensic assessments is that in profiling there is generally no opportunity for directly assessing the individual concerned. Most forensic assessments involve a comprehensive assessment of the client (Gudjonsson, 1992, 1996a). This has the advantage of being able to conduct an objective assessment through direct observations and by using tests with known reliability and validity. Profiling, in contrast, is based on predicting offender characteristics on the basis of offence characteristics from the crime scene. Such an indirect way of conducting assessments is likely to be unreliable, because it typically involves intuition, psychodynamic ideas, limited repertoire of behaviour to extrapolate from, and methods of unknown reliability and validity.

Profilers, notably FBI analysts, increasingly have an advisory role in the USA, where the rules of evidence are different. The case of *Daubert v Merrill Dow Pharmaceuticals, 1993* asserts rule 702 of the Federal Rules of Evidence, which allows an expert opinion based on 'scientific, technical, or other specialized knowledge' if it 'will assist the trier of fact to understand evidence or to determine a fact in issue' (see Friedman, 1994, for a more detailed discussion). This status has not been accorded in Britain, although at least one profiler has been required to give what might be termed 'evidence of context' to explain to a court how and why officers happened to be in a certain place at a certain time watching for a certain kind of behaviour when they came to arrest the accused and find material evidence elsewhere. That appearance in court was a rarity for British profilers. Out of the 90 studied cases that went to court, profiling was an issue in only six and only two profilers reached the courtroom.

CONCLUSIONS

Forensic psychologists are often involved at the pre-trial, trial and sentencing stages of a case. Profilers are almost exclusively involved pre-trial. Acting purely as profilers, they have little potential for taking part at the trial stage and no potential for taking part at the sentencing stage. Their role is not to deliver expert evidence, still less to deliver any evidence which goes towards establishing the guilt or innocence of a particular person. Instead, their part is to offer new ideas on a case which might assist the officer in charge with decisions concerned with the management of investigative options and resources in pursuit of admissible evidence. To some this might seem more of a therapeutic or a reassuring role than a scientific one.

Profiling is neither a readily identifiable nor a homogeneous entity and its status is properly regarded as a professional sideline not amounting to a true science. Most profilers in Britain are psychologists and psychiatrists, and there are disagreements between them over whether profiling is best performed using statistics derived from police case data or clinical expertise without such data. Little has been published to shed light on what profilers actually do or how they do it. The substance, focus and style of the written product of British profilers varies greatly between individuals. Most profiling in Britain is done on an amateur basis, and some profilers appear reluctant to provide written advice.

Success in British profiling is very difficult to determine, but seems to have little to do with high rates of accurate prediction, directly assisting in solving cases, or leading to the identification of offenders. Instead, it seems to be to do with the introduction of new thoughts, arising from an intelligent second opinion, and the development of investigative philosophy — formulating and testing theories about the case and the offender — through the process of consultation and debate with the profiler.

CHAPTER 5

Standard Investigatory Tools and Offender Profiling

John A. Stevens

The skills and expertise of detectives who investigate serious crimes have always attracted widespread interest and comment. The multitude of fictional cases on television, in books and films have characterized the detective as an individual ranging from the bumbling incompetent to the awe-inspiring super-sleuth, often neglecting reality for the sake of a good story. In recent years the detective's role has been the subject of intense public scrutiny, often prompted by sensationalized media reports. Frequently, some new aspect of science that acts to support the detective's work draws public attention or else it is an unusual case. In contrast, routine, professional aspects of detection are seldom highlighted.

The purpose of this chapter is to explain the reality of the detective's role and how serious crime is investigated and detected. Publicity and public interest are important and a good detective will use them to advantage to obtain maximum information about the offence and the offender. However, irresponsible reporting and fictionalized accounts can present highly inaccurate and distorted perspectives on the detective's role and investigative procedures suggesting skills, expertise and techniques which simply do not exist.

'*Offender profiling*', which is the term applied to a range of methods that are used to develop advice for crime investigators based upon inferences drawn from behavioural characteristics of offenders, has suffered from such exposure. Some initial success has resulted in expectations, at times, bordering on the magical. Crime is not solved by magic. Crime is solved by sheer hard work and determination on the part of highly skilled and professional police officers, often working with equally professional colleagues in the scientific, medical and legal fields.

Profiling is only one of many tools available to detectives who frequently undertake complex, difficult and often frustrating tasks. There are no short cuts. Evidence has to be painstakingly gathered, assessed, presented and then proved in a court of law. That is the reality of the investigation of serious crime, and no matter what new techniques lie in wait around the corner, that is how it will remain. That is not to say that new techniques are not welcomed. Indeed, the skills of policing are continually evolving to meet the unusual demands which are faced in the detection of serious crime. Frequently, it is the unusual or the most difficult situations which provoke the development of new skills.

Despite the now famous quotation that the arrest of the serial killer Peter Sutcliffe, the Yorkshire Ripper, came about *as a result of good coppering*, it still led the Home Secretary to make the following announcement in the House of Commons on 19 January 1982:

> The Ripper case gave rise to the longest criminal investigation ever conducted in this country, imposing a great strain on all concerned. It would have been surprising if in this unprecedented situation there were no mistakes. What we should now do is to respond constructively to the considerable experience gained in the course of it in order to ensure that future investigations of crimes such as this are carried out as effectively and as quickly as possible.

The learning process began when a review of the Sutcliffe case was conducted by Sir Lawrence Byford, HM Inspector of Constabulary. The recommendations of the review were made in a document which is now more commonly referred to as the 'Byford Report' and specifically addressed each of the following:

1   The requirements of the investigation of a 'series' of major crimes.
2   The training of Senior Investigating Officers and personnel working in major incident rooms.
3   The conduct of investigations involving crimes which cross force boundaries.
4   The harnessing for such investigations of the best detective and scientific skills in the country.
5   The use of computer technology.

Each one of these issues, which are explained in more detail below, had a marked impact upon the subsequent investigation of serious and series crime. They set a national standard for *all* major inquiries to follow, especially when linked to other cases, and are still used as a benchmark today.

SERIES CRIME INVESTIGATION

Once a Senior Investigating Officer (SIO) has been appointed to take charge of any serious crime, an early consideration should be whether or not it is linked to any other previously reported offence and could involve a serial offender. This will require early liaison with the National Crime Intelligence Service, National Identification Bureau and the Scottish Records Office, since they maintain up-to-date indices on victims, modus operandi and descriptions. The Forensic Science Service can similarly search for forensic links on DNA, blood, fibres, firearms, tyre marks and shoe impressions, whilst all forces have access to a local facility which can compare finger/palm impressions from other scenes. In 1995, the National Crime Faculty was established at the Police Staff College at Bramshill. The staff of the Faculty are also available to liaise with SIOs and, in addition, databases are being established there which will serve to compare new cases with old.

One of the most notable cases to benefit from the identification of links between the crimes was that involving the abduction and murders of three young girls; Susan Maxwell at Coldstream in July 1982; almost a year later, Caroline Hogg from Portobello; and Sarah Harper from Morley in Leeds in March 1986. In each case, these young children had been transported and their bodies found at considerable distances, and in different police force areas, from the locations of their abduction. This pattern of abduction consequently led the forces where the bodies were found, namely Staffordshire, Leicestershire and Nottinghamshire, to assist Lothian & Borders, Northumbria and West Yorkshire, the forces which covered the abduction sites, in the investigation of a serial killer.

In August 1986, a conference was convened at the Home Office for the senior Police Officers involved in unsolved child murder, including the cases of Maxwell, Hogg and Harper. There was an obvious need to examine similar cases. This meeting resulted in a team operating under the overall command of Mr Don Dovaston, the Assistant Chief Constable at Derbyshire Police Headquarters, working to develop a database which is now well known to police and academic circles by the acronym CATCHEM (Centralized Analytical Team Collating Homicide Expertise and Management). Research from the CATCHEM database has analysed the salient points of all child murders dating back to 1960 and now provides a comprehensive 'library' to facilitate the comparison of current crime with previous similar crimes or occurrences. Such comparison facilitates 'series' identification and also provides guidelines for setting operational priorities and parameters.

SENIOR INVESTIGATING OFFICER TRAINING

In addition to detective skills, SIOs in command of the investigation of a series of major crimes also require particular management skills to meet the demands of very large scale enquiries, as do the senior members of his/her team. To this end, the National Crime Faculty at Bramshill in Hampshire provides the Management of Serious and Series Crime Course[1] to those Chief Officer, Superintendent and Chief Inspector ranks who are involved in major incident investigation. Importantly, the principles of offender profiling are outlined and the benefits of this emerging science are explained to those officers who may most of all need to draw upon this area of expertise.

CROSS-BOUNDARY INVESTIGATIONS

In the event of an investigation being linked with another major crime enquiry, the Assistant Chief Constable with the responsibility for Crime should be informed through the Head of the Criminal Investigation Department (CID). The Assistant Chief Constable will then arrange a conference at the earliest opportunity for all SIOs. The purpose is to discuss any *points of similarity*[2], to confirm links and to decide upon the course of action that needs to be taken.

It is vital to the success of any major investigation that the enquiry is approached on an organized and methodical basis from the start. Prior to the post-war amalgamations of police forces, it was common practice for forces faced with protracted homicide enquiries to seek assistance from the Metropolitan Police, who normally supplied a Detective Superintendent and a Detective Sergeant. The primary task of these officers was to set up a major incident room and, in consequence, a standard procedure evolved. Subsequent force amalgamations produced larger police forces with a higher incidence of major crime. These new forces developed their own expertise and consequently made fewer and fewer demands on the Metropolitan Police. Unfortunately, individual forces developed their own systems of major incident room procedure which, although suitable for their own purposes, were not capable of being easily merged when a crime became linked with another in a different force area. National standard administrative procedures for major investiga-

---

[1] The course delivers input concerning policy and guidelines for serious and series crime. Equally, it is a welcome opportunity for the participants to receive presentations and review some of the difficulties encountered in some of the more notable crimes, together with the best practice which has evolved nationwide. Presentations are made on forensic and other scientific expert support which is available to the SIO and the Investigation Team.

[2] Points of similarity may occur in any aspect of the offence, for example, the location, time, method of contact, sexual paraphilias or weapons used. Similarities are not necessarily exact matches and may simply be aspects of two or more offences which are comparable in some way.

tion were needed; and such a standard system was agreed by the Association of Chief Police Officers (ACPO) and implemented on 1 January 1984. This standard system facilitates the merging of cross-border offences, enables an officer with incident room experience to assist in any incident room in the country, and has made possible the introduction of computerization in major crime investigation.

In the event of a series transcending police force boundaries, as in the case of Maxwell, Hogg and Harper, the Chief Constables or Assistant Chief Constables of the forces concerned will liaise to consider the appointment of an Officer in Overall Command (OIOC) who will be at least one rank above the most senior SIO. This officer, who will normally be from one of the forces involved, will have authority to direct *all* aspects of the investigation in the police areas affected. He/she will have no other responsibility and will have a senior Police Management Team to assist him/her in the enquiry. One of the more recent and most publicized cases which led to the appointment of an OIOC followed the murder of Julie Dart from Leeds and the kidnapping of Stephanie Slater in the West Midlands. Mr T. M. Cook, the Deputy Chief Constable of West Yorkshire, was appointed to this position and, after a difficult and protracted enquiry, his investigation led to the arrest and conviction of Michael Sams in July 1993.

SUPPORT SKILLS

In addition to management support, the OIOC also has an Advisory Team who will assist on a regular consultancy basis. Usually this team includes a senior forensic scientist who, following the Byford report, has become known as 'The Byford Scientist', and any other *ad hoc* specialists appointed at the discretion of the OIOC. Typical examples include a pathologist, odontologist, forensic archeologist, fire investigation specialist, ballistics expert, marine expert, computer expert, communications specialist and legal advisor. It could also include a consultant forensic psychologist or any other expert in the field of psychological/behavioural science. One of the most crucial elements of the Sams investigation was clearly the appointment of Dr Roger Cook as the senior forensic scientist who worked full time on the OIOC's Advisory Team.

COMPUTER SUPPORT

The enormous amount of information that such incidents generate require computer technology to assist in storage, assessment and rapid retrieval. The nationally accepted major incident room computer system that will be used for such incidents is known as Home Office Large Major Enquiry System (HOLMES), which will be used in most investigations except, for example, the 'domestic' type murder or manslaughter where the offender is known and has been arrested. In the case of linked incidents, the OIOC will set up a separate HOLMES facility to those already in operation. This becomes known as the Central Research Incident (CRI). It will be used to research the databases of each major incident with a view to identifying and pursuing an investigation into anyone and anything linked to more than one of the cases under investigation.

Following recent developments in computer technology, several 'bolt-on' pieces of computer software are now available to the SIO to research and automatically analyse any information contained in a HOLMES database. Most of these systems, which are currently referred to as IT Analysis Workbenches, use a system called ANACAPA to dynamically chart any links and areas of activity within major crime investigation. Such tools are extremely useful when briefing incident room and enquiry staff, the Crown Prosecution Service in relation to evidential details of the case, or conducting reviews of an enquiry. Much can be learned from this process and it provides an objective analysis of the enquiry.

Mention has already been made of the CATCHEM database, which contains information on all child murders spanning almost three and a half decades. As well as *linking* cases, the database can also draw up statistically sound inferences to provide meaningful guidance to SIOs investigating similar cases. It is therefore used as a *decision support system* to enable SIOs to prioritize and validate selected lines of enquiry. The CATCHEM system has provided guidance in the search for bodies and missing persons where foul play is suspected; criteria for filtering suspects where initial intelligence has failed to indicate the person responsible; and guidelines when considering a mass blood sampling exercise when suspect blood or other body fluids are recovered at the scene of a crime. It is not only in this country that the success of CATCHEM has been recognized. The British Police Service has close links with its counterparts in Europe and elsewhere in order that work undertaken with offender profiling techniques can be closely followed. In particular, the Netherlands has undertaken its own research programmes and shared results and experiences with us. This led, in 1991, to the provision of direct support in the case of the murder of an 11-year-old girl, Jessica Laven, who was reported missing after visiting a local swimming pool in the town of Hoorn, in the Netherlands.

Derbyshire Police compiled a report which was provided in September 1991 and which led the SIO in Hoorn, Dick Brussee, then Deputy Chief of Police, to extend the geographical area of his enquiries.

This kind of guidance has proved successful where investigators have followed the statistical inferences derived from CATCHEM to locate both bodies and offenders. In the Laven case, the offender, Michel Stokx, was identified following a television appeal.

The offender profile provided by Derbyshire Police, utilizing the statistical inferences of CATCHEM, matched Stokx on nine out of ten points. This type of accuracy, and the accurate guidance on body deposition sites provided by CATCHEM, instils confidence in its use. As any major enquiry gathers pace, the possible areas of enquiry can multiply and extend to unmanageable proportions. CATCHEM permits an initial acceptable prioritization. Like all offender profiling techniques, however, it is only part of the overall process leading to the elimination of suspects and an identification of the most likely offender.

OFFENDER PROFILING

The previous paragraphs have described in basic detail the standard investigative tools available to the SIO in identifying linked offences and the procedures to be followed when investigating a serial offender, especially one who operates across police force boundaries. However, unless a suspect has come to attention in each of the *linked* cases under investigation, such tools can be limited when it comes to *identifying* the serial offender or offenders. As a consequence, there has developed a growing interest in the scientific application of offender profiling in order to analyse whatever information is available to an investigation in order to:

1   Predict characteristics of the offender.
2   Establish whether the crime appears to be part of a series.
3   Develop advice on the running of certain aspects of the enquiry, e.g. how to take best advantage of any media interest in the case.

It is helpful to see offender profiling, in this context, as one of a number of analytical tools for use in an investigation. The huge publicity generated by its application to a few very high profile cases has tended to misrepresent offender profiling as a panacea for difficult investigations. Fiction, such as the film *Silence of the Lambs*, tends to reinforce this misrepresentation. Offender profiling is not a magical concept which will categorically identify the offender nor, unfortunately, is it ever likely to be so. Instead, it exists to help a SIO to structure an enquiry and prioritize any list of suspects. In its widest sense, offender profiling can provide skilled, professional advice on interview strategy of both witnesses and suspects and can assist with the management of difficult major investigations, particularly where preceded by kidnap and ransom demands. The Julie Dart and Stephanie Slater cases benefited from such advice.

Profiling relies upon offenders giving away details about themselves through their behaviour during the offence. When coupled with forensic analysis and the assessment of witness statements, the parameters for suspect elimination can be set. Major enquiries can throw up hundreds of suspects and it is important that appropriate prioritization takes place to allow the most effective use of the SIO's most valuable resource, detective expertise.

THE USE OF OFFENDER PROFILING

The first acknowledged success from offender profiling was in Leicester where, in a bizarre case of murder, a clinical psychologist provided a psychologically-based interview strategy following the arrest of a suspect, Paul Bostock. The psychologist advised detectives to structure the interviews by working around Bostock's weaknesses, fantasies and sexual behaviour, and this strategy proved successful.

Leicestershire Police again received useful advice from a psychologist in 1986, when a 15 year-old called Dawn Ashworth was raped and killed near the village of Narborough. This case was linked to the rape and murder of another 15 year-old called Linda Mann in November 1983 in the same village. During the massive murder hunt which followed, Leicestershire Police arrested a young kitchen porter who had been seen several times near the murder location. Whilst in custody, this man, who had a history of molesting children, confessed to the murder of Dawn Ashworth but emphatically denied killing Linda Mann. Believing they had also found the killer of Linda Mann, the police enlisted the assistance of the Forensic Science Laboratory. Using the then new scientific discovery of DNA profiling, police were able not only to eliminate this kitchen porter from both murders but also to prove that one man had committed both crimes.

The complex scientific process of DNA profiling, discovered by Dr Alec Jeffreys, compiles a genetic print which is characteristic of an individual. This was used in tandem with a psychological profile that was used to set the parameters for taking samples of blood for DNA testing. The extensive blood sampling exercise which followed came to be known as the 'blooding' and eventually led to the arrest of Colin Pitchfork, who became the first person to be convicted of murder on the strength of DNA evidence.

The earliest acknowledged operational police use of external psychological expertise in this country actually preceded the Bostock and Pitchfork cases when, in the mid 1980s, the Metropolitan Police approached the FBI in the USA to profile a serial rapist operating in the West London area of Notting Hill. Between September 1979 and September 1983, there were 15 attacks on women, in their own homes, in the Kensington and Notting Hill areas of West London. An enquiry team worked on those attacks until 1985 without success. There were no further attacks linked to this series until May 1987, when a woman was raped in a basement flat in Notting Hill and the attack bore many similarities to some of the previous attacks. A new enquiry team was set up in 1987. A second attack took place in July, again in Notting Hill, with striking similarities to the earlier offence in May.

The first enquiry team had recognized that the offences in Kensington and Notting Hill were probably committed by different persons, a fact that was corroborated by the FBI Psychological Profiling Unit report. Nevertheless, it was decided to treat this series, at that point, as one enquiry and this proved cumbersome. Lines of enquiry were developed which were time-consuming and unhelpful. The second enquiry team concentrated only on the eight actual Notting Hill attacks and support for this tactic came from accumulated forensic science samples. About three-quarters of the population secrete their blood group into their bodily fluids and are known as 'secretors'. Consequently, in many cases blood group can be identified from semen. A blood test on a 'non-secretor' is termed inconclusive.

The samples from the Notting Hill cases were inconclusive in that no blood group was found, so it was reasonable to assume the attacker was from a non-secretor blood group. This differed from the Kensington samples which showed an 'A-secretor' blood group. The investigations (post-1987), amongst other lines of enquiries, sought an explanation for the gap of four years between the offences, giving priority to military service, diplomatic service, imprisonment, employment away from the area, and further education away from the area. Police observations were kept in the locality, which was only a half square mile of enclosed communal gardens, and house-to-house enquiries were in progress. To assist these traditional enquiries, the SIO consulted with two psychologists, who gave profiles of a possible offender which, with the earlier FBI profile, meant three separate profiles were now in existence. There were differences between them; but, as it turned out, none of the profiles directly contributed to the arrest of the man known as the 'Notting Hill Rapist'. The SIO in the Notting Hill case had samples from both 1987 rapes tested by the DNA profiling process, which proved both were committed by the same man. Suspects for the rapes had samples of blood taken for DNA profiling and one, Tony Frederick McLean, proved a match. He was subsequently sentenced to life imprisonment on each of three rapes.

These cases indicate the emerging involvement of offender profiling in sexual murder cases. Perhaps the watershed case is that of John Duffy, who was known as the 'Railway Murderer'. His conviction in 1988 brought to an end a terrifying series of attacks on women in London and the Home Counties stretching back to 1982. The investigation into the series of rapes and murders cost £3 million and involved four forces; Metropolitan, Surrey, Hertfordshire and British Transport Police.

Duffy, a former British Rail carpenter, was a suspect from the start of the police investigation — but he quickly became hidden amongst 4900 other suspects as the enquiry progressed. The police turned to a psychologist to see if a profile could assist them in their enquiries. Using a computer programme and directed by the psychologist, police officers analysed the statements taken in 27 cases of rape. Investigating officers had realized that the attacker had committed many of the attacks near railway lines and therefore knew the railway system very well. This information was taken a stage further by building up a picture of the attacker's own *mental map* of London and looking for a psychological focus of the map. This was done by *time-slicing* the attacks and examining their progressive locations. The earlier attacks were closer to West Hampstead; and it was hypothesized that, as the offender's confidence and experience grew, he would move further from his home base. It was, therefore, possible to surmise that the attacker lived within three miles of West Hampstead.

The profile prepared by the psychologist suggested that the attacker was trying to form some sort of relationship with the women he attacked; that he was either married or living with a woman, but that the relationship was a turbulent one with no children. This information proved to be of interest as the picture of Duffy's mentality emerged from his trial. During the hearing, his ex-wife said that Duffy had told her he was raping other women because she had rejected him. It also emerged that Duffy had not been able to father children because of his very low sperm count.

Although the psychological profile assisted, it would perhaps be wrong to attribute success in the Duffy case solely to the profile. Officers had assembled a list of 4900 suspects after forensic scientists identified blood from samples taken from the body of one of the murder victims, Maartje Tamboezer. They had also discovered a footprint near the scene of the murder which showed that the killer had size 4 feet — which narrowed him down to 1% of the adult male population in Britain. Duffy had been interviewed by two Metropolitan officers about one of the attacks in July 1986, but gave an alibi. The officers were not happy with the interview and told a senior officer who made arrangements to see Duffy again. Before he could do so, Duffy paid a friend to slash his chest and checked himself into a mental hospital saying he had been mugged and was suffering amnesia.

The Tamboezer murder was linked with another murder, that of Alison Day at Hackney because of the use of a garrotte as a method of killing in both cases. The Day murder was, in turn, tentatively linked with the rapes in north and south London. The statement of one rape victim, Miss X, showed the victim had been wiped with tissues which were then burned. Tamboezer's clothing had been burned, so the possibility existed that the same person had raped Miss X and killed Alison Day and Maartje Tamboezer. The rape of Miss X was re-investigated and an enquiry team were tasked to visit every place where they could obtain information about the suspect — described as a White man, 5'4" tall, with ginger/fair hair and a spotty or acne-pitted complexion.

An enquiry team visited a local intelligence office in a police station at Hampstead and returned with the file on John Duffy and a photograph taken at the time of his arrest for a burglary in 1985. He fitted the description given by Miss X and there were additional points which made him a good suspect. Probably of most importance were the discoveries that he had allegedly raped his ex-wife at knife-point in a north London park and that his blood group matched semen found in the body of Tamboezer. The photograph also showed Duffy wearing a hooded sweatshirt, and several of the rapes in north London had been committed by hooded attackers. In addition, at the time of his arrest for the burglary he had with him a balaclava, another feature of the suspected rapes. Finally, his home address was in the area predicted in the profile prepared by the psychologist. Duffy was the subject of surveillance by the police and was then arrested. He was convicted in 1987 of two murders and five rapes.

As a result of the Duffy case, ACPO Crime Committee set up a Subcommittee to examine offender profiling [3]. Its members include experienced detectives and senior members of the Home Office Police Research Group. The immense publicity which surrounded and followed Duffy's trial created a demand for offender profiling which has seen it employed in over 300 major investigations during the last nine years. The mixture of detective expertise, behavioural science theory and statistical facts all contribute to offender profiling and involve police, acad-

---

[3] The author chaired the ACPO Subcommittee on Offender Profiling for a period of 10 years before leaving Northumbria Police to take up a position with Her Majesty's Inspectorate of Constabulary.

emic, medical, psychological and forensic science sources. In 1991, it was apparent to everyone on the Subcommittee that there were encouraging signs of progress from the work that it had organized; useful relationships had been established between the police and a number of psychologists; the concept was being developed as part of the senior CID courses at the Police College; and investigating officers were enthusiastic and more importantly, using profiling techniques. Whilst the signs were encouraging, there was no evidence that a coherent and usable system was emerging and it became clear that an evaluation of the work to date was required. With the agreement of ACPO, the Home Office commissioned a review. Its purpose was simple: to establish what was the operational value of offender profiling to the end-user, the detective. Four objectives were set:

1   To clarify the nature of profiling and the expectations of those likely to use or finance this development as an operational facility.
2   To critically examine the work up to that time.
3   To examine existing detective approaches to determine whether they consistently use models or processes to investigate crime and, if so, what they were.
4   To outline the options available to progress profiling and make recommendations on the most appropriate options.

In June 1992, the confidential report was presented to the Joint ACPO/Home Office Policy Committee. The review found that there was positive potential for the development of offender profiling as an operational tool. This confirmed the unanimous view of the ACPO Committee arrived at four years earlier. The review made 26 recommendations, the five main ones being:

1   Offender Profiling is essentially viable.
2   Work should begin towards providing an operational system.
3   The project should be owned by the police but managed by the Police Research Group in the Home Office. Ownership is important to ensure that all future work is tied to service delivery and not academic research.
4   National data sets should be created to permit sufficient statistical analysis to enhance profiling.
5   The feasibility of an artificial intelligence-based expert computer system should be explored using CATCHEM, Dutch profiling work on rape, clinical research at Broadmoor Hospital, research then being conducted at Surrey University, and the Metropolitan Sexual Assaults Index.

The subsequent research programme was developed by the Police Research Group (PRG). The overall objectives of the programme were:

1   To establish whether offender profiling can significantly enhance the investigative efficiency of the experienced detective.
2   To manage the development of an appropriate mechanism to deliver any benefits of offender profiling to the Police Service.

These objectives have been achieved through an number of individual but connected projects. In relation to the first objective, over 200 cases have been collated, where profiling advice has been given. These are in the process of being evaluated and some of the findings have been published (see Gudjonsson & Copson, Chapter 4 of the present Volume).

The statistical validation of offender profiling methods to date has been hampered by a lack of data sets sufficiently large to stand up to rigorous analysis. Part of the research programme involved creating a database of solved stranger rape cases to allow such analysis to take place. Whilst the rape database was being built, the CATCHEM database was used to test which statistical techniques are appropriate in order to analyse data for offender profiling. Research by statisticians from the Universities of Edinburgh and Heriot-Watt has already shown that reasonably reliable statistical models can be developed to predict outline characteristics of an offender from details of the offence and victim.

These projects have already identified that offender profiling has much to offer and work has commenced to develop suitable mechanisms to deliver those benefits to the Police Service. It is true to say that, in the past, offender profiling was provided on an *ad hoc*, consultancy basis from individuals with relevant experience. The National Crime Faculty has now developed a more formal system of training and advice which will be supported by relevant, computerized databases. To ensure such a system meets the needs of the detective, research has been undertaken to identify key investigative problems encountered during a particular class of major crime enquiries. The research will also identify the methods that experienced detectives use to address these problems.

This structured research and development programme is vital for the future credibility of offender profiling. To date, much of the operational use has taken place within rape and sexual murder cases which are horrific and often sensationally reported in the press. The modern media exerts enormous pressure on police forces engaged in major crime investigations and, in particular, on the SIO tasked with solving the case. We are fortunate in Britain to have detectives of outstanding ability and dedication who continually succeed in solving difficult and tragic cases. The SIO's greatest strength lies within the investigative team, in experienced police officers who are seeking and evaluating every piece of information in a manner which can ultimately be presented to a judge and jury. The HOLMES computer, standard working practices in major incident rooms, painstaking examination of scenes of crimes and the subsequent forensic analysis including DNA profiling, together with offender profiling, are all important tools which are available to the SIO and the investigation team.

It is the responsibility of the SIO to make the appropriate use of these tools, as well as anything else which can be properly used to bring the case to a conclusion and then to allow the court to decide on the evidence presented. What cannot be ignored is that the SIO works in the real world and, whilst it may be academically good practice to await the result of a research programme before using a concept, in practice this is not always possible. The SIO has to look at all options and make his/her decision on all the facts known to him/her at the time, conscious that his/her decisions and judgement will be considered within a legal framework at a later date.

This chapter has concentrated on the use of standard investigative practices and offender profiling techniques on the most serious crimes, but there is potential for profiling to be used on other crimes such as house burglary. Within my old force, Northumbria Police, the development of a Statistical House Offender Profiling (SHOP) database, using similar techniques to CATCHEM, is producing significant results in dealing with serial burglars. On the arrest of a house burglar, the details of both the offender and the offence are entered on a simple but very effective database. Modus operandi, location, proximity, time and victim–offender relationship are just a few examples of the information that can be researched.

In one Area Command within Northumbria Police which has been operating SHOP since 1 January 1993, the details of over 200 active house burglars have been accumulated and are the subject of statistical analysis. This analysis has confirmed that almost three-quarters of the offenders carry house-breaking implements with them to the scene, and that they repeatedly re-offend within half a mile from their homes. Such is the effectiveness of the system that the modus operandi and offending behaviour of many offenders can be differentiated or hallmarked and used in conjunction with a computerized Crime Pattern Analysis system to profile the offence. Whenever an offender appears in the system more than four times, he/she is tagged as a serial house burglar and becomes the subject of closer scrutiny and profiling research. This research has confirmed the habitual behaviour and associated pre-planning of such offenders even when they commit their crimes with friends and relatives. Vulnerable property, victims and periods of the day have become subject to much more effective targeting by resources from the police and other agencies. This has led to a significant impact on reported crime.

In conclusion, the term 'offender profiling' covers a range of methods used to develop advice for investigators, based upon both systematic studies of behaviour exhibited during the commission of criminal acts and the more particular approach of drawing out inferences about an offender from the circumstances of an offence. I believe that some areas of this work have been sensationalized to the detriment of the in-depth research which has been going on for many years. However, it will be some time before we have a system which is a fully functional tool for operational detectives.

The overriding aim is to provide investigators with information which will help them in the management of major crime — what the most likely options are and where resources should be targeted. Offender profiling is an additional tool in the detective's armoury and has to be used in conjunction with other investigative approaches. offender profiling advice does not amount to probative evidence; a profile is no proof of guilt. It is not and never will be a magic wand to point directly to the persons who have committed offences, but it can be an extremely effective aid to an investigation — an aid which, in cases of serial offenders, can make a dramatic impact upon the duration and the overall success of an investigation.

CHAPTER 6

What Help Do the Police Need with their Enquiries?

Dick Oldfield

INTRODUCTION

This chapter is based upon a number of research projects carried out through the Police Research Group's Offender Profiling Research Programme[1], as was introduced in the previous chapter (Stevens, 1997, Chapter 5 of the present Volume). It explores:

- What expertise is required to investigate serious crime, such as 'stranger' murder and rape.
- How detectives in the UK currently develop their expertise and the inherent limitations with this method, hence
- What additional support detectives need with serious crime investigation.
- Where this additional support might come from.

WHAT EXPERTISE IS REQUIRED TO INVESTIGATE SERIOUS CRIME?

It would be easy to conclude from an examination of detective fiction that the only expertise that a detective needs to investigate a serious crime is the skill to work out 'whodunnit'. Of course, detectives do need an ability to identify lines of enquiry that are likely to implicate the offender. But these analytical skills need to be supported by a range of complementary skills to ensure that an investigation can be managed to

---

[1] The Police Research Group is part of the Police Policy Directorate of the UK's Home Office.

a successful conclusion. These complementary skills include the ability to manage resources, communication skills, interviewing skills, legal knowledge, case preparation skills and many more. In other words, investigative expertise is multifaceted and a Senior Investigating Officer (SIO) must have access to the full range of these skills if he/she is to manage an enquiry in the best way possible.

However, not only is investigative expertise multifaceted — it is also multilayered. Adhami & Browne (1996) used a four-layer model based on a standard knowledge-based systems methodology (KADS) to describe this detective expertise (see Figure 6.1).

The Domain Layer

Expertise from the *domain layer* of the model is used to identify the basic building blocks of a crime investigation. For example, a detective's domain expertise will identify the physical components of the crime such as the *victim*, the *suspect*, the *scene* and the *weapon*. It will also identify more conceptual components such as the *motive* for the crime.

Expertise from the domain layer is also used to identify the relationships between these components of the crime. For example, the domain layer will generate simple relationships such as 'the victim *was* at the scene' or 'the offender *had* a motive'.

An investigator's skill lies with the identification of *all* the salient components of a crime and the relationships between them. Some of

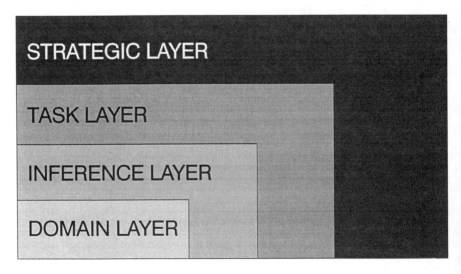

Figure 6.1. The KADS four-level model of expertise (from Adhami & Browne, 1996, with permission).

these will be a lot less obvious than the examples used above. For example, the *absence* of certain injuries to a victim could be an important component of a crime that might be missed by an inexperienced investigator.

Whilst these examples concentrate on aspects of the crime itself, the investigator must be able to identify the domain components and their relationships in each of the multiple facets of the investigative process. For example, components such as the *media, accommodation, finance, Police and Criminal Evidence Act (PACE), disclosure, technical support* and *staff morale* all need to be identified and managed if an investigation is to lead to a successful conclusion.

The Inference Layer

The second layer of Adhami & Browne's model of investigative expertise is the *inference layer*. It is with this level of expertise that a detective will draw inferences about the crime from the contents of the previous (domain) layer. For example, the domain layer may have identified that:

- The *victim's* body was *dumped* by a *road* in a *remote location*.

Using expertise from this second layer, the detective might infer that:

- The *offender* has *access* to a *vehicle*; and
- The *offender* is *familiar* with the *remote location*.

It is important to note that these inferences build upon the contents of the domain layer. It follows that if a salient feature of a crime is missed within the domain layer (e.g. if the *absence* of defence wounds on the victim's body went unnoticed), then the investigator could not use this piece of information to draw inferences in this layer. This dependency exists for each of the subsequent layers within the model, as each layer builds upon the contents of the previous one.

The Task Layer

The third layer in the model is the *task layer*. It is through the expertise associated with this layer that the investigator can turn the inferences drawn from the previous layer into actions that will help progress the investigation towards a successful conclusion.

Continuing the earlier example, the inferences that were drawn were that the offender had access to a vehicle and that the offender was familiar with the location of where the body was dumped. On the basis of these inferences, a detective can 'task' the investigation team to prioritize all suspects who meet these criteria. The actual actions that are generated will very much depend on the nature of the investigation. It may be that these criteria are used only to revise the investigation's policy on the elimination of suspects. Alternatively, they might define a sufficiently small group of people to make, for example, a mass DNA 'blooding' feasible.

This simple example again concerns itself with inferences and tasks associated with the crime itself. It must be remembered that an investigating officer must have a broad knowledge of those actions that are both useful and practical for *all* of the facets of serious crime investigation.

The Strategic Layer

The expertise in the final *strategic layer* in this model is used to coordinate those actions generated within the task layer. It is likely that the task layer will generate far more actions than there are resources to carry out. Hence, investigators must employ their strategic skills to prioritize and coordinate those that are to be actively pursued, and to hold others pending for further consideration at a later time.

Strategic decisions are required in all facets of investigation management. Important decisions will have to be made concerning the overall direction of the enquiry, suspect elimination criteria, media policy, overtime issues, whether HOLMES should be used, etc.

Once again, the strategic layer builds upon the products of the previous layers. In other words, the whole strategy of an investigation depends on *all* of the expertise previously discussed. So, if a mistake or oversight has been made in any of the previous layers of expertise then it will be propagated throughout the rest of the model and the whole direction of the investigation can be affected.

During the course of a crime investigation, there will be numerous amendments to, and interactions between, the layers of this model. Not all of the domain components will be available, or will have been correctly identified, at the outset of the enquiry. For example, it may take some weeks to analyse the physical samples obtained from the scene, witnesses may be slow in coming forward and antecedent checks may only gradually reveal aspects of the victim's life that are relevant to the crime. Changes will occur within the other layers, too. Some of the inferences will be found to be incorrect and alternatives will have to be developed in their place. Tasks will be found to be unmanageable or too expensive, and new possibilities may be suggested to the SIO part-way through the investigation. Changes in strategy may have to be considered if, for example, it is discovered that the crime under investigation is part of an established series committed by a single offender. Hence the model will be very dynamic throughout the course of an investigation, with any change in a lower layer of the model having a 'knock-on' effect to the layers above it. The SIO must have the ability to keep on top of these changes without losing sight of the objective of the exercise, that is, to identify and build the case against the offender.

HOW DO DETECTIVES DEVELOP THEIR INVESTIGATIVE EXPERTISE?

Through their interviews with senior detectives[2], Adhami and Browne (1996) found that there were a number of sources of 'investigative expertise'. In particular, a detective's approach to a particular case may be influenced by:

- 'Know-how' developed as a result of personal involvement with previous cases.
- 'Good practice' disseminated through standard procedures and training programmes.
- Knowledge developed through access to informal networks and other known cases.
- Insight developed through wider reading and specific academic studies; and/or
- Experiences in a defined domain, such as dealing with the media or managing finances and resources.

It was found, though, that it was the first of these sources that appeared to be the primary source of detective expertise in the UK. Their skills did not generally come from books, courses at university or from police training colleges, but mainly through *personal experience* of a wide variety of crimes over a number of years, either first-hand or by working with more experienced detectives in an apprenticeship role. In other words, detective expertise is largely dependent on experience. The more experience a detective has had with a certain crime type, the more investigative expertise he/she is likely to have developed.

This reliance upon a detective's personal involvement to develop investigative expertise has both strengths and weaknesses. For example, it works adequately for those *types* with which a detective has a lot of experience, namely high volume crime such as burglaries or car

---

[2] Fifteen senior detectives, each with considerable experience in the role of SIO, were nominated by the ACPO Offender Profiling Committee as subjects for this study.

thefts. Every detective becomes very familiar with these crimes and, consequently, their expertise has the opportunity to develop.

This method is also fine for those *aspects* of the investigation that are *common* to all crime investigations. For example, regardless of the *type* of crime being investigated, most investigations will involve a certain amount of communication with fellow officers, interviewing of witnesses and suspects, action management, exhibit handling and case preparation. The skills that a detective develops with these aspects of the investigative process will be applicable to the next investigation that he/she undertakes, regardless of the nature of the crime.

However, this reliance upon personal experience is not adequate for those aspects of an investigation that are *peculiar* to the type of crime under investigation, especially where the type of crime does not occur very often. Take, for example, sexually-oriented child homicide in the UK. Fortunately, this type of crime is relatively rare in this country; usually there are no more than a dozen cases per year. But because it is rare, only a few detectives have had any direct experience of its investigation. Fewer still, if any, have experience with two or more separate sexually-oriented child homicides. Indeed, it is probable that the detective who will be put in charge of the next crime of this type in the UK will not have any experience of sexually-oriented child homicide. If this is the case, then he/she will not have experienced those aspects of the investigation that are peculiar to that type of crime. It follows that, without this previous *experience*, the detective will have limited *expertise* in the management of those crime-dependent aspects of the investigation.

It is important, therefore, to identify which aspects of investigative expertise are crime-type dependent, as it is in these areas that detectives are most likely to require support. In their pilot study, Adhami & Browne (1996) used a series of structured interviewing techniques and scenario-based analyses to elicit the expertise of experienced SIOs in each of the four levels of their model (see Figure 6.1). The sessions focused on what approaches and expertise were used by the detectives to determine the characteristics of unknown suspects. This expertise was then evaluated, (a) by an examination of consistency between the detectives, and (b) through testing, where possible, against a representative set of relevant solved cases (i.e. the CATCHEM database described in the previous chapter of this Volume). Their results suggested that the expertise that is strongly associated with the *type* of crime under investigation lies predominantly in the 'domain' and 'inference' layers. Further, the expertise in the 'task' and 'strategic' layers tends to be more relevant to crime investigation in general.

Together, these findings suggest that detectives are most likely to have problems with their domain and inference expertise associated with *low volume* serious crime. It therefore follows that UK detectives may need additional support with the identification of the salient features of low-volume serious crime — and with the inferences that can be drawn from those features.

HOW CAN ADDITIONAL INVESTIGATIVE EXPERIENCE BE DEVELOPED?

The problem appears to be that detectives do not have the opportunity to develop domain or inferential expertise in low-volume serious crime, as they do not have many (or any) personal experiences of that type of investigation. This problem could be solved by:

- Increasing detectives' personal experience of these low-volume serious crimes.
- Training detectives with appropriate domain and inference skills for those crime types.
- Providing some form of consultative support for the domain and inferential processes to the investigators of such crimes.

With the first of these options, the only legitimate way of increasing detectives' personal experience of low-volume serious crime is to decrease the number of detectives who have the opportunity to investigate those few crimes. In effect, detectives would have to *specialize* as investigators of particular types of low-incidence crime. Indeed, various specialist 'squads' do exist within some of the larger UK forces. These serve to concentrate the experience of these crimes onto a relatively small group of officers and, thus, allow their expertise to develop in that area. However, this option is not practical, or even desirable, for many forces in the UK. For example, with certain crime types, such as sexually-oriented child homicide, their incidence is so low within individual forces that even specialist investigators would not experience many, or any, within their careers.

The second and third options (training and consultation) both assume that someone has a greater understanding of the expertise required for the investigation of low-incidence crime than the detectives who are to be taught or advised. Such an understanding could be developed:

- Through consultation with 'experts' from other fields who have domain and inferential knowledge relevant to low-volume serious crimes.
- By collating and analysing many examples of individual detective experiences with these crimes.

- Providing and supplementing any research relevant to the development of domain and inferential knowledge for this type of crime investigation.

CONSULTATION WITH 'EXPERTS'

Other chapters of this book (see Gudjonsson & Copson, Chapter 4; Stevens, Chapter 5; Jackson, van den Eshof, & de Kleuver, Chapter 7 of the present Volume) discuss how *consultation* with experts from the behavioural sciences might be useful to detectives and I do not wish to replicate their contents here. However, it is relevant to note an interim finding of Copson's evaluation of the operational usefulness of 184 instances of such consultations in the UK (Copson 1995; Gudjonsson & Copson, 1997, Chapter 4 of the present Volume). Copson finds that the detectives *perceived* the benefits of the consultations that they received as being associated with the *strategic* understanding of the crime and its investigation, rather than with the *inferential* aspects of the underlying investigative process. Whilst this finding needs considerable clarification, it does suggest that experts may have only a limited contribution to make to the detectives' requirement for more domain and inferential expertise.

Collating Individual Detective's Expertise

Whilst individual detectives gain little, if any, experience of low-volume serious crime, detectives in the UK *collectively* have to investigate a significant number of cases each year. A possible way of developing support for individual detectives is to provide them with access to this 'pool' of experience whenever they need it.

This is one of the responsibilities of the UK's newly formed National Crime Faculty. The Faculty has been established to provide, amongst a range of other services, a 'gateway' for operational investigators into the corporate knowledge of UK detectives. Already, the Faculty is in the practice of assembling, at the request of an SIO, a team of advisers for his/her enquiry which includes two detectives with recent experience of the type of crime under investigation. Informal feedback suggests that benefit is gained from these exercises both by the SIO *and* by the two visiting detectives who, through their participation, will usually have doubled their personal experience of the investigation of that crime type.

In addition to these 'consultative groups', the Faculty has plans to begin debriefing all officers who have been involved in the investigation of low-volume serious crimes and to collate their experiences in a form that can be used to advise future investigations of a similar type. It is recognized that initiative on its own has limitations. Adhami & Browne conclude from their pilot study that it will not be possible to develop a single model of the inference layer of investigative expertise that would be generally acceptable by detectives. Debriefing all these detectives is likely to yield a large number of heuristics, but these 'rules of thumb' will be of variable quality and difficult to validate. The experience of the Dutch with the development of an expert system to classify rape attacks appears to bear this out (van der Heijden, van den Eshof & Schrama, 1990; Jackson, van den Eschof & de Kleuver, Chapter 7 of the present Volume). Nevertheless, it is considered that such an initiative will help to retain some investigative expertise within the service rather than letting it all disappear with detectives when they retire, as it does at present. At the very least, the initiative will provide a reference of practice that has been 'tested in the field' and a rich source of hypotheses to test through a structured research programme which is the subject of the final section of this chapter.

DEVELOPING DOMAIN AND INFERENTIAL KNOWLEDGE FROM EMPIRICAL RESEARCH

The collective experience of low-volume serious crime is not only recorded in the minds of those detectives who were responsible for their investigation. Details of each of these crimes will have been documented in case papers, in computer files and in audio and image libraries by the police, criminal record departments, scenes of crime officers, forensic scientists, prison psychologists, probation officers and others. Unfortunately, these records are generally widely distributed across tbc country and are not readily available for research purposes.

However, a few projects have attempted to draw some of these sources together and to analyse them in order to identify useful patterns in the data that might assist the police with the investigation of subsequent crimes. These research projects have generally sought to develop hypotheses from the sources of 'expertise' discussed earlier (i.e. from the behavioural sciences and/or detective expertise) and to test them against the available data.

For example, as discussed in the previous chapter (Stevens, 1997, Chapter 5 of the present Volume) Derbyshire Constabulary has collated and coded details of all sexually-oriented child homicides that have occurred in the UK since 1960. This data set was originally collected as part of an active investigation into a series of child homicides. However, the experienced detectives working on this aspect of the enquiry noticed that there were some interesting, and potentially useful, irregularities in the data. For example, there appeared to be patterns in the relationships between the offender and the victim, the criminal careers of the offenders and the location of the offenders' residences in relation to the sites from which the children were abducted (Bailey, 1989). Some of these patterns appeared to support their detectives 'gut feelings' about these crimes. Equally, several of the patterns appeared to go against what the experienced detectives expected. For example, detectives believed that anyone who had committed a murder of this type would have previously come to the notice of the police for some lesser sexually-oriented crime. The data suggested that, in fact, only 46% had.

The Police Research Group's research programme used the CATCHEM data set to explore which statistical techniques were appropriate for the analysis of this type of data. Aitken et al. (1995), examined a range of techniques to evaluate how they could be used to predict details of an individual offender from the details of his offence[3]. The findings of the study suggested that there was the potential for the development of 'predictive models' to assist the police with active investigations, but it also revealed the limitations of many of the previous quantitative studies in the field. In particular, problems were found with:

- Data sets that were *not consistently coded*, were *not representative* or were *too small*.
- Statistical techniques that were inappropriate for the data being analysed, particularly with *serial* and *multiple* crimes.
- The methods used to test the *reliability* of the predictive models.

Aitken et al. (1995) demonstrated how statistical models could be developed from an analysis of solved cases to predict characteristics of the offender of a new case. As expected, a clear trade-off was identified between the *detail* of the predictions that could be made about the offender and the *reliability* of those predictions. With a sample of 320 solved cases of sexually-oriented child homicide, only outline offender characteristics could be predicted independently with an acceptable level of reliability. The 'real-life' problem of *simultaneously* predicting a number of offender characteristics did not appear to be attainable with this size of data set using statistics alone. However, a technique was identified which combined subjective expertise of sexually-oriented child homicide (in this case elicited from an experienced detective) with

---

[3] The sample was exclusively males who had been convicted of only one of the subject crimes ($N = 320$).

the CATCHEM data to produce a simple model that predicted a combination of outline offender characteristics with some reliance. It was anticipated that more detailed predictions would be possible when larger data sets designed specifically for the purpose became available.

The first data set compiled specifically for the Police Research Group offender profiling research programme is described by Davies (Davies, 1997, Chapter 12 of the present Volume). The analyses of the geographical aspects of offending and the criminal careers of the offenders further demonstrate the benefits that are likely to accrue for SIOs from the careful analysis of past cases (see also Davies & Dale, 1995; Davies, Wittebrood & Jackson, in press). This stranger rape data set was also used as the basis of a study of patterns within serial rape offences (see Grubin, Kelly & Ayis, in press). The project investigated whether it was possible to develop a technique to identify, from the behavioural characteristics of the offences alone, which of the crimes had been committed by the same offender. This study broke down the behaviour displayed by the offender within each offence into four components or *domains* related to the *control*, *sexual* and *escape* aspects of the attack, and the personal role or *style* of the attacker (see Table 6.1).

Using a group-means-based cluster analysis, a typology was then created for each of these domains; four *types* were identified for each of the domains. For example, within the 'escape' domain the clustered behaviours ranged from 'Type 1' offences, where the offender appeared unconcerned about escape to 'Type 4' offences where the offender took great precautions, such as wearing a mask and gloves, and/or destroyed semen after the attack.

The study then examined the offences committed by individual serial offenders to establish the extent to which they behaved consistently within each domain (e.g. if the offender was Escape Type 1 in his first rape, was he also Escape Type 1 in subsequent rapes within the series?). Further, the study examined consistency within series across the

Table 6.1. Offence domains of a 'stranger' rape (from Grubin, Kelly & Ayis, 1997, with permission)

Control domain	Behaviours directed towards gaining control of the victim so that the sexual aspect of the attack can take place
Sex domain	Behaviours associated with the sexual component of the attack
Escape domain	Behaviours associated with leaving the crime scene or avoiding capture
Style domain	Behaviours that reflect the offender's personality or offence style, but are not directly necessary for the success of the attack

domains (e.g. if the offender's first offence was Escape Type 1, Sex Type 4, Control Type 1 and Style Type 2, were similar combinations of domain types displayed within subsequent rapes in the series?). The results of the analysis were encouraging.

Of the 50 offenders who had committed two or three rapes, 46 (92%) were consistent throughout their series within at least one of the domains. Similarly, of the 31 offenders who had committed four or more rapes in their series, 21 (68%) were consistent throughout the series within at least one of the domains. Overall, of the 81 serial offenders in the data base, 83% had at least one domain for which they were always of the same type throughout their series. Further, 26% of the serial offenders had two or more crimes within their series which matched across all domain types.

To illustrate the findings, Table 6.2 details the behavioural consistency (or otherwise) of the seven offenders in the data set who had committed a series of six rapes.

CONCLUSION

This study by Grubin, Kelly & Ayis (in press), as with all of the earlier studies mentioned, require replication with larger, independent data sets to ensure that they are of operational significance. To this end, the Police Research Group has expanded its research into serious crime and has set up a new research team within the National Crime Faculty. This collaboration promises to lead to the development of objective advice to assist with many of the decisions that have to be made in the domain and inferential layers of the investigative process. However, the 'science' of offender profiling is still very much in its infancy, and there is much work to be done to develop its empirical base before it can be accepted as a reliable tool for the operational detective.

To summarize, detectives develop the vast majority of their investigative expertise from personal experience, either first-hand or through an apprenticeship role. Consequently, the level of a detective's expertise is largely related to the number and range of crimes that he/she has investigated. Expertise is developed in different aspects of the investigative process such as the *strategic* management of the crime enquiry or the *inference* of offender characteristics from the available information about the crime and the victim.

Some of this expertise is transferable from one type of crime investigation to another. For example, expertise in effective communication within an enquiry team or in the preparation of evidence into a prosecution file will be applicable to all serious crime enquiries. Some exper-

Table 6.2. The behavioural types of the offences committed by offenders with series length 6 (from Grubin, Kelly & Ayis, 1997, with permission)

Offender	Crime	Control	Sex	Escape	Style
12	1st	4	3	3	4
	2nd	4	*	1	4
	3rd	4	3	4	4
	4th	4	3	3	4
	5th	4	1	1	1
	6th	3	2	3	4
17	1st	2	3	2	4
	2nd	*	3	2	1
	3rd	2	2	2	3
	4th	2	1	1	1
	5th	2	1	1	1
	6th	2	2	2	1
57	1st	4	1	4	2
	2nd	4	4	4	4
	3rd	2	4	4	2
	4th	4	1	3	4
	5th	4	4	4	4
	6th	4	4	4	4
58	1st	2	2	2	4
	2nd	4	2	2	4
	3rd	4	4	2	2
	4th	2	2	1	3
	5th	4	4	2	2
	6th	4	4	1	3
83	1st	4	1	2	3
	2nd	4	3	3	1
	3rd	4	1	4	2
	4th	4	1	4	3
	5th	4	3	4	3
	6th	4	3	1	2
89	1st	4	1	4	1
	2nd	2	1	1	1
	3rd	1	1	1	1
	4th	2	1	3	3
	5th	3	3	1	1
	6th	1	1	1	1
139	1st	4	1	4	2
	2nd	4	1	4	2
	3rd	4	1	4	2
	4th	4	1	4	2
	5th	4	1	4	4
	6th	4	3	4	2

* Indicates that there was insufficient data to type the crime in that domain.

tise, however, is relevant only to the specific type of case in which it was developed. In particular, *inferential* expertise, which helps an investigator to speculate as to what type of person committed the crime under investigation, appears to be crime-type specific.

As a consequence, detectives are unlikely to have much inferential expertise in crime types with which they have little or no experience. As some of the UK's most serious crimes (e.g. sexual homicide of children) are very low in volume, there is a need for additional support for detectives in this area. Some of this support may be provided from 'experts' from other disciplines and is made clear in other chapters of this Volume. Studies discussed in this chapter have shown that some inferential and domain knowledge can be developed through the combination of detective expertise, behavioural science theory and statistical validation against solved cases.

CHAPTER 7

A Research Approach to Offender Profiling

Janet L. Jackson, Paul van den Eshof & Esther E. de Kleuver

INTRODUCTION

Within Dutch police organizations, the 1980s brought an increasing awareness and emphasis to the key role that could be played by crime analyses in police investigations. This interest led to several initiatives, one of which was the setting up of an offender profiling unit within the National Criminal Intelligence Division of the National Police Agency. The task of this unit was to respond to requests from regional police forces for help and advice with criminal investigations, particularly those involving serious contact crimes.

When the service finally went into operation in September 1991, the unit's guiding principles and work methods bore a strong resemblance to FBI methods. However, from the beginning of the enterprise it was also recognized that to be effective, the unit had not only to be accountable to those it served, namely the Dutch police, but should also be actively involved in the scientific forum (see Davies, 1997, Chapter 11 of the present Volume). This meant that research, including evaluation studies, should be carried out and the findings made public to ensure critical debate and opportunities for development.

In this chapter, the principles guiding the work of the unit and an indication of the type of caseload it has dealt with will first be described. Data will then be presented from four studies. The first two attempt to provide an empirical answer to the question of what, if any, are the differences between experienced detective work and offender profiling. The final two studies will be more evaluative in nature. One will explore the usefulness of examining the criminal antecedents of rapists. The fourth study describes a consumer evaluation report which explores the extent that regional police forces are satisfied with the service they receive from the profiling unit.

Setting Offender Profiling within a Dutch Context

There are two basic principles underlying the development of the Dutch profiling unit, each of which has consequences for its pattern of work. These are:

1   *Offender profiling is a combination of detective experience and behavioural scientific knowledge.* Given this perspective, it is not surprising that close links were quickly established with the Behavioural Science Unit of the FBI (as it was then called) and still continue to be maintained. A further consequence of this view is that the unit should be organized on multidisciplinary lines. The team comprises a police profiler (trained at the FBI Academy at Quantico) working closely together with a forensic psychologist who is also a qualified lawyer[1].

2   *An offender profile is not an end in itself, but is purely an instrument for steering an investigation in a particular direction.* Within Dutch police practice, offender profiling is not viewed as a product in itself, but simply as another management instrument to further the work of the detective team. This principle means that the profiler's description of a possible offender must always be coupled with practical advice and suggestions about how to proceed with the investigation in hand.

Working within these guidelines, the Dutch profiling unit has dealt with requests for assistance from a broad spectrum of regional forces as well as a number from colleagues from police forces in neighbouring countries. The cases presented cover a wide range of crimes, but are specifically contact crimes (see Table 7.1 for examples). Table 7.2 shows the types of advice involved[2].

While it may be assumed that a profiling team's basic task is to produce profiles, such a job description would hide both the depth and breadth of support that can and is offered. The team offers a variety of expertise similar to that subsumed under the broader label of 'criminal

---

[1] Since the initial preparation of this manuscript, a second psychologist, who is also a law graduate, has now joined the team.
[2] Given that the unit was initially described as being a profiling unit, it is perhaps surprising to note that of the 55 types of advice given, only 16 were actually profiles.

Table 7.1. Caseload, period 1 September 1991 – 31 August 1994

Type of case	Frequency
Sexual homicide cases (SH)	20
Murder cases (M)	11
Rape cases (R)	10
Disappearances (D)	3
Threat cases (T)	4
Sexual abuse cases (SA)	5
Arson cases (A)	2
Total number of cases	55

Table 7.2. Type of advice given, period 1 September 1991 – 31 August 1994

Type of advice	Frequency
Profile (P)	16
Investigative solutions (IS)	46
Personality assessment (PA)	9
Crime assessment	2
Interview techniques (IT)	15
Threat assessment	2

investigative analysis' as used by the FBI. This includes advice such as investigative suggestions, personality assessment and interview techniques which may often be as, or even more, useful to the investigating team than an actual profile (see Bekerian & Jackson, 1997, Chapter 12 of the present Volume). Moreover, given the guiding principles behind the unit, the actual assistance that the team gives is seldom, indeed if ever, simply of one type but is generally a combination (e.g. a sexual homicide case may actually produce a profile, practical investigative suggestions, and also advice on interviewing techniques).

Do Experienced Detectives and Profilers Operate Differently?

The first study was carried out in 1989 when the plans for the unit were still in a preparatory phase. Decisions had not yet been made regarding the type of profiling approach that would be most useful for, and fit most easily into, the practical work situation of Dutch investigating officers. This initial study examined whether there were any differences between offender profiling and traditional detective work. The justification for this premise was as follows. When experienced detectives are faced with a new crime scene, they interpret or make sense of the situation by applying their previously acquired knowledge about similar types of offence and also about the types of people frequently encountered as offenders, victims and witnesses in similar crimes. Thus, when faced with a new crime, detectives use their prior experience to establish a theory of what has probably taken place and the type of person for whom they should probably be looking. In this respect, it was hypothesized that the cognitive strategies adopted by experienced detectives would be qualitatively similar to the strategies assumed to be used by profilers and should be equally capable of being formalized as a set of *if–then* statements or production rules, e.g. *if* the victim was sexually assaulted and was older than 60, *then* the perpetrator was a man between 20 and 25[3]. However, it was also acknowledged that differences in terms of specific experience could arise. For example, the crime selected for study was stranger rape, and it is possible that some detectives, even though they may have many years of investigating experience, may nevertheless have had minimal exposure to this particular form of crime. As a result, their prior knowledge would probably be very non-specific and therefore of limited value in making sense of a new case.

STUDY 1: AN EXPLORATION OF DETECTIVES' THEORIES OF STRANGER RAPE

The first study examined the underlying theories of stranger rape held by 30 detectives from various forces throughout the country. All had had some experience of investigating serious sexual crimes (see van der Heijden, van den Eshof & Schrama, 1990, for a more complete description of the study). The main focus of the study was to explore whether detectives build up a detailed picture of possible suspects in the course of a criminal investigation and, if they do, to examine which features of the crime scene are particularly important in developing this description.

The study included three tasks. The first involved completing a questionnaire containing some general questions about the way the detectives normally conducted a rape investigation. The second required the detectives to recall and reconstruct a case in which they had personally been involved. In particular, they were asked to focus on how information relating to the case had been gathered and what steps were taken on the basis of the available information. We will not discuss the results of these tasks further but will concentrate on the third and final task. The detectives were presented with nine elements of a crime scene (based on

---

[3] That profilers operate in this fashion is, at this point, an assumption based on personal communication between the researchers and FBI profilers rather than an empirical fact.

the FBI crime scene criteria) and were asked to indicate whether, and how, each could be used to deduce certain characteristics of the probable offender. The crime elements that were presented included:

1 The selection of the victim.
2 The characteristics of the victim.
3 The modus operandi of the offender.
4 The attitude of the offender towards the victim.
5 The manner in which the offender reacted to certain behaviour of the victim.
6 The language used by the offender.
7 Violence used by the offender.
8 The state in which the victim was left behind.
9 Forensic evidence at the crime scene.

The detectives were also presented with a list of possible characteristics of the offender which they could, if they wished, use in their deductions. These included:

1 Age.
2 Social characteristics (e.g. civil status, profession).
3 Cultural background.
4 Neighbourhood and place of residence.
5 Character traits.
6 Possible mental disturbances.
7 Outward appearance (e.g. body height, clothes).
8 Habits (e.g. visits to bars).
9 Possible other details (e.g. antecedents).

The most striking result of this phase of the study was the sheer number of possible characteristics of the offender that the detectives said they could deduce from the elements of the crime scene. When their individual responses were reformulated into if–then statements or rules by the researchers (see van der Heijden, van den Eshof & Schrama, 1990, for the procedure used), the number totalled 700. In particular, many offender characteristics were deducted from the modus operandus (141), the violence and the language used by the offender (119 and 104 respectively) and forensic evidence left at the crime scene (101). In contrast, only a few if–then statements related to either the way in which the offender selected his victim (16) or to victim characteristics (45).

This large number of rules appears, at first glance, to confirm that detectives do make inferences about the likely suspect based on elements of the crime scene. However, a more detailed examination of the actual rules formalized from the detectives' statements raises questions about their utility. Many of them would actually be of extremely limited use for investigation purposes. For example, 85 rules related to ethnicity, race and skin colour. Given that such information is frequently reported by the victim in stranger rape cases, such rules have little practical value. Moreover, a study of the content of many of these rules suggested that they were based more on general stereotypical information than on actual domain-specific knowledge gained through experience (see van der Heijden, van den Eshof & Schrama, 1990).

A further problem related to the level of specificity in many of the statements. For example, some deductions were overly general, like reference to 'young' or 'old' perpetrators without delineating the actual age ranges included in these broad categories. Other statements went in the other direction and were in fact too specific, suggesting that they were based on one particular case and would only be useful when applied in the future to an offence virtually identical to the original. An example would be, 'A button left at the scene of the crime would indicate that the offender is younger than 18 years'. While this statement was no doubt a true experience from a particular crime, its predictive usefulness is extremely doubtful.

In summary, the study showed that detectives, experienced in dealing with serious sexual crimes, can and do draw inferences and conclusions from elements of the crime scene (particularly from the modus operandi, the violence and language used by the offender, and forensic evidence left at the crime scene). Moreover, their deductions could be formalized as if–then statements or production rules. In this respect, there may seem to be little difference between the strategies used by detectives and those assumed to be used by profilers. However, the quality of the if–then statements or rules that could be formalized from the detectives inferences and conclusions was very mixed. A very large number of rules were formulated but they alternated between being too global or too specific, with neither type having much general predictive value.

One further study was conducted. According to the criteria of nontriviality and precise formulation, 257 if–then rules were selected from the original corpus of 700 (see Table 7.3 for some examples). The detectives who had taken part in the first study were once again asked to participate (22 accepted and 4 others were added to the group). The total set of selected rules were presented to the 26 detectives in random sequence on two occasions. On the first presentation, the detective's task was to judge how often each of the rules applied in practice, using a five-point scale (never, rarely, sometimes, often, and always). The task on the second presentation was to rate how much experience the respondent had personally had with each rule (the choice was: no personal experience; yes, one personal experience; and yes, several personal experiences).

The judgements of the detectives failed to produce much consensus and instead underlined the individual idiosyncracy of the original corpus of rules. On average, the detectives rated 4% of the rules to be never applicable[4], 25% seldom applicable, 48% sometimes applicable, 22% often applicable and only 1% to be always applicable. Group differences, presumably as a result of experience, were also found. Detectives from the larger metropolitan forces were more likely to judge particular rules to be applicable than those from provincial regions.

Unfortunately, a similar mixed picture, with large individual as well as geographical differences between detectives, appeared in relation to practical experience with the rules. On average, 51% of the rules were judged never to have been personally experienced; 26% to have been experienced once; and 23% to have been personally experienced on several occasions.

In summary, the results of these initial studies show that it is possible to extract and formalize the knowledge and practical experience of detectives involved in serious sexual crimes. It appears that they do apply knowledge which can be formalized as if–then rules in order to deduce certain offender characteristics from crime scene characteristics. However, the rules selected did not achieve a large degree of consensus and would therefore be of little practical value. Moreover, there seemed to be little similarity between the rules that were produced by

Table 7.3. Example of rules presented to the detectives

If the offender and victim met in a local bar, *then* the offender lives in the
   neighbourhood
If the offender makes himself unidentifiable, *then* he knows the victim
If the crime is always committed around the same early hour of the morning,
   then the offender has a paper round or works on shifts
If the offender drives to a quiet lane, *then* he lives in the neighbourhood
If the offender pressurizes the victim not to go to the police *then* he has
   antecedents
If the offender shows consideration to the victim, *then* he is married or has a
   relationship

---

[4] These rules were probably formulated by detectives who participated in the first study
but not in the second.

our detectives and those found in FBI publications on offender profiling (see Hazelwood & Burgess, 1987) and presumably taught in profiling courses. Our original hypothesis of no difference between the deductions assumed to be made by FBI profilers and those of experienced detectives was therefore not confirmed. In an attempt to explore possible similarities and differences between the two groups further, a case study was carried out.

STUDY 2: AN EXPERT/NOVICE APPROACH TO OFFENDER PROFILING

The second study was carried out as a preliminary examination of the processes involved in producing an offender profile. Since the number of subjects taking part in the study was extremely small ($N = 3$), it must be viewed as a case study. While such an approach may be criticized on the grounds of generalizibility, given the scarcity of expert profilers (only one in the Netherlands), the choice of methodology open to us was limited.

The specific approach adopted was one frequently used by cognitive psychologists to explore expertise in specific domains, namely an expert/novice paradigm. It involves all participants producing verbal protocols, that is, talking aloud as they attempt to solve a particular problem. One of the most stable findings from such studies (e.g. VanLehn, 1989) is that, in general, strategy differences are found, with experts adopting a top-down and novices a bottom-up approach. A top-down strategy refers to processing and interpretation of information being affected by what an individual brings to a stimulus situation (e.g. expectations determined by context, and concepts acquired from past experience). This is in contrast to novice behaviour which is predominantly bottom-up. In bottom-up processing, the knowledge base relating to the particular domain under consideration is very limited and can therefore not guide further processing. Instead, the novice has to rely solely on processing new information as it emerges. A further robust finding from expert/novice studies is that, in general, experts perform faster than novices (VanLehn, 1989).

Two *experts*, the Dutch FBI-trained profiler and a detective from the Rotterdam police force with experience in investigating serious sexual crimes, took part in the study. The third subject was a *novice*. He was a psychologist with some experience of reading police files, although mainly for civil offences. The material used in the study included all the available documentation relating to a sexual murder which took place seven years earlier but still remains unsolved. The case involves a young boy of 11 who was sexually assaulted and murdered at one site (crime scene 1) and whose body was subsequently dumped at a second site (crime scene 2). The three subjects were given access to all of the available information and were asked to 'think aloud' as they worked through the files and attempted to develop a *picture* or *description* of the possible perpetrator. Neither the detective nor the psychologist had read any published literature relating to offender profiling. All three were filmed as they worked through the files (which took each of them almost a full working week). The specific experimental questions that were to be explored in this study were:

- What are the processes involved in producing an offender description or profile?
- Are there substantial differences (quantitative and/or qualitative) between the processes used (top-down/bottom-up) and the interpretations made by a professional profiler, an experienced detective and an intelligent novice ?

A fuller description of this study can be found elsewhere (e.g. Jackson, Herbrink & van Koppen, in press). For the present argument, we will concentrate on discussing the differences found between the two *experts*.

Since detective skills have seldom been considered within an expert/novice paradigm, let us first speculate on how strategy differences might apply in the criminal investigation domain. As an expert in crime, the experienced police detective would be expected to adopt a top-down approach. In other words, when he comes to examine a crime scene, his knowledge of previous crimes as well as knowledge of the ways and workings of criminals allow him not only to organize his thinking and actions within a particular framework but also to anticipate and fill in gaps in his information. As an expert, the detective has at his command a large portfolio of information and episodes from which to construct a theory of the crime and of the likely perpetrator that will fit the critical events of the crime; he will then use this theory as a basis for actively searching for further evidence which, by inference, should exist if the chosen theory is a valid one. In short, a detective's skill may rely to a great extent on the depth and breadth of his/her specific knowledge base which is used to search for, process and interpret new facts and information in a top-down fashion. In this respect, an experienced detective should not differ from a trained profiler whose approach, based on the study of, and working experience with, a large number of criminal cases is also presumed to be top-down oriented.

Transcripts of all sessions were made and an analysis of these showed that, not surprisingly, the first step for both experts was one of data assimilation, the gathering of information relating to the case. The processes they used to analyse these data, however, were rather different. As the profiler read and analysed the data (the WHAT), it was clear from his verbal protocol that he was simultaneously trying to build up a picture of the type of person the perpetrator was (the WHO). While he read everything very carefully, his analyses were guided in a top-down fashion by a mental checklist which included domain-specific knowledge based on probability judgements. This checklist related to factors such as knowledge of different offender types, generating selection rules, matching the current crime with previous crimes and predicting post-crime behaviour. He used this knowledge to interpret and structure the data he was assimilating. A working hypothesis was then made and an initial reconstruction of the crime was developed. Further reading of the file resulted in refinements being made to his working hypothesis and an elaboration of the reconstruction. Based on these, he developed an initial summary of the case, listing some of the characteristics of the probable offender (the WHO).

The starting point for the detective was the crime itself. This was the problem that had to be solved and as he studied the files, he focused on details (the WHAT) that could be used as evidence to convict the perpetrator. Unlike the profiler, he constructed a picture of the crime very quickly and only then did he formulate working hypotheses which he then sought to confirm. From his verbal reports, it was clear that his reading of the autopsy reports and study of the crime scene pictures was guided by a search for the motive for the crime (the WHY) and that this variable was important in arriving at a possible WHO. While he did produce a description of the possible suspect for us, his main concern was with matching the evidence he had acquired to a list of potential suspects[5]. His goal was clearly to find the offender and to produce enough corroborating evidence to convict him.

A summary of the most important elements of the reconstruction for both the profiler and detective are shown in Table 7.4. An inspection of this table shows that while there are many similarities, some differences appear (e.g. location of crime scene 1, which was the initial encounter). Such differences are important since they are closely related to the descriptions/profiles that were made. For example, in describing the possible legal and arrest history of the perpetrator, the profiler, who stated in his reconstruction that the offender is cruising around looking for victims, described him as having a prior record. For the detective, on

---

[5] This list had been devised during the initial police investigation and included a number of persons with previous convictions for similar types of crimes

the other hand, the meeting with the victim was more of a chance encounter and he assumed that the crime was probably the first and possibly the last the offender would carry out. These differences would obviously affect the criminal investigation process. Unfortunately, until the perpetrator is found, it is impossible to judge which of these reconstructions and related predictions are the correct ones.

Summarizing our data leads to the following conclusion. There are differences between the profiler and the experienced detective. They approached the case very differently: they had different goals and used different strategies to reach them. The profiler brought with him a wide range of experience of similar cases and used this knowledge in a top-down fashion to analyse, structure and interpret the case information. He then used this information to predict the probable personality and behavioural characteristics of the offender. The detective worked in a more bottom-up fashion, assimilating more and more details and attempted to corroborate and weigh up their value as evidence at each step. Our detective had many years of investigative experience in a metropolitan area and came to us with high recommendations. In spite of

Table 7.4. A summary of the most important elements of the construction for both the profiler and detective

---

Profiler
Offender is cruising, looking for a victim
Unexpected encounter with boy — uses ruse — boy goes willingly
Crime Scene 1 — somewhere outdoors
Partially undressed (top half)
Oral sex — sperm in mouth
During or shortly after sexual encounter, strangled — with hands
Redressed
Transportation to crime scene 2 (known to offender) — to prevent discovery of
  body
Offender leaves scene quickly
Discards garment

Detective
Offender uses ruse (e.g. ask directions) to get boy into car. Boy goes willingly
Crime Scene 1 — car
Garment off
Forced to have oral sex — sperm found in mouth
Boy escapes
Offender catches him — face down in the dirt — kills him probably with a rope
Transportation to crime scene 2 (known to offender) — to prevent discovery of
  body
Interrupted — escapes in panic
Throws garment away

this, he did not appear to have an organized body of specific knowledge that he could use in a top-down fashion to guide and organize his exploration of a novel case or to predict the type of person who should be sought.

GENERAL CONCLUSIONS FROM THE TWO STUDIES

The main conclusion we draw from our work to date is that there are a number of important differences between traditional detective work and offender profiling.

One of the main characteristics of offender profiling is that it is based on inferences drawn from considerable experiences both of and with similar types of case. This experience is achieved by extensively studying the main characteristics of a large number of solved crimes. Solved crimes produce data which can then function as statistical probabilities or testable hypotheses rather than facts. This probabilistic way of thinking is virtually unknown in everyday police practice. For detectives, facts are all-important. Forensic evidence is more secure if it is based on established data and not on probabilities.

Further differences between the profiler and the detective are also the result of specific training. For example, in the FBI training course followed by the profiler, a lot of emphasis was placed on studying the rich behavioural information incorporated in crime scene characteristics and how these data can be extrapolated and used to further an investigation. The results of this training were found in the mental checklist the profiler used to generate information leading to a working hypothesis. In contrast, traditional research work, such as experienced by the detective, is more likely to focus primarily on the search for clues such as fingerprints, traces of blood, hair and fibres that will be useful for technical, forensic research and information from witness statements. These data are combined to form a reconstruction of the case and only then are testable hypotheses produced.

The verbal protocols also showed that experience with specific training programmes increased the ability of the profiler to deal with, and to have available in memory, combinations of data represented in classes or categories of crimes. In contrast, the detective failed to employ higher-order classes and considered individual details, which added an extra burden on his memory processes. Examples of the representations or classifications that the profiler used are the typologies which have been developed to describe rapists and child molesters (e.g. Hazelwood, 1995; Lanning, 1995). These were clearly unknown to the detective.

EVALUATION OF OFFENDER PROFILING PRACTICES

An offender profiling approach appears to add additional information to standard police investigations. It is important, however, to continue to monitor and evaluate progress. To date, our research has concentrated on three questions:

1   How valid are certain probability rules used in offender profiling?
2   What percentage of offenders are apprehended as a result of a profile?
3   Are the police satisfied with the service they are given by the profiling unit?

Let us consider each of these in turn.

STUDY 3: AN EXAMINATION OF THE CRIMINAL RECORDS OF CONVICTED RAPISTS

The principles used by the Dutch profiling unit to derive offender profiles in rape cases lean heavily on the knowledge and experience of the FBI Behavioural Science Unit, formalized as probability rules. However, there has been little empirical research testing the validity of these probability rules in general, and certainly none within the Dutch context. The goal of the present study was therefore to explore the validity of certain rules relating specific characteristics of the offence (rape) to certain characteristics of the perpetrators, namely their previous criminal records or antecedents (see van den Eshof, de Kleuver & Ho Tham, in press, for a more detailed report). This was done by means of an in-depth study of official police records. Before describing the study in some detail, however, let us first place this type of criminological research within a theoretical framework.

Traditionally, criminological studies have analysed variables (such as family interaction styles, age at first conviction, and number of previous convictions) in order to predict either future delinquent careers (e.g. Farrington, 1986; Glueck & Glueck, 1930; Loeber & Stouthamer-Loeber, 1986), or recidivism (e.g. Grenier & Roundtree, 1987; Hassin, 1986; Nijboer, 1975; Wormith & Goldstone, 1984). Many of these studies have focused on the question of whether or not criminals specialize in their careers (predictive research). Whilst accepting the usefulness of this approach, van de Bunt (1988) has suggested that such studies are also of relevance to another goal, namely that of furthering police investigations (crime detection research). He claims that much of current police practice now proceeds on the presupposition that recidivists are specialists and that new police investigative strategies based on this specialization hypothesis are currently being developed.

The difference in emphasis between predictive and crime detection research is mirrored in the type of questions addressed by each. The traditional experimental question in prediction studies is, 'given the particular characteristics of a certain person, what conclusions can be drawn with regard to his/her future criminal career?'. This question is in fact reversed for studies aimed at furthering police investigations, becoming, 'given (the nature of) a certain crime, what conclusions can be drawn with regard to the criminal experiences of the perpetrator?'.

The focus of the present study is on the latter crime detection type of question. First, however, let us consider what is known about criminal careers. Although other theories exist, in general there is most support for the theory which suggests that criminals commit a diversity of delinquent activities over the course of their criminal careers (see, for example, Briar & Pilavian, 1965; Farrington & Lambert, Chapter 8 of the present Volume; Davies, 1997, Chapter 11 of the present Volume; Smith & Smith, 1984). Although not much research has yet considered the criminal careers of rapists, the results that do exist support the general view that antecedents are better described by diversity than by specialization. For example, in a study which looked at the assault of female strangers, Heritage (1992) found that a large percentage of the perpetrators had antecedents for crimes other than sexual ones: 79% had committed property crimes. Moreover, violent crime and acts of criminal damage or disorderly conduct were present in the criminal records of almost half the offenders. Hazelwood & Warren (1989) analysed the records of 41 serial rapists and they too found many different types of crimes to be present in the rapists' criminal histories. The most frequently occurring non-sexual offences included burglary and breaking and entering (cf. Davies, 1997, Chapter 11 of the present Volume).

A further relevant finding from the literature for the relationship between the characteristics of the rape and the perpetrators' criminal record are that rapists without any criminal record are very rare indeed. For example, in their study of imprisoned rapists in England, Grubin & Gunn (1990) found the total to be 14%; in an American survey, Knight & Prentky (1987) found the percentage to be 6%; Heritage (1992) reported that only four rapists in his sample had no criminal record (5%); the equivalent figure for Hazelwood and Warren (1989) was one rapist (2%).

These results present interesting findings about the criminal history of rapists, but, unfortunately, none of the studies discussed have attempted to link antecedents with specific crime characteristics. Since this is precisely the type of information that is required for offender pro-filing, the present study describes an attempt to examine these links. The materials used were official police records of solved assault and rape cases. Those selected for study had to meet the following requirements:

- The victim and perpetrator were not to be acquainted. However, it is conceivable that the perpetrator's tactics included getting to know the victim and engaging in a short relationship. Such cases were included in the analysis.
- The perpetrators were to have been found guilty of at least one com-pleted rape. According to Dutch law, this requires the penetration of a body orifice (vagina, anus or mouth)
- The victim was to be 16 years or older at the time of the crime.

A total of some 322 cases involving 112 rapists were analysed. The results are based on 112 completed rape cases committed by 112 differ-ent perpetrators, 71 Dutchmen and 41 persons who were born abroad (since it is not clear at what age they actually came to live in the Netherlands, this group is excluded from further analysis). The last completed crime of each perpetrator was selected. At the time of these crimes, the perpetrators' ages ranged from 14 to 57 years, with an aver-age of 28 years.

To place the data within the context of previously published studies, a number of characteristics relating to the antecedents of the sample were first examined. On average, the perpetrators had 10 antecedents prior to the rape, although just under 18% of them had no previous record. This percentage is higher than that found by either Grubin & Gunn, Knight & Prentky or Heritage. (If the group who were born abroad are included, the percentage having no previous record rises to 23%). Another impor-tant aspect that should be taken into account when considering the num-ber of antecedents is that of age. For instance, the chance that a young offender had antecedents was relatively small compared to that of older offenders. Among the group of 18-year-olds, for instance, only 15% had antecedents for sexual crimes, while of the 26-year-old group, almost 53% had antecedents for sexual crimes (see van den Eshof, de Kleuver & Ho Tham, in press).

Almost 70% of our sample had antecedents for property crimes, a fig-ure which is similar to both that of Grubin & Gunn (72%) and Heritage (79%). Other types of antecedent offences and crimes were the use of violence and traffic violations, which is also consistent with the litera-ture. Traffic violations were almost always serious offences or crimes, such as driving while under the influence of alcohol, failing to stop after an accident, and joyriding. More than 44% had antecedents for sexual crimes, which is similar to the findings of both Heritage (40 – 50%) and Grubin & Gunn (43%).

These results are therefore in agreement with other published studies, namely that the criminal antecedents of rapists are diverse and not specialized. In fact, when we compared the criminal careers of our sample of rapists with a sample of 204 Dutch bank robbers (van den Eshof & van der Heijden, 1990), who ranged in age from 17 to 53 years (average age 27), no differences in specialization were evident. Instead, it was the similarity in career patterns that was most striking. Apart from the crimes on which the sample selection was based, namely robbery or rape, there were few differences between the two groups in terms of criminal antecedents (see Figures 7.1 and 7.2), although other aspects of their lifestyles did vary significantly. The bank robbers were professional criminals who had usually committed more than one bank robbery, mostly in cooperation with others. In contrast, the rapists were mainly isolated, single men who raped one or more women whom they did not know (according to Groth's typology of rapists, most of them were 'power reassurance rapists'; Groth, Burgess & Holmstrom, 1977; see Badcock, 1997, Chapter 2 of the present Volume).

The conclusion to be drawn from this examination of the data is therefore that criminal antecedents alone do not provide sufficient data on which to base the offender profiling of rapists. To put it more strongly, if there is little difference between the antecedent patterns of robbers and rapists, how can antecedents be of use to offender profiling?

The purpose of this study, however, was to examine the degree to which certain characteristics of the offence relate to criminal backgrounds. In particular, the aim was to test the validity of a number of if–then rules, expressed as probabilities, that could be used by the Dutch profiling team. Given that the rules actually used in producing a profile have to take the interaction of a large variety of crime characteristics into account, they are necessarily complex. As a first step, a number of possible rules have been simplified into the following testable hypotheses:

1   Offenders who use expressive violence more often have antecedents which involve the use of violence than offenders who use instrumental violence.
2   Offenders who use a great deal of violence more often have antecedents which involve the use of violence than offenders who inflict little violence.
3   Offenders who take many precautions more often have antecedents than offenders who take few precautions.
4   Offenders who have reached an orgasm more often have antecedents than offenders who have not.

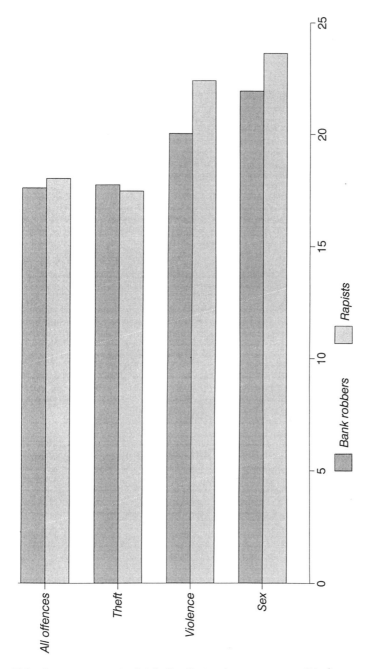

Figure 7.1. Average age at which the first crime was committed: comparison between bank robbers and rapists.

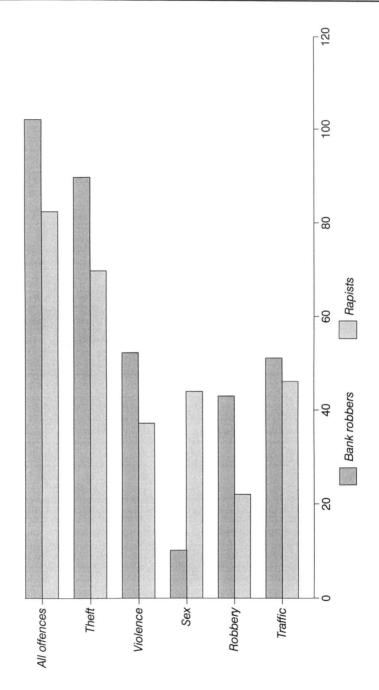

Figure 7.2. Percentage of antecedents per type of crime: comparison between bank robbers and rapists.

5 Offenders who have engaged in several different sexual acts more often have antecedents than offenders who have engaged in only a few sexual acts.
6 Offenders who have committed rape within a home more often have antecedents for burglary than those who have committed rape outside.

The first two hypotheses focus on the use of violence. According to the literature (Warren, Reboussin, Hazelwood & Wright, 1991; Knight & Prentky, 1987) two qualitatively different types of violence can be distinguished:

- *Expressive violence* is used to describe situations where the perpetrator applies more violence than is necessary to keep the victim under control (i.e. the purpose of the violence is not primarily control but more to meet psychological needs).
- *Instrumental violence* is used to describe situations where the goal of the violence is solely to keep the victim under control. The level of this type of violence can vary with victim type: the perpetrator may use a high level of instrumental violence (to keep the victim under control) or a low level (when the victim offers little resistance).

The results show that offenders who used expressive violence when committing a rape more often had antecedents for violence than those who used instrumental violence. This suggests that the purpose of the violence (whether intended as an instrument for achieving control, or expressive of psychological needs) seems to be of significance. In contrast, there were no differences in antecedents between those who used a great deal of violence and those who used little. Thus, the amount of violence used did not yield any information about antecedents while type of violence did.

The third, fourth and fifth hypotheses relate to the criminal experience of the offender, with the important question being whether or not an analysis of the crime scene can predict the level of experience (the total number of antecedents) of the offender. Hypothesis (3) is based on the notion that offenders who are experienced criminals have learned how to obstruct criminal investigations. To explore this hypothesis, the relationship between the taking of precautionary measures and previous antecedents was examined. Our definition of precautions included the use of a disguise, wearing gloves, covering the victim's face, gagging the victim, putting objects out of order and removing traces. When offenders who had used either no or only a small number of precautions were compared with those who had used many, the results revealed no difference in criminal experience.

The idea behind the fourth and fifth hypotheses is that perpetrators who are experienced criminals are less nervous during the actual crime, with the result that their sexual activities are not hindered in any way. An examination of these two hypotheses, however, showed that they could not be supported. Neither those criminals who reached an orgasm nor those who engaged in several different sexual acts had more antecedents than offenders who showed none of these behaviours. Thus, those aspects of sexual behaviour at the crime scene explored here could not predict the criminal experience of the offender.

The final hypothesis involves the difference between rapes that take place within a home and those that occur outdoors. The results showed a significant relationship between indoor rapes and antecedents for breaking and entering: perpetrators who have committed rape within a home more often have antecedents for burglary than perpetrators who have committed rape outdoors. What is perhaps even more remarkable, however, is that no relationship whatsoever was found between indoor rapes and antecedents for any other property crimes apart from burglary (cf. Davies, 1997, Chapter 11 of the present Volume).

Let us now summarize the findings of this study. In one respect, the information we have presented may appear inconsistent. The pattern of rapists' criminal antecedents hardly seems to deviate from that of another group, bank robbers. On the other hand, the study has shown that it is possible, be it to a limited extent, to use specific information relating to a rape case to predict something of the offender's past criminal history. We are of the opinion that much of the criminological research into criminal antecedents has to date been too general to be of real use for offender profiling. If more research examining the relationships between specific characteristics of certain crimes and the characteristics of the perpetrator were to be carried out, this could be extremely productive for offender profiling.

We would suggest that this type of research we have just described is very important if offender profiling is to achieve an acceptable status in the scientific and police worlds. In our view, the relationships between crime scene characteristics and offender characteristics that are the basis of offender profiling should not be blindly accepted but should regularly be tested by independent research.

ARE PROFILES EFFECTIVE?

A completely different type of evaluation, but one that is obviously also of prime importance, is to study the effectiveness of profiling techniques.

What sort of success rate[6] do such techniques yield? An answer to this question is hard to find. As do most professionals, individual profilers tend to report their success stories and keep their less successful ventures to themselves. Apart from autobiographical accounts, there is very little literature on this subject[7] (but see Copson, 1995; Gudjonsson & Copson, 1997, Chapter 4 of the present Volume). Scientific research exploring the effectiveness of offender profiling is not an easy task. The use of police files is problematic (see, for example, Farrington & Lambert, 1997, Chapter 8 of the present Volume; Davies, 1997, Chapter 11 of the present Volume): a retrospective study inevitably encounters difficulties in deciphering which information was actually used to make decisions. The ideal would be a prospective study in which the researcher would follow the activities of the investigating team in real time with the aim of exploring how much the profile and additional advice contributed to the solution of the crime. Given that one case would not be sufficient on which to base conclusions, this type of research will not only be time-intensive but will have to span several years.

STUDY 4: A REPORT OF CONSUMER SATISFACTION

Success of profiling can be defined as the number of hits scored by profiles. However, one can criticize such a definition as being too restrictive. Given that the work of our profiling unit covers a wider scope of assistance than merely producing profiles, perhaps our definition should also be extended to incorporate the perceived value of advice in relation to investigative suggestions, crime assessment and interviewing techniques (see also Gudjonsson & Copson, 1997, Chapter 4 of the present Volume). A second point worth discussing is who should judge the success, or the effectiveness, of the help that is offered by a profiling team? Surely, if we wish to judge the effectiveness of a service we should approach the consumers of that service directly and ask them for their views? While this may seem a fairly obvious step, surprisingly it is one that has rarely been systematically explored.

In spite of widening the scope of our search to include the broader term 'criminal investigative analysis', at the time we carried out our

---

[6] Defined as the number of hits (i.e. the number of offenders convicted) as a result of using the profile.

[7] Such a study is currently being prepared in the Netherlands. All the profiles that have been made by the Dutch profiling team have been collected and, as new information relating to a case becomes available, this is being collated. As yet, there are still insufficient data on which to base general conclusions.

study, it was only possible to find one published study that discussed consumer satisfaction in any depth (Pinizzotto, 1984). References to the need for such studies were made in some FBI literature. For example, Dietz (1985) stated:

> 'Many success stories and a consumer satisfaction survey indicating that many police departments receiving profiles find them helpful have generated great enthusiasm.' (*Please note, however, that the author does not refer to any published article in this respect.*) 'Nonetheless, the Unit is aware that the accuracy of profiling has not yet been measured.'

Later, McCann (1992) wrote, in relation to current research developments:

> 'Another area of potential value is the design of so-called *consumer satisfaction* studies........Under this research paradigm, resulting profiles can be assessed for their accuracy and validity by those who make use of the profiles, namely criminal investigators and police agencies.'

He did not, however, refer to any studies which explored consumer satisfaction.

Given that the only way to improve a service is to get this type of feedback, a consumer evaluation study was carried out in the Netherlands (for a full report of the study, see Jackson, van Koppen & Herbrink, 1993). Although almost 40 cases had been presented to the profiling team by this time, they were in various stages of completion. In order to achieve some level of conformity, the cases selected for evaluation had to meet several selection criteria. These included the following: the complete set of case papers (i.e. the police files, forensic reports, crime scene photographs, etc.) had to be available to the profilers; a final report (or profile, if made) had been completed and delivered to the police force; and sufficient time had elapsed for the investigating team to act on the advice given. Twenty cases met these criteria. They varied from sexual homicide to threat and were not only spread geographically over different regional police forces in the Netherlands but also included two cases in Belgium. The actual breakdown of the cases was as follows: 8 sexual homicides; 4 murders; 4 rapes; 1 disappearance; 2 threat cases, and 1 child sexual abuse series. One prominent member (e.g. SIO) from each case was contacted and an interview was arranged. The questions guiding the interview include the following:

- How did the team know about the services offered by the profiling group?
- Why did the team decide to get in contact with the profiling group?

- What were the team's expectations in contacting the profiling group, and what sort of help/advice were they hoping to get?
- How did the team experience the contact at a personal level?
- How did they rate the usefulness of the advice/help they were given — did it meet their expectations, or were they disappointed or surprised that the help was in a different direction than they had anticipated?
- Would they ask for similar help in the future, or did they have ideas about other sorts of support/advice systems that would be either equally or more beneficial to officers in the field?

Trained profilers have high demands in relation to the amount of information they require in order to produce a profile, and when this is not available, no profile is forthcoming. This was also the case in our study: of the 20 cases examined, only six were found by the team to be suitable for profiling. As far as the other 14 were concerned, in some there was already a suspect in custody. In others, there were simply not enough data available. In yet another, a disappearance case, there was no crime scene. As can be seen in Table 7.5, however, other types of investigative help were available.

The evaluations of the interviewees were divided into three categories: very useful, reasonably useful and not very useful. The broad conclusion to be drawn from the ratings was that the majority of detectives interviewed could be viewed as satisfied customers: of the 42 evaluations made, only two were viewed in a completely negative light. Of

Table 7.5. Breakdown of advice for different crimes

	Sexual homicide	Rape	Murder	Other	Total
Profile	1	1			2
Profile + IS*	3			1	4
IS			1		1
IT + IS		1	1		2
PA + IT	1				1
PA + IS	1	1	1		3
CA + IS	1			1	2
PA + IT + IS	1	1	1		3
TA + IS				2	2
Total	8	4	4	4	20

(Other = 1 sexual abuse case, 1 disappearance case, 2 threat cases)
* IS = investigative suggestions; TA = threat assessment; CA = crime assessment; PA = personality assessment; IT = interviewing techniques.

the seven respondents who had received help on interviewing techniques, all judged the advice to be very useful; of the eight personality assessments given, six were rated as being very useful and two as reasonably useful; 12 of the 17 investigative suggestions given were rated as being very useful, four as reasonably useful and only one as not very useful. In summary, therefore, the great majority of advice falling under the broader label of criminal investigative analysis was rated very highly indeed.

Transcripts of the interviews revealed another important function of the expert team, that of teaching. Irrespective of the crime they had been investigating, the majority of those interviewed remarked spontaneously that the contact with the crime analysis group had been something of a *general learning experience*. They described how much they had learned from the experience of simply discussing the case with experts who were not directly involved in the case, how many new ideas and work strategies they had acquired and how useful these would be in future investigations. While hard to quantify, this teaching role is an important measure of consumer satisfaction and this type of help was greatly appreciated by the Dutch detectives.

But what of profiles? Did the positive satisfaction with other types of advice extend to profiles? We have already mentioned that only six of the 20 cases studied actually resulted in a profile being produced. The sample sizes are therefore too small to produce any firm conclusions. Nonetheless, judgements in relation to the six profiles were mixed, with two being judged as positive, three as intermediate and one as negative.

Another means of evaluating profiles of course would be to look at hit rate. However, as we have previously mentioned, measuring hit rate is not an easy task. For example, in one specific case where a profile was made and the perpetrator was subsequently arrested, there is a major difference of opinion between the profiler and the investigating team about what actually contributed to the success. Apart from problems inherent in retrospective reports (e.g. the confounding of subjective recollections by factors such as the time interval between case and interview, intervening thoughts, actions and wishes that become incorporated in current memory of what happened, and hindsight bias), other problems became evident. The majority of cases that were referred to the profiling team were old and, in effect, the police investigations had already come to a dead end. The possibilities that a profile would be able to breathe new life into the case were therefore limited. In fact, in a couple of the cases, the investigating team was disbanded in the time that a profile was being prepared and as a result, the suggestions arising from the profile were not followed.

One specific criticism of profiles that was expressed is of fundamental importance. This relates to the generality of the profile and thus to the lack of specific detail. A number of those interviewed indicated that they had expected far more detailed information, perhaps not at the level of a name, address and telephone number, but certainly more than the very general information they were given (e.g. demographic information, educational level, family characteristics, and age and type of vehicle).

SUMMARY

The results of the first study suggested that the theories adopted by detectives may be either too global or too specific to be of much value in furthering investigations. What is needed is a prototype that would be positioned somewhere between the two extremes of global and specific. Do the profiles of the trained profiler meet these requirements? In the view of some of the detectives interviewed, this appeared not to be the case. Instead, the profiles presented to them were judged to be too global. One explanation for their judgement, and one that we would support, is that when profiles are considered as a separate entity, they seldom, if ever, offer enough foundation or impetus to steer or guide an investigation in a new direction. However, as already indicated, a guiding principle of the Dutch profiling unit is that offender profiling should *never* be viewed as a separate entity. It is a management instrument. This implies that the description of a possible offender should always be coupled with practical advice and suggestions about how to proceed with the investigation in hand. Our consumer study clearly showed these types of assistance to be rated very positively by the detectives and they were judged to be useful in guiding the investigations along new lines.

This feedback from the consumers has been incorporated within the work of the unit. As a result, making profiles is now the exception rather than the rule. Apart from the standard criteria (e.g. type of crime; availability of sufficient information), decisions as to whether or not to make a profile are now also based on an evaluation of its ability to steer the investigation in a new direction (cf. Stevens, 1997, Chapter 5 of the present Volume). In other words, can a profile add anything extra to the knowledge that the investigating teams either already have at their disposal or glean through discussions with the profiling team? Furthermore, to eliminate the waste of time and effort that arises when the advice that accompanies a profile is not acted upon, discussions first take place with the detective team to ensure that sufficient resources and manpower are available to undertake the recommendations that may accompany a profile. Finally, more effort is being made to encourage detectives to approach the profiling team at an earlier stage in their investigations with particular types of crimes, and not to wait until they are at a dead end.

The work of the Dutch unit continues to grow. Requests for assistance have not only increased but are now being made at an earlier stage in investigations. Courses and lectures are being organized not only to increase the analytical skills of detectives faced with low-volume serious crimes, such as rape and murder, but also to make them aware of the merits and possibilities of investigative support.

Complimentary to such operational assignments are the ongoing research activities of the group. These are carried out both alone and in collaboration with academics from other institutes in the Netherlands. Research is critical if offender profiling is to achieve an acceptable status in the scientific and police worlds. For example, the relationships between crime scene characteristics and offender characteristics that are the basis of offender profiling should not be blindly accepted, but should regularly be tested by independent research. Only by such efforts can we begin to talk about the 'science' of profiling.

CHAPTER 8

Predicting Offender Profiles from Victim and Witness Descriptions

David P. Farrington & Sandra Lambert

OFFENDER PROFILING

Offender profiling is a psychological technique designed to assist in the identification and detection of offenders (see Canter, 1989; Canter & Heritage, 1990). Its aim is to predict characteristics of the offender in a particular case from characteristics of the offence, characteristics of the victim, and reports by victims and witnesses. The objective is to narrow down the range of people who could possibly be the offender by specifying a combination of characteristics that the offender is likely to possess.

Offender profiling is particularly useful in detecting offenders whose records are already stored in a criminal record system. Hence, the increasing tendency of some English police forces to deal with offenders using unrecorded warnings (see, for example, Farrington & Burrows, 1993) will make it harder for a profiling system to be effective. Offender profiling will also be particularly useful to the extent that offenders are consistent in their commission of particular types of offences and choice of particular types of victims. To the extent that offenders are versatile or random in their offending, the value of offender profiling will be limited.

Much previous work on offender profiling has been essentially clinical in nature and has dealt with particular cases, notably sequences of unsolved serious crimes such as rapes or murders thought to have been committed by the same person (Copson, 1995). Typically, an independent psychologist has been engaged to examine all the evidence and make predictions about the likely personality and behavioural characteristics of the offender. In contrast, we have adopted a more statistical approach (see also Aitken et al., 1995) and have focused on the more common offences of burglary and violence.

Our aim is to investigate how far existing data collected by police forces might be used as the basis for a computerized system of offender profiling[1]. This naturally leads us to consider how existing data collection methods might be improved, both by increasing the accuracy of existing data and by collecting additional data.

THE PRESENT RESEARCH

Our research was designed to address the following questions arising in offender profiling:

1   How reliable are police-recorded descriptions of offenders?
2   How are offender characteristics inter-related?
3   How can offender profiles be developed?
4   How accurate are victim descriptions in predicting characteristics of offenders?
5   How accurate are witness descriptions in predicting characteristics of offenders?
6   How are offenders apprehended?

Comparisons will be made throughout between burglary and violence offenders and offences.

Our research is empirical. We primarily use information that is available in existing police records, and hence our conclusions are limited by the adequacy of these records. Ideally, our research should be based on criminological theories about which types of people commit which types of offences and choose which types of victims, and the theories should guide us in deciding which data to collect about offenders, offences and victims. Unfortunately, adequate theories for our purposes do not exist. Many theories have been proposed to explain why persons who are male, younger or Afro-Caribbean have a relatively high prevalence of recorded offending (e.g. Farrington, 1987). However, such theories do not make specific predictions about types of offences and types of victims. Also, while there is a great deal of research and theory on the predictors and correlates of prevalence (differences between offenders and non-offenders), there is much less work on the predictors and correlates of recidivism, which is more relevant to our concerns.

---

[1] We are very grateful to Gloria Laycock and the Home Office Police Research Group, and to Barrie Irving and the Police Foundation, for supporting and funding this research, and to the Nottinghamshire Police for their splendid cooperation.

In order to compare information recorded at the time of the offence with later-discovered characteristics of the offender, our research was based on offences leading to convictions. Whether convicted offenders are similar to undetected offenders is not entirely clear, although self-report studies (e.g. West & Farrington, 1973) suggest that they are comparable in many respects. Hence, it should be possible to generalize our conclusions to undetected offenders.

Our research is based on case files entering the Nottinghamshire[2] Criminal Record Office (CRO) after conviction. These case files are extensive and voluminous. Most of the documents are destroyed after the essential information is computerized for Nottinghamshire CRO purposes, but we were able to extract data for our purposes before the CRO staff worked on it. The information about previous offences in the files and in computerized records was not sufficiently detailed for our purposes.

Information was extracted and computerized for 655 different offenders whose files reached the Nottinghamshire CRO during the 9-month period March 1 – November 30, 1991. Our original aim was to extract data about all offences of burglary or serious violence committed in Nottinghamshire and leading to a conviction, where the identity of the offender at the time of the offence was unkown by victims, witnesses or police. Obviously, problems of detecting offenders do not arise in cases where someone knows the offender (as is true in the majority of cases of serious violence, which are between acquaintances, relatives, friends or intimate cohabitees). All the included offences involved offenders who were strangers to the victim. For statistical purposes, we needed several hundred of each type of case (burglary or violence).

Our original aim of including all cases of burglary or serious violence could not be achieved. This was because the flow of eligible burglary cases was about twice as great as the flow of eligible violence cases. Consequently, we randomly excluded up to half of the burglary cases to keep the numbers manageable. Our sample includes a small number of offences committed just outside the county, because they were dealt with by the Nottinghamshire police and hence eventually reached the Nottinghamshire CRO.

---

[2] Nottinghamshire, in the Midlands of England, consists of a predominantly rural county surrounding the large city of Nottingham. The population of Nottinghamshire in 1991 was about 1 000 000. Nottinghamshire was chosen as the site for this project because previous research had been conducted there by Farrington & Dowds (1985). In 1991, Nottinghamshire had the highest per capita rates of violence, sex and theft offences in England and Wales (Home Office, 1993). However, as Farrington & Dowds showed, part of the reason for this high crime rate was the assiduous recording of crimes by the Nottinghamshire police.

The offenders in our sample comprise 345 burglars and 310 violent offenders (166 convicted of causing actual bodily harm or Section 47 assault, 35 convicted of wounding/causing grievous bodily harm or Section 18/20 assault, 39 convicted of affray, violent disorder or common assault, and 70 convicted of robbery). Seventeen offenders were convicted of both burglary and violence during this time period; they were included in the number of violent offenders. An additional 316 burglars were excluded (271 at random and 45 because a victim or witness knew the offender). Similarly, 889 violent offenders were excluded (815 because a victim or witness knew the offender and 74 where the victim was a police officer and the violence occurred during an arrest). Hence, problems of detection occurred for only 310 out of 1199 violent offenders (25.9%), but for 633 out of 678 burglars (93.4%).

The data consists of w offenders, x offences, y victims and z witnesses for each incident. This makes the analysis very complicated. Generally, the problems have been overcome by basing analyses on N pairs. For example, in comparing victim descriptions of offenders with police-recorded characteristics of offenders, the analysis was based on N victim–offender pairs. However, it must be realised that the same victim can appear in more than one pair, just as the same offender can appear in more than one pair.

CHARACTERISTICS OF BURGLARY AND VIOLENCE OFFENDERS

The police information on characteristics of the 655 offenders was extracted from the C10 (description and antecedent history) form, which was completed at the time of arrest (see Farrington & Lambert, 1994). This C10 form contained information about the offender's name, date of birth, place of birth, sex, ethnic appearance, nationality, height, weight, build, accent, eye colour, voice, hair colour, hair length, facial hair, marks/scars/abnormalities, dress, address, occupation, education, marital status and children. The Nottinghamshire C10 form was similar to the national NIB74 form, which was accompanied by coding instructions and categories. For example, the coding instructions for ethnic appearance specified White European, Dark European, Afro-Caribbean, Asian, Oriental, Arab or Mixed-race.

Sex was recorded in every case. Most offenders were male (95.4% for burglary and 90.6% for violence). However, there were significantly more females among the violence offenders. Ethnicity was recorded in almost all cases (97.4%). The vast majority of offenders were said to be White (567), with 36 Afro-Caribbean, 27 Mixed-race and eight Asian (of Indian, Pakistani or Bangladeshi ethnic origin). There were no Oriental, Arab or other ethnic origins. Ethnicity was not significantly related to the type of offence, although more of the violence offenders were Afro-Caribbean or of Mixed-race (12.3% as opposed to 7.7% of burglars). The age of the offender was recorded in every case. While this ranged from 10 to 59, the majority of offenders (472 out of 655, or 72.1%) were aged 14–24. Violence offenders were significantly older: 59.0% of them were aged 21 or over, compared with only 34.2% of burglars.

Height was recorded in every case except one and was not significantly related to the type of offence[3]. Most offenders (65.5%) were between 5 feet 6 inches and 5 feet 11 inches tall. Weight was recorded in 97.1% of cases, and violence offenders were significantly heavier. Most offenders (58.5%) were between 9 stones 1 pound and 12 stones. Similarly, build was recorded (in three categories) in 98.8% of cases, and violence offenders had a significantly larger build. Hair colour was recorded in almost all cases (99.1%), with about half of the offenders (47.0%) having dark brown hair. Hair length was recorded in most cases (91.3%), with three-quarters of offenders (75.1%) having hair above the collar. Hair style was only recorded in about half of the cases (50.7%), and most of these offenders (66.0%) had curly/permed or straight hair. The presence or absence of facial hair was recorded in nearly all cases (98.3%), and 30.0% of these offenders had a beard, moustache or marked stubble.

Eye colour was recorded in almost all cases (98.6%), with most offenders having blue/grey (44.3%) or brown (45.0%) eyes. The offender's accent was recorded in 96.5% of cases, with the vast majority of these (86.4%) having a local (Nottinghamshire) accent. Only 33 (5.2%) had other English accents (e.g. Geordie), 23 (3.6%) had other British accents (Welsh, Scottish or Irish) and 30 (4.7%) had non-British accents. Violence offenders were significantly more likely to have non-local accents (20.1% as opposed to 7.8%).

The offender's voice was classified in 82.1% of cases (e.g. medium, deep, soft), and whether or not the offender was tattooed was recorded in almost all cases (99.2%). Over one-third of offenders (36.5%) were tattooed. Scars or birthmarks were noted in 186 cases (28.4%); presumably, they were absent in all other cases. Facial features (bulging eyes, teeth missing, gold teeth, marked acne or pitted complexion, wearing glasses) were noted in only 13 cases, and again presumably they were not present in other cases. The offender's dress at the time of arrest was recorded in almost all cases (98.6%) but in the vast majority of these (90.9%) the dress could only be classified as sloppy/casual.

---

[3] From now on, only significant differences between burglary and violence offenders will be noted.

The offender's place of birth was recorded in almost all cases (97.6%), with three-quarters of these offenders (76.5%) born in Nottingham or Nottinghamshire. Violence offenders were significantly more likely to have been born outside Nottinghamshire (29.8% as opposed to 17.9%). Nationality was almost always recorded (98.8%), but only five offenders were not British. The offender's address was almost always recorded (97.9%) with most offenders living in central or suburban Nottingham.

Living circumstances were recorded in 91.9% of cases, and over half of the offenders (55.0%) lived with their parents. Marital status was recorded in almost all cases (99.1%), and about three-quarters of offenders (76.6%) were single. More of the burglary offenders were single. About a quarter of offenders (23.4%) were recorded as having children, and violence offenders were significantly more likely to have children. The offender's occupation was recorded in almost all cases (98.9%), and about half of these (50.6%) were unemployed at the time of arrest. There was a significant tendency for burglary offenders to be more often unemployed (60.6% as opposed to 39.6%) or still in education (24.1% as opposed to 14.9%). The offender's education was recorded in 87.8% of cases, but only 15 of these offenders (2.6%) had been to grammar or private schools or in further or higher education.

RELIABILITY OF POLICE DATA ON OFFENDERS

As the C10 form was used as the criterion against which information from victims and witnesses was compared, it was important to investigate the reliability and validity of the information it contained. Reliability refers to the extent to which the information from different sources is concordant, while validity refers to the extent to which information from a particular source agrees with an external criterion. Unfortunately, it was impossible to establish validity, as there was no external criterion against which to compare the C10 data. For example, it was not possible to interview offenders within the scope of this research. However, reliability could be assessed by studying cases where the same offender had two or more C10 forms completed independently (because of two or more separate arrests during the 9-month study period). Cases of obvious duplication of C10 forms (e.g. by photocopying) were excluded.

In total, 56 offenders had more than one C10 form completed, allowing a total of 177 comparisons of C10 forms. Each form was compared with each other form for each offender; hence, if an offender had N forms, this would generate $N(N-1)/2$ comparisons. Most offenders (38) had only two forms.

Table 8.1 summarizes the results of these comparisons. The features listed on the C10 form were divided into those which were potentially observable by a victim or witness (e.g. sex) and those which were not (e.g. place of birth). The table shows four statistics: the percentage agreement between the two forms, the percentage of comparisons with data recorded (i.e. not missing) on both forms, the highest percentage of cases in one category of the table, and the value of Kappa, which is a statistical measure of agreement which takes account of chance expectation (see Cohen, 1960).

All four statistics are shown because they all indicate different features of the data. The percentage agreement between the two forms is a simple measure of concordance, but it is possible to have a high per-

Table 8.1. Reliability of police data on offenders

Variable (No. of Categories)	Agreement (%)	Recorded (%)	Highest (%)	Kappa
Observable features				
Sex (2)	100.0	100.0	98.9	1.00
Ethnicity (2)	96.4	78.5	82.7	0.86
Age (5)	86.7	97.7	36.2	0.81
Height (5)	69.5	100.0	27.1	0.59
Weight (6)	73.1	81.9	39.3	0.63
Build (2)	77.3	99.4	75.6	0.00
Hair colour (6)	54.7	97.2	29.1	0.49
Hair length (3)	86.5	83.6	84.5	0.26
Facial hair (3)	92.5	83.1	88.4	0.51
Eye colour (5)	82.6	94.4	45.5	0.75
Accent (3)	97.0	93.8	93.4	0.69
Voice (4)	46.4	54.8	28.9	0.17
Tattoo (2)	84.8	96.6	53.8	0.68
Scar/birthmark (4)	65.0	100.0*	51.4	0.28
Facial feature (2)	98.3	100.0*	97.7	0.39
Dress (3)	95.3	96.6	94.7	0.95
Non-observable features				
Place of birth (5)	66.0	91.5	48.8	0.34
Address (3)	77.6	96.0	45.9	0.60
Living circumstances (6)	70.4	91.5	50.6	0.51
Marital status (3)	98.8	95.5	95.3	0.85
No. of children (4)	98.3	100.0*	94.4	0.82
Occupation (4)	84.9	93.8	59.6	0.83

Based on 177 pairs of C10 forms (police data on offenders).
* Absence of information assumed to be negative information.
% Recorded in both forms.
% Highest in any category of the table.

centage agreement by chance, if a high proportion of the cases tend to fall in one category. This is why Kappa is included as a measure of improvement over chance agreement. According to Fleiss (1981), a Kappa value of 0.40 or greater shows good agreement in comparison with chance expectation, and a Kappa value of 0.75 or greater shows excellent agreement. Variables containing a great deal of missing data are likely to be of limited usefulness in detecting offenders. Similarly, variables with a high proportion of cases in one category are likely to be of limited usefulness in narrowing down the range of potential offenders. Clearly, the most useful variables are those with a high percentage agreement between the forms, a high percentage of data recorded and a high value of Kappa. We have focused particularly on variables with at least 75% agreement, at least 75% of data recorded, and a Kappa value of at least 0.40. It should also be realized that these quantities depend on the number of categories of a variable.

As (a) sex was always recorded, there was no missing data; (b) there were 175 male–male pairs of forms and 2 female–female pairs in this comparison; (c) no offender was recorded as male on one form and female on the other, yielding 100% agreement between the forms on sex (and hence Kappa = 1.00); (d) however, since 98.9% of cases were in the male–male category, knowing that an offender was male did not help very much in narrowing down the range of possible offenders (although knowing that an offender was female did). The percentage of males is higher among these repeat offenders than in the whole sample (93.1% of whom were male), presumably because males tend to be more frequent offenders than females on average and because only the most frequent offenders had two or more arrests for burglary and/or violence during the 9-month period of the research.

Ethnicity was recorded very accurately, as shown by the 96.4% agreement between the forms. The only discrepancy concerned one multiple offender who was coded as Afro-Caribbean on five forms and as White on one form. Kappa had a high value of 0.86 for ethnicity. The 86.7% agreement figure for age is also an under-estimate of reliability, as is the Kappa value of 0.81, because some offenders were older at a later arrest than at an earlier one. There was only one case where an offender apparently had a younger age at a later arrest, and no cases where an offender was more than one year older at a later arrest.

There was also good agreement between the forms on height, despite the fact that offenders were rarely measured carefully. Height on the two forms agreed within 2 inches in 76.8% of the cases. The categorical measure of agreement for height (69.5%) and the Kappa value of 0.59 are under-estimates of reliability, because some younger offenders had grown by the time of their later arrest. For adults aged 17 or over, the height on the two forms agreed within 2 inches in 90.4% of cases, and within 3 inches in 96.2% of cases.

Like height, weight was not measured carefully but was typically self-reported by offenders. The categorical measure of agreement was 73.1% and Kappa was 0.63. Only 61.4% of the forms agreed on the offender's weight within 7 pounds. Unlike height, this low level of agreement was not caused primarily by younger offenders becoming heavier at the later arrest. Indeed, the weight on the second form was more likely to be lower than the first weight than higher (45 lower, 40 higher, 60 exactly the same). Also, the agreement was lower when the analysis was restricted to adults aged 17 or over.

The 77.3% agreement on build between the forms seems high, but this was because most (75.6%) of these repeat offenders were coded as small on both forms, and none was coded as large. The Kappa value of zero indicates only a chance level of agreement between the forms on build. Hence, build was not recorded reliably in these comparisons. The percentage agreement was lower for hair colour (54.7%), but this was partly because of the large number of categories (6) and because of the relatively even distribution of offenders over them. The Kappa value of 0.49 indicates quite good reliability. Hair length had a higher percentage level of agreement (86.5%) but a lower value of Kappa (0.26). Hair style was not included in this analysis because of the large amount of missing data.

There was a high level of agreement (92.5%) between the forms in recording facial hair, and quite a high value of Kappa (0.51), but most offenders (88.4%) were recorded on both forms as having no facial hair. Hence, having no facial hair does not help in narrowing down the range of possible offenders. There was a high level of agreement (82.6%) and a high value of Kappa (0.75) for eye colour, and also for accent (97.0% agreement, 0.69 Kappa). However, the percentage agreement (46.4%) and Kappa (0.17) for voice were much lower, suggesting that this rating may have been rather subjective and unreliable.

Tattoos were recorded more reliably (Kappa= 0.68) than scars/birthmarks and facial features (Kappa= 0.28 and 0.39 respectively). There was a high level of agreement (95.3%) on dress between the forms and a high value of Kappa (0.95), but this was because the vast majority of offenders were classified as sloppy/casual in their dress. Hence, dress was not a useful variable in discriminating between the offenders. Also, dress is potentially a very changeable factor. While it might be useful in searching the area for the offender immediately after the crime, it is unlikely to be very useful in a system of offender profiling.

Analyses of non-observable features showed that nationality was not a useful variable. All of these repeat offenders who were recorded on both forms were listed as British. Similarly, education could not be studied because all of these offenders had a comprehensive or secondary education. The level of agreement on place of birth (66.0%) was low because of inconsistency in recording.

The percentage level of agreement (77.6%) and Kappa (0.60) for the offender's address at the time of arrest are perhaps less than expected. This is because of the relatively high mobility of these repeat offenders in this relatively short (9-month) period. This high mobility poses some problems for offender profiling. Any profiling system is likely to include predictions about the offender's address at the time of the current offence, and the records will only specify the offender's address at the time of the last offence. The percentage level of agreement for living circumstances (70.4%), and the Kappa value of 0.51, are also affected by residential mobility.

The percentage level of agreement and Kappa were high for marital status (98.8%, 0.85) and the number of children (98.3%, 0.82), but this was largely because the vast majority of these repeat offenders were single and had no children. Hence, these variables were not very useful in narrowing down the range of possible offenders. The percentage level of agreement (84.9%) and Kappa (0.83) were both high for occupational status, suggesting that this variable was recorded reliably and was stable over the 9-month period of this research.

In the remainder of this chaper, we will focus especially on the 12 most important observable features of offenders: sex, ethnicity, age, height, build, hair colour, hair length, facial hair, eye colour, accent, tattoos and facial abnormalities.

INTER-RELATIONSHIPS AMONG POLICE-RECORDED OFFENDER CHARACTERISTICS

Table 8.2 shows the inter-relationships among the 12 most important observable police-recorded variables. The p values are based on two-way cross-tabulations. This table is based on 655 different offenders (345 burglary, 310 violence). Where an offender had more than one C10 form completed, the information on the first C10 form was used, except where data were missing or obviously incorrect. In order to avoid problems of small expected values in tables, some adjacent categories of variables have been combined.

We will summarize some of the key results shown in Table 8.2. Female offenders were more likely to be non-White, younger, smaller and to have black, long hair[4]. Females were less likely than males to have tattoos. Afro-Caribbean and Mixed-race offenders tended to be younger, to have

---

[4] Not surprisingly, females had less facial hair than males.

Table 8.2. Inter-relationship of observable features

Variable (no. of categories)	SEX	ETH	AGE	HT	BU	HC	HL	FH	EC	AC	TAT	FF
Sex (2)	X	0.0004	0.075	0.0001	0.042	0.031	0.0001	0.024	–	–	0.013	–
Ethnicity (4)		X	0.091	–	–	0.0001	0.038	0.001	0.0001	0.0003	0.0001	0.0009
Age (5)			X	0.0001	0.0001	–	0.0002	0.0001	–	0.0001	0.0001	–
Height (4)				X	0.013	–	0.062	0.0001	–	–	0.0001	–
Build (3)					X	–	0.004	–	–	–	–	–
Hair colour (4)						X	0.009	0.014	0.0001	–	0.0001	–
Hair length (4)							X	0.001	–	–	–	–
Facial hair (3)								X	0.027	–	0.0001	–
Eye colour (4)									X	–	0.0001	–
Accent (4)										X	–	–
Tattoo (2)											X	0.090
Facial feature (2)												X

The figure in each cell gives the significance level (based on chi-squared).
– = Not significant.
Key:
ETH = ethnicity; HT = height; BU = build; HC = hair colour; HL = hair length; FH = facial Hair; EC = eye colour; AC = accent; TAT = tattoo; FF = facial feature.

black, long hair, to have beards, and to have brown eyes. Non-White offenders were less likely to have local accents and less likely to have tattoos, but they were more likely to have unusual facial features. Younger offenders tended to be smaller, with shorter hair, less facial hair and fewer tattoos, and they were more likely to have local accents.

Smaller offenders tended to have shorter hair, less facial hair and fewer tattoos. Black-haired offenders tended to have long hair, facial hair and brown eyes, but tended not to have tattoos. Long-haired offenders tended to have facial hair, and facial hair was also associated with brown eyes and tattoos. However, brown-eyed offenders were relatively unlikely to have tattoos.

As some of these features were correlated (e.g. ethnicity and hair colour), a factor analysis was carried out on the 12 features (all dichotomized) to investigate how many different underlying dimensions they reflected. Three important factors were extracted, accounting for 16.0%, 13.9% and 10.6% of the variance, respectively[5]. The highest loadings of features on the first factor were non-White ethnicity (0.73), brown eye colour (0.77) and black/dark brown hair colour (0.69). It is reasonable to conclude that this factor reflects ethnicity. The highest loadings on the second factor were older age (0.76), facial hair (0.56), larger build (0.47) and non-local accent (0.44). This factor seems to reflect age. The highest loadings on the third factor were male sex (0.79), tall height (0.53) and short hair length (0.54). This factor seems to reflect sex. Hence, the three most important variables underlying the 12 observable features were sex, ethnicity and age.

DEVELOPING AN OFFENDER PROFILE

An offender profile essentially combines values of variables for an offender. For example, the profile of one offender might consist of the values of sex, ethnicity, age, height, etc. An offender profiling system stores the profiles of offenders convicted in the past. A key issue is selecting the number and type of variables to include in this profile.

As the number of variables increases, the number of unique profiles increases disproportionally, and the number of offenders in the system with each profile decreases. For example, offenders fall into only two sex categories, male and female, with 610 males and 45 females in this project. Hence, 610 offenders (93.1%) share the same male profile. With the two variables sex and ethnicity (in four categories), there are eight pos-

---

[5] Varimax rotation was used.

sible profiles, the largest (White males) comprising 536 persons and the smallest (Afro-Caribbean females and Mixed-race females) each containing only six persons. Already, one profile (Asian females) contained no offenders.

Combining three variables (sex, ethnicity and age, in seven categories), there are 56 possible profiles. Only 35 contained offenders in this project. The largest category comprised 177 White males aged 17–20, while eight profiles already contained only one offender and, of course, 21 contained none. Adding a fourth variable, height (in five categories), the number of different possible profiles increased to 280, although only 84 contained offenders. Table 8.3 shows the relationship between sex–ethnicity–age and height. The largest number of offenders (72 out of 637 known on all four variables, or 11.3% of offenders) were White males aged 17–20 with heights between 5 feet 9 inches and 5 feet 11 inches. Only 15 profiles contained 13 or more offenders (2% of offenders), and only 20 profiles contained seven or more offenders (1% of offenders). Conversely, 64 profiles contained less than 1% of offenders and hence defined a relatively small number of offenders. Profiles containing very few offenders in a system are the most useful for identifying likely offenders.

Adding the three-category build variable produced 840 possible five-variable profiles, of which 137 contained offenders, with 37 offenders (5.9% of 631 known) in the largest category. Adding the seven-category hair colour variable produced 5880 possible six-variable profiles, of which 267 contained offenders, with 19 offenders (3.0% of 624 known) in the largest category. Adding the six-category hair length variable produced 35 280 possible 7-variable profiles, of which 323 contained offenders, with 14 offenders (2.4% of 572 known) in the largest category. Adding the four-category facial hair variable produced 141 120 possible eight-variable profiles, of which 382 contained offenders, again with 14 offenders (2.5% of 565 known) in the largest category. It can be seen that, as variables are added, the proportion of offenders with missing data on at least one variable increases.

Eventually, of course, as more variables are added to the profile, each profile would contain only one offender, so that each offender would be defined by a unique combination of values of variables. However, it would be undesirable to go to this extreme in an offender profiling system. As the number of variables in the profile increases, so also does the probability of a victim or witness getting at least one of them wrong, so that the offender would not be identified correctly.

Basically, there is a relationship between the proportion of persons in the system identified as possible offenders (which we will term the 'system proportion' or SP) and the probability of an identified person being

Table 8.3. Sex, ethnicity, age and height

Sex	Ethnicity	Age	5ft	5 ft 1–5 in	5 ft 6–8 in	5 ft 9–11 in	6 ft+	Total
M	W	10–13	11	5	1	1	0	18
M	W	14–16	7	15	31	24	9	86
M	W	17–20	0	12	56	72	36	176
M	W	21–24	0	2	26	50	42	120
M	W	25–29	0	0	22	22	18	62
M	W	30–39	1	1	19	16	13	50
M	W	40+	0	3	5	9	6	23
M	B	10–13	2	0	0	0	0	2
M	B	14–16	0	1	3	3	0	7
M	B	17–20	0	0	1	3	5	9
M	B	21–24	0	0	1	3	1	5
M	B	25–29	0	1	0	1	2	4
M	B	30–39	0	0	3	0	0	3
M	H	14–16	0	0	1	3	1	5
M	H	17–20	0	0	0	3	6	9
M	H	21–24	0	0	2	2	2	6
M	H	25–29	0	0	0	1	0	1
M	A	14–16	1	2	0	0	0	3
M	A	17–20	0	0	1	1	0	2
M	A	30–39	0	0	0	2	1	3
F	W	10–13	0	1	0	0	0	1
F	W	14–16	1	6	1	0	0	8
F	W	17–20	0	6	1	3	0	10
F	W	21–24	0	1	2	0	1	4
F	W	25–29	0	2	1	0	1	4
F	W	30–39	0	2	1	0	0	3
F	W	40+	0	1	0	0	0	1
F	B	10–13	0	1	0	0	0	1
F	B	14–16	0	3	0	0	0	3
F	B	17–20	0	0	1	0	0	1
F	B	21–24	0	1	0	0	0	1
F	H	10–13	1	0	1	0	0	2
F	H	14–16	0	1	1	0	0	2
F	H	17–20	0	0	0	1	0	1
F	H	25–29	0	0	1	0	0	1

M = male, F = female, W = White, B = Afro-Caribbean, H = Mixed-race, A = Asian.

a true offender (which we will term the 'true positive probability' or TPP). As the number of variables in a profile increases, the average SP (termed ASP) for each case will decrease, but so will TPP. These ideas will be illustrated in the next section.

ACCURACY OF VICTIM DESCRIPTIONS OF OFFENDERS

There were 652 possible comparisons of victim reports and offender characteristics for burglary and 417 for violence. The records indicated

Table 8.4. Agreement between victim descriptions and offender characteristics

Variable (no. of categories)	Agreement (%)	Recorded (%)	Highest (%)	Kappa
Burglary				
Sex (2)	98.0	7.8	94.1	0.79
Ethnicity (2)	100.0	5.2	85.3	1.00
Age (6)	68.8	4.9	31.3	0.57
Violence				
Sex (2)	98.5	93.0	90.2	0.91
Ethnicity (4)	95.5	60.9	82.5	0.85
Age (7)	48.5	55.4	14.3	0.36
Height (5)	53.6	56.4	18.3	0.38
Build (3)	55.3	48.0	22.1	0.33
Hair colour (7)	58.8	46.5	29.4	0.50
Hair length (6)	76.8	38.1	57.0	0.75
Facial hair (4)	71.0	16.8	31.9	0.59
Accent (4)	68.2	5.3	45.5	0.44
Facial feature (2)	95.0	100.0*	94.0	0.25

Based on 652 victim–offender pairs for burglary and 417 victim–offender pairs for violence.
* Assuming that absence of information indicates negative information.
% Recorded by victims.

in only 14 cases that burglary victims said that they could positively identify their offenders. In contrast, 127 violence victims said that they could positively identify their offenders. This probably reflects differences in the nature of the crimes.

Table 8.4, modelled on Table 8.1, shows the level of agreement between victim descriptions and offender characteristics. It includes characteristics about which there was information in the records from at least 5% of victims. Generally, few burglary victims could provide any descriptive information about their offenders (7.8% information about the offender's sex, 5.2% about ethnicity, and 4.9% about age). The percentage level of agreement between the victim description and the offender characteristic was very high for sex and ethnicity. The percentage level of agreement was less for age, but Kappa was still quite high (0.57).

Many violence victims could provide descriptions of their offenders (e.g. information about the offender's sex in 93.0% of cases). Again, victims were very accurate in reporting the sex and ethnicity of their offenders. The age and height of the offender were reported in more than half of the cases, and the victim was moderately accurate (over 50% agreement, Kappa = 0.36 for age and 0.38 for height).

The offender's build was also recorded in about half of the cases (48.0%), and the victim was again moderately accurate (55.3% agreement, Kappa = 0.33). Hence, our earlier conclusion that build was not recorded reliably, based on the low agreement between C10 forms, seems incorrect. The multiple offenders who had more than one C10 form disproportionally had a small build. However, this was not true of violent offenders, who were equally distributed over the 3 categories of build (small, medium and large).

Hair colour was reported by violence victims in about half of the cases (46.5%), and this report was quite accurate (58.8% agreement, Kappa = 0.50). Hair length was reported even more accurately (76.8% agreement, Kappa = 0.75). The presence or absence of facial hair was rarely recorded explicitly (16.8%) but again the victim's report was quite accurate (71.0% agreement, Kappa = 0.59). The accuracy of the victim's report is quite impressive, bearing in mind that it was obtained independently of police information about the offender's characteristics.

The offender's accent was only recorded in 5.3% of cases. Since the victim said that the offender had a non-local accent in about half of these cases, this suggests that the offender's accent was primarily reported and recorded when it was unusual. The victim was again quite accurate in assessing the offender's accent (68.2% agreement, Kappa = 0.44). Violence victims rarely reported facial features such as bulging eyes (one), teeth missing (three), gold teeth (one), acne/pitted complexion (eight) or glasses (six), and these reports were not especially accurate in comparison with the police data (Kappa = 0.25).

Violence victims provided information on the offender's eye colour in only six cases and on the offender's tattoos in only six cases. While the reports of tattoos were accurate, the reports of eye colour were not. Violence victims often reported the offender's dress (48.9%), but this was classified as sloppy/casual in 93.1% of these cases. Dress is not a very useful variable in these analyses, partly because of the absence of an adequate classification system and partly because it is easily changed.

Violence victims also provided information on the offender's mood at the time of the offence in 67.4% of cases. The most common offender moods were angry/aggressive (56.2%), unreasonable (12.8%), argumentative (10.7%), cold/calculating (5.7%) and firm/manipulative (5.7%). Victims reported that the offender was under the influence of alcohol in only 26 cases (6.2%), but this is undoubtedly an under-estimate because the question was not systematically asked or answered.

As an illustration of the use of victim descriptions in an offender profiling system for violent offences, an attempt was made to predict the sex–ethnicity–age profile of the true (police-recorded) offender from the sex–ethnicity–age profile of the offender as described by the victim. Full information about the sex, ethnicity and age of both victim-described and true offenders was available for only 196 of the 417 victim–offender comparisons. In order to show the full relationship between victim-described and true offender profiles in Table 8.5, sex, ethnicity and age have all been dichotomized. Hence, there are only eight possible offender profiles. For example, the victim said that the offender was a young White female on six occasions; on five of these, the victim was correct, while on the other occasion the true offender was an older White female. Most errors concerned the offender's age, as was noted before (see Table 8.4).

The concepts of average system proportion (ASP) and true positive probability (TPP) will now be illustrated using Table 8.5. The system proportion (SP) for the identified young White females is 0.0255 (5/196), since there are five of these stored in the system (2.55% of all stored offenders). Five of the six identified young White females were correct (true positives), so the true positive probability, TPP= 0.833 (5/6). Over all eight profiles, the weighted average SP (ASP) = 0.326, and TPP = 0.714 (140/196).

A profile that identifies 32.6% of stored offenders on average is not operationally useful, as it is important to narrow down the range of possible offenders far more than this. One reasonable approach would be to set a maximum value of ASP (e.g. identifying 1% of the stored offenders) and a minimum value of TPP (e.g. accurately identifying 10% of the offenders) in deciding on the optimal number of variables and categories in a profile. The relative values of ASP and TPP could also be adjusted

Table 8.5. Offender profiles: victim descriptions vs. offender characteristics

	\multicolumn{3}{Victim description}			\multicolumn{8}{Offender profile}								Total
	Age	Eth	Sex	1	2	3	4	5	6	7	8	
1	YO	WH	FE	5	0	0	0	1	0	0	0	6
2	YO	WH	MA	0	33	0	0	1	24	0	0	58
3	YO	NW	FE	0	0	10	0	0	0	0	0	10
4	YO	NW	MA	0	0	0	7	0	0	0	2	9
5	OL	WH	FE	0	0	0	0	3	2	0	0	5
6	OL	WH	MA	0	19	0	0	1	72	0	0	92
7	OL	NW	FE	0	0	0	0	0	0	3	0	3
8	OL	NW	MA	0	0	0	5	0	1	0	7	13
Total				5	52	10	12	6	99	3	9	196

Age: OL = older (21 or over); YO = younger (20 or less).
Eth (ethnicity): WH = White; NW = non-White.
Sex: MA = male; FE = female.

according to the relative costs of identifying false positives (i.e. incorrectly identifying the offenders) and benefits of identifying true positives. However, many factors would need to be taken into consideration.

If we repeat these analyses for the full sex (two categories) – ethnicity (four categories) – age (seven categories) profile[6], the ASP came to 0.132 and the TPP to 0.459. Hence, each sex–ethnicity–age profile of the offender (according to the victim) identified 13.2% of stored offenders in the system on average, and 45.9% of sex–ethnicity–age profiles reported by victims were correct.

It seems useful to divide profiles into common and rare ones. Rare profiles may be more useful in an offender profiling system than common ones. There were 27 different sex–ethnicity–age profiles of offenders in this analysis, but 22 of these contained five or fewer offenders (less than 3% of all offenders). The ASP for these rare profiles was 0.019, with a TPP of 0.509. Therefore, each rare profile identified 1.9% of offenders on average. For the five common profiles, the ASP was 0.178 and the TPP was 0.439. Hence, the accuracy was slightly (but non-significantly) greater when using rare profiles than when using common ones (50.9% vs 43.9%, respectively).

ACCURACY OF WITNESS DESCRIPTIONS OF OFFENDERS

There were 440 possible comparisons of witness reports and offender characteristics for burglary and 610 for violence. In 70 cases, burglary witnesses said that they could positively identify the offenders; 167 violence witnesses said that they could positively identify the offenders. Table 8.6 shows the level of agreement between witness descriptions and offender characteristics. Like Table 8.4, it only includes characteristics about which at least 5% of witnesses provided information.

For both burglary and violence, there was a very high level of agreement between witness reports of sex and ethnicity and the corresponding offender characteristics. It is likely that many of the missing cases involved reports of males and Whites, and that police officers sometimes did not bother to specify such common categories in the records of witness (and indeed victim) statements. Some statements included sentences such as 'the youth ran off' without specifying the youth's sex, but there was probably the implicit assumption in virtually all cases that the youth was male. Witnesses were also quite accurate in their reports

---

[6] Which had 56 categories in principle but 27 in practice for this comparison (because of missing values).

Table 8.6. Agreement between witness descriptions and offender characteristics

Variable (no. of Categories)	Agreement (%)	Recorded (%)	Highest	Kappa
Burglary				
Sex (2)	99.0	46.6	99.0	0.99
Ethnicity (4)	96.2	31.6	82.6	0.88
Age (6)	59.4	23.0	22.8	0.45
Height (5)	46.2	21.1	18.3	0.26
Build (3)	58.7	17.0	33.3	0.32
Hair colour (5)	65.1	14.5	34.9	0.49
Hair length (4)	89.8	14.5	83.1	0.56
Violence				
Sex (2)	98.0	81.3	88.3	0.89
Ethnicity (4)	95.7	54.1	82.0	0.86
Age (7)	54.9	43.3	14.8	0.44
Height (5)	53.0	44.8	20.9	0.34
Build (3)	60.7	40.8	23.0	0.41
Hair colour (7)	60.9	38.4	30.5	0.53
Hair length (6)	72.0	33.1	59.3	0.43
Facial hair (4)	72.9	9.7	32.2	0.60
Facial feature (2)	95.2	100.0*	94.3	0.27

Based on 440 witness–offender pairs for burglary and 610 witness–offender pairs for violence.
* Assuming that absence of information indicates negative information.
% Recorded by witnesses.

of the offender's age, height, build, hair colour, hair length and facial hair (see Table 8.6).

The offender's accent was rarely reported, although burglary and violence witnesses were accurate in nine out of 11 cases (six specifying non-local accents). Similarly, the offender's tattoos were rarely reported. Witnesses were correct in all five cases where they said that the offender was tattooed, but there were 10 other cases where the witness said the offender was not tattooed and the police records indicated that the offender was tattooed. Facial features such as teeth missing (four), gold teeth (one), acne/pitted complexion (four) and glasses (11) were rarely reported, and the police records agreed with the witness in only six of these 20 cases. Witnesses often reported the offender's dress (in 33.0% of cases), but this could only be classified as sloppy/casual in 90.8% of these cases.

As an illustration of the use of witness descriptions in an offender profiling system, an attempt was made to predict the sex–ethnicity–age profile of the true offender from the sex–ethnicity–age profile of the offender as described by the witness. In this analysis, sex had 2 categories, ethnicity had 4 categories, and age had 7 categories. Full information about the sex, ethnicity and age of both witness-described and true offenders was available for only 315 of the 1050 witness–offender comparisons. Burglary and violence witnesses were combined in this analysis partly to increase the numbers and partly because their accuracy was similar (TPP = 0.554 for burglary and 0.530 for violence). Over all witness-offender comparisons, the ASP came to 0.118 and the TPP to 0.537. Hence, each sex–ethnicity–age profile identified 11.8% of stored offenders in the system on average, and 53.7% of sex–ethnicity–age profiles reported by witnesses were correct. The accuracy of witnesses was slightly but not significantly greater than the accuracy of victims (chi-squared = 2.59, 1 d.f., NS).

Again as an illustration, profiles were divided into common and rare ones. The rare profiles were those containing six or fewer offenders (less than 2% of all offenders; 18 profiles), while the common ones were those containing seven or more offenders (nine profiles). The ASP for the rare profiles was 0.011, with a TPP of 0.571. Therefore, each rare profile identified 1.1% of offenders on average. For the nine common profiles, the ASP was 0.141 and the TPP was 0.529. Again, therefore, the accuracy was slightly (but non-significantly) greater when using rare profiles than when using common ones.

HOW WERE OFFENDERS APPREHENDED?

In considering how to improve the detection of offenders, it is useful to determine how offenders are currently detected. As explained before, all cases where the identity of the offender was known were excluded from our analyses. We had detailed records of a total of 742 arrests of our 655 offenders; this number is slightly less than the number of C10 forms (750) because police statements about arrest were missing in eight cases. In 694 of the 742 cases where police statements were found (93.5%), it was possible to establish the main reason why the offender was apprehended. Table 8.7 shows these reasons separately for burglary and violence arrests.

The most common ways in which burglars were arrested were: they were caught in the act (14.5%); through an informant (12.5%); they were caught near to or leaving the scene of the crime (12.0%); they were traced through property left at the scene of the crime or through the disposal of stolen goods (10.5%); they were seen acting suspiciously in the area, for example carrying stolen goods (7.7%); they were caught for another crime and admitted this burglary (7.0%); or through an accu-

Table 8.7. Reasons for arrest

Reason	Burglaries (%) (N = 401)	Violence (%) (N = 293)
Caught in the act	14.5	10.6
Detained at scene of crime	4.2	16.0
Caught near scene of crime	12.0	5.8
Victim description	2.0	14.7
Witness description	6.7	13.3
Vehicle description/number plate	3.2	10.6
Surveillance/caught returning to crime	2.5	0.3
Offender followed to home/work	1.0	3.4
Acting suspiciously in area	7.7	1.4
Forensic evidence	4.5	0.7
Traced through property left or disposed	10.5	1.0
Enquiries in local area	4.5	6.5
Informant	12.5	2.0
Implicated by co-offender	5.5	3.8
Caught for another crime	7.0	4.4
Recorded on video	0.0	2.0
Gave themselves up	1.2	2.0
Found at co-offender's home	0.5	0.0
Other	0.0	1.4

Based on 694 arrests where the reason was recorded.

rate description by a witness (6.7%). The most important ways in which violence offenders were arrested were: they were detained at the scene of the crime (16.0%); through an accurate description by a victim (14.7%), through an accurate description by a witness (13.3%); through a description of a vehicle or a number-plate (10.6%); they were caught in the act (10.6%); or as a result of enquiries in the local area (6.6%). Clearly, victim and witness descriptions were far more important in apprehending violence offenders than burglars, no doubt because violence offenders were more often seen by victims and witnesses.

In view of the frequency of catching offenders at or near to the scene of the crime, it was not surprising to find that the time interval between the first report of an offence and the apprehension of the offender was typically quite short. Over half of the violence offenders (60.7%) were arrested straight away or within one hour, as were 43.0% of burglars. Another 9.1% of violence offenders and 6.0% of burglars were arrested within one day. A further 13.3% of violence offenders and 19.9% of burglars were arrested between 2 and 10 days after the offence, and 9.1% of violence offenders and 14.5% of burglars were arrested between 11 and 30 days after the offence. Only 7.8% of violence offenders and 16.2% of burglars were arrested more than 30 days afterwards. It is reasonable to conclude that the likelihood of an offender being arrested declines steeply with time after the commission of the offence, especially for violence offences. One of the aims of an offender profiling system would be to increase the probability of detecting the offender at least one day after the crime, when the immediate trail had gone cold.

OTHER ANALYSES RELEVANT TO OFFENDER PROFILING

An important issue is how far offenders are specialized as opposed to versatile. In principle, offender profiling is likely to be more useful if offenders are specialized. Farrington & Lambert (1994) investigated specialization in the present data by searching the previous criminal records of all 655 offenders. They found that 89.2% of burglars and 72.1% of violent offenders had a previous criminal record (this refers to the criminal record at the time of the first arrest recorded in the period of our research). Since only 10.8% of burglars and 20.9% of violent offenders would not have been found in existing records, this suggests that offender profiling is potentially useful as a technique for assisting in the detection of offenders. Burglars were significantly more likely than violent offenders to have previous recorded offences. As many as 36.2% of burglars and 23.6% of violent offenders had 10 or more previous recorded offences.

Just over half of the burglars (51.1%) had one or more previous burglaries, in comparison with about a quarter (25.1%) of the violent offenders. Similarly, nearly half of the violent offenders (46.8%) had at least one previous violent offence (wounding, grievous bodily harm, actual bodily harm, affray, threatening behaviour or robbery), in comparison with about one-third (32.4%) of the burglars. Hence, restricting offender profiling to offenders with a recorded offence of the same type (e.g. searching for burglars only among recorded burglars) would make it impossible to identify about half of the offenders. More of the violent offenders also had a previously recorded offence of breach of the peace or public disorder (17.5% as opposed to 10.5% of burglars). These figures agree with criminological research (e.g. Stander et al., 1989) showing that there is some specialization in burglary and violence superimposed on a fair degree of versatility in offending.

Farrington & Lambert (in press) compared offence characteristics with offender characteristics, finding many regularities. A factor analysis of offence characteristics showed that the important underlying dimensions could be measured by the basic variables of location, site (e.g. burglary of a residence, violence in the street), time of day and day of the week. They compared location–site–time–day offence profiles with address–sex–ethnicity–age offender profiles. The relationships were measured in a randomly chosen construction sample and predictive accuracy was tested in a validation sample. In the validation sample for violence, ASP = 0.247 and TPP = 0.480. Hence, on average these offence profiles identified 24.7% of offenders stored in the system and were correct 48% of the time.

Farrington & Lambert (in press) also compared victim characteristics with offender characteristics, finding similarities for violence especially in sex, age and address. They compared address–sex–age victim profiles (since the ethnicity of the victim was rarely recorded) with address–sex–ethnicity–age offender profiles in construction and validation samples. In the validation sample for violence, ASP= 0.262 and TPP= 0.511. Hence, on average these victim profiles identified 26.2% of stored offenders and were correct 51.1% of the time.

Farrington & Lambert (in press) also investigated how far offenders repeated similar types of offences and similar type of victims. For offenders who committed more than one offence, the location–site–time–day offence profiles agreed very well for violence (Kappa = 0.80) but not for burglary (Kappa = 0.21). For offenders with more than one victim, the address–sex–age victim profiles did not agree very well for either violence (Kappa = 0.24) or burglary (Kappa = 0.23).

CONCLUSIONS

Our research has shown the existence of numerous relationships that could form the basis of an offender profiling system. The following features at least could and should be included:

1 *Offender features*: address, sex, age (date of birth), ethnicity, height, accent, build, hair length, hair colour, facial hair, tattoos, distinctive physical features.
2 *Offence features*: location, site, time, day, date, method, instruments or weapons, method of escape, disguise, offender under influence of drink or drugs.
3 *Victim features*: address, sex, age, ethnicity, marital status, occupation, activity at the time of the crime, victim under influence of drink or drugs.
4 *Victim report of offender*: all offender variables except address.
5 *Witness report of offender*: all offender variables except address.

The distinctive physical features (e.g. bulging eyes, teeth missing) are worth recording even though they do not apply to many cases, because they might help to identify the offender in these few cases.

We have made some progress in developing offender and offence typologies, but further work requires more extensive and more complete data. It is important to develop offender and offence typologies based on far more variables and categories than we have used. However, there are a number of problems that our research has highlighted and that need to be overcome, in addition to the major problem that many detected offenders (especially juveniles) are given unrecorded warnings (Farrington, 1992).

At present in Nottinghamshire, there is unsystematic and incomplete coverage of many items of interest, for example those on the C10 (description and police antecedents) form. We think it is unlikely that the Nottinghamshire police are very different from other forces in this respect. The problem is that much of the information on the C10 form is never used again, so there is little incentive for police officers to spend a great deal of time completing the form. Indeed, the Nottinghamshire police did start completing these forms more carefully when they saw that we were making use of them. This problem might be overcome by redesigning the form into a series of checklists, making it easy to ring the appropriate alternative each time. Also, the police could be trained in completing the forms and encouraged to record all items (e.g. height) as accurately as possible. It may be a mistake to rely too much on offender self-reports. Once offenders realize that the information on the C10 form might help to detect them in the future, they might be motivated to provide inaccurate information.

An obvious problem with the C10 form at present is that the information on it is different or impossible to retrieve. This problem can be overcome by routinely computerizing the data on the revised form. This is being done in the PHOENIX computerized criminal record system since May 1995, but it is unclear how easily the data can be retrieved and used. The CRO operators could type in variables from ringed checklists on the C10 form when they type in details of the offence for storage in the CRO system. Data on changeable variables (e.g. height or address) would then be routinely up-dated. In the interests of completeness, the C10 form could be filled in and computerized for all detected offenders, including those dealt with by cautions or unrecorded warnings. Similarly, information about the offence, the victim, and descriptions of the offender by the victim and witness could be coded and computerized using systematically completed checklists of questions. This would ensure that every topic (e.g. whether the offender was under the influence of alcohol or drugs) would be systematically covered.

Further research is needed on many topics connected with offender profiling. An important topic is the rate of change of variables such as address, height and build over time. A major problem is how offence data, victim data, and victim and witness information on the offender can best be combined to predict the profile of the offender. Different profiling systems could be compared using ASP and TPP. One of the greatest challenges is how best to cope with a variable number of victims, a variable number of witnesses, a variable number of offenders, and a variable number of separate incidents. We have recorded co-offending but not really addressed it in our analyses; any offender profiling system will probably have to search for individuals rather than co-offending groups, especially as co-offending groups are typically short-lived (Reiss & Farrington, 1991).

Research is also needed on how best to classify physical features of the offender, dress, tattoos, and so on. The classification systems currently in operation seem to be based on common sense rather than systematic research, but there could be relevant scientific literature on physical characteristics that could be applied; for example, there is the scientific field of anthropometry (concerned with the measurement of bodily features) and there is a great deal of psychological literature on the related topic of face identification. Research could also be carried out on improving questions to offenders, victims and witnesses; for example, questions about being under the influence of alcohol or drugs could be made more specific, and hence more reliable and valid.

Research is also needed on the usefulness of additional information that might be collected. For example, on the C10 form, information could be collected about the offender's drug and alcohol problems, psychiatric problems, and about his/her family background (e.g. number of siblings, coming from a one-parent family). Detected offenders might be given psychological tests, for example to measure their antisocial attitudes or impulsiveness. Left- or right-handedness, face shape and handwriting could be recorded. Records could be searched to determine the convictions of offenders' parents, siblings and other family members, to detect criminal families. The crime rates of the areas in which offenders live could be measured and coded. The distances between locations of offences and addresses of offenders could be determined more easily by reference to a geographical database. In connection with burglary, research is needed on how best to classify characteristics of households, dwellings and business premises, and on correlations between these characteristics and features of offenders.

More fundamental research could also be carried out, designed to develop theories about why there are correlations between certain offender characteristics, offence characteristics and victim characteristics. Existing criminological theories are of limited relevance, because few criminologists have been interested in investigating correlations between physical characteristics of offenders and specific details of offences. This more fundamental research should include interviews with offenders and victims. The theories should help to guide research on offender profiling by specifying particular characteristics of offenders, offences and victims that should be measured. Research is also needed on typologies of offenders. Studies are also required on the prediction of recidivism by offenders, so that recidivism probabilities and rates of offending can be taken into account in an offender profiling system. The data collected and maintained in the system could be used for this purpose, and also to study specialization and escalation in offending over time.

To a considerable extent, our research on offender profiling has been exploratory, but we feel that the relationships between offender, offence and victim characteristics are sufficiently promising to justify a larger-scale expenditure of resources on more extensive data collection. We believe that it is useful to focus on common offences such as burglary and violence. If the detection rate of these offences could be improved by developing an offender profiling system, that would be to the benefit of law-abiding members of society.

CHAPTER 9

Geographic Profiling

D. Kim Rossmo

INTRODUCTION

When the throat of Victorian prostitute Polly Nichols was slashed in Buck's Row on August Bank Holiday, 1888, horrified London newspapers warned of a 'reign of terror' (Rumbelow, 1988). Jack the Ripper was certainly not the first or last of his type, but the unsolved mystery of the Whitechapel murders still symbolizes our lack of understanding of such dangerous predators. Equally important, the very nature of their crimes makes these criminals difficult and challenging to apprehend.

One of the most problematic aspects of predatory violent crime is the volume of tips and suspects generated through their investigation. Traditional police methods are not always sufficient and detectives need alternative tactics to assist them in these types of cases. Geographic profiling, a strategic information management system designed to support investigative efforts in cases of serial murder, rape and arson, is one such approach.

INVESTIGATIVE DIFFICULTIES

For heaven's sake catch me before I kill more. I cannot control myself (message written in lipstick on the living room wall of Frances Brown, victim of serial murderer William Heirens; Kennedy, 1991).

The investigation of serial violent and sexual crime is complex and difficult. Most murders are solved because they involve intimates and the search for the offender begins with the victim's family, friends and acquaintances. There is no such victim–offender relationship, however, 'n stranger sexual crime.

The police must therefore delineate likely groups of potential suspects, a process referred to as 'framing' (Kind, 1987) or establishing the 'circle of investigation' (Skogan & Antunes, 1979). Such an effort typically involves the inspection of those parties with relevant criminal or psychiatric records, the accumulation of intelligence and the collection of suspect tips from members of the public. Because these investigative efforts can produce large numbers of potential suspects, often totalling into the hundreds and even thousands, problems with information overload usually develop.

'Although a modern police force can fill rooms with details of possible suspects, they still have the enormous problem of finding the vicious needle in their haystack of paper' (Canter, 1994).

The still unsolved Green River Killer case in Seattle, Washington, involved the murder of 49 prostitutes. To date the police have only had the resources to investigate two-thirds of the 18 000 names in their suspect files (Montgomery, 1993). Detectives have gathered 8000 tangible items of evidence from the crime scenes and a single television special on the case generated 3500 tips. In Britain, the nationwide search for the Staffordshire serial murderer amassed details on 185 000 people over the course of 11 years before the child-killer was finally caught (Canter, 1994).

The Narborough Murder Enquiry, a massive four-year manhunt, obtained close to 4000 blood samples for DNA testing prior to eventually charging Colin Pitchfork with the deaths of two teenage girls (Canter, 1994; Wambaugh, 1989). The Yorkshire Ripper inquiry accumulated 268 000 names, visited 27 000 houses, and recorded 5 400 000 vehicle registration numbers (Doney, 1990; Nicholson, 1979).

A corollary to the problem of information overload is the high cost associated with any extensive, long-term investigation. The final tally for the Atlanta Child Murders case was more than $9 million (Dettlinger & Prugh, 1983), while the Yorkshire Ripper inquiry cost an estimated £4 million (Doney, 1990). The Green River Task Force has so far accumulated expenses of approximately $20 million (Montgomery, 1993).

It is important for police detectives to know which crimes are connected so that information between related cases can be collated and compared. An inability to recognize connections and confusion over which crimes should form part of a series has occurred in several investigations. This problem has been termed 'linkage blindness' (Egger, 1984).

Several other investigative difficulties exist that complicate efforts to connect linked crimes and to identify and apprehend serial killers, rapists and arsonists (Egger, 1990; Holmes & De Burger, 1988; James, 1991

O'Reilly-Fleming, 1992). Such problems include: (a) the learning process inherent in serial offending; (b) false confessions; (c) copy-cat crimes; (d) public fear, media interest and political pressure; (e) personnel logistics; (f) multiple agency coordination; and (g) resource and cost issues.

GEOGRAPHIC PROFILING

Several investigative approaches to these problems have been developed by police agencies, including psychological profiling and computerized crime linkage analysis systems (Copson, 1995; Johnson, 1994). Geographic profiling is an information management strategy designed to support serial violent crime investigation (Rossmo, 1995a). This service is provided by the Vancouver Police Department's Geographic Profiling Section to police forces and prosecuting offices (MacKay, 1994; Thompson, 1996). The first such profile was prepared in 1990 and to date, requests have come from a variety of federal, provincial, state and local law enforcement agencies across North America and Europe, including the Royal Canadian Mounted Police (RCMP), the Federal Bureau of Investigation (FBI), and New Scotland Yard. The cases have involved crimes of serial murder, serial rape and sexual assault, serial arson, bombings, bank robbery, sexual homicide and kidnapping.

The location of a crime site can be seen as an important clue, one that can provide valuable information to police investigators. Geographic profiling focuses on the probable spatial behaviour of the offender within the context of the locations of, and the spatial relationships between, the various crime sites. A psychological profile provides insight into an offender's likely motivation, behaviour and lifestyle, and is therefore directly connected to his/her spatial activity. Psychological and geographic profiles thus act in tandem to help investigators develop a *picture* of the person responsible for the crimes in question. It should be noted that not all types of offenders or categories of crime can be geographically profiled. In appropriate cases, however, such a spatial analysis can produce practical results.

A psychological profile is not a necessary precursor for a geographic profile, although the insights it may provide can be quite useful, particularly in cases involving a small number of offences. Geographic profiling has both quantitative (objective) and qualitative (subjective) components. The objective component uses a series of scientific geographic techniques and quantitative measures to analyse and interpret the point pattern created from the locations of the target sites. The subjective component of geographic profiling is based primarily on a reconstruction and interpretation of the offender's mental map.

The main quantitative technique used in geographic profiling is a computerized process termed criminal geographic targeting (CGT) (Rossmo, 1993, 1995b). By examining the spatial information associated with a series of crime sites, the CGT model produces a three-dimensional probability distribution termed a 'jeopardy surface', the 'height' of which at any point represents the likelihood of offender residence or workplace (see Figure 9.1). The jeopardy surface is then superimposed on a street map of the area of the crimes (see Figure 9.2); such maps are termed 'geoprofiles' and use a range of colours to represent varying probabilities. A geoprofile can be thought of as a fingerprint of the offender's cognitive map.

The system's underlying algorithm was developed from research conducted at Simon Fraser University in the area of environmental criminology (Rossmo, 1995c). The process relies on the model of crime site selection proposed by Brantingham & Brantingham (1981), and is also informed by Cohen & Felson's (1979) routine activities approach. The CGT algorithm employs a distance-decay function $f(d)$ that simulates journey to crime behaviour. Each point (x, y), located at distance d from crime site i, is assigned a probability value $f(di)$. A final value for point (x, y), representing the likelihood of offender residence, is determined by summing the N values for that point produced from the N different crime sites. The predictive power of the model is related to the number of crime sites — the more locations, the better the performance.

By establishing the probability of the offender residing in various areas and displaying those results on a map, police efforts to apprehend

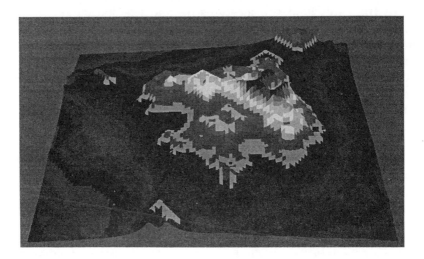

Figure 9.1. Jeopardy surface for series of armed robberies in Vancouver, Canada.

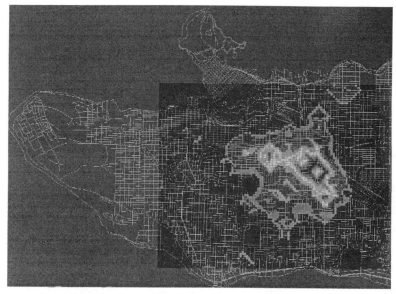

Figure 9.2. Geoprofile for series of armed robberies in Vancouver, Canada

criminals can be assisted. This information allows police departments to focus their investigative activities, geographically prioritize suspects, and concentrate patrol efforts in those zones where the criminal predator is most likely to be active.

The Profiling Process

A geographic profile fits into a typical criminal investigation in the following sequence:

1 Occurrence of a crime series.
2 Employment of traditional investigative techniques.
3 Linkage analysis determining which crimes are connected.
4 Preparation of a psychological profile.
5 Construction of a geographic profile.
6 Development of new investigative strategies.

The preparation of a geographic profile involves the following operational procedure: (a) examination of the case file, including investigation reports, witness statements, autopsy reports and, if available, the psychological profile; (b) inspection of crime scene and area photographs; (c) discussions with investigators and crime analysts; (d) visits to the crime sites when possible; (e) analysis of neighbourhood crime statistics and demographic data; (f) study of street, zoning and rapid transit maps; (g) analysis; and (h) report writing (Holmes & Rossmo, 1996).

In addition to the offence locations and times involved in a crime series, some of the other elements that need to be considered in the construction of a geographic profile include crime location type, target backcloth, and offender hunting style. These three considerations are the most important and are discussed in detail below. Other factors include location of arterial roads and highways, presence of bus stops and rapid transit stations, physical and psychological boundaries, zoning and land use, neighbourhood demographics, routine activities of victims, and displacement.

Crime Locations

Most of the geography of crime literature treats the concept of crime site as a single location. Depending upon the type of crime, however, there may be various locations connected to a single offence. Each of these has a potentially different meaning to the offender and, consequently, distinctive choice properties (Newton & Swoope, 1987; Ressler & Shachtman, 1992). In homicide, for example, such location types include (a) victim encounter, (b) attack, (c) murder, and (d) body dump sites. While these particular actions could all occur at one place, in many cases they are divided up between two or more different locations.

Eight possible crime location sets can result from combinations of these four different crime site types. For example, Canadian sex killer Paul Bernardo encountered and attacked his victims on the street, strangled them in his home, and then dumped their bodies at remote sites (Burnside & Cairns, 1995; Pron, 1995). The specific location set for a given crime is a function of victim selection and encounter site characteristics, but it also implies something about the offender, how he/she searches for victims, and the associated level of organization and mobility. Generally, the greater the organization and mobility of the offender, the greater the potential complexity (i.e. the more separate locations) of the crime location set. Research has also shown a high level of consistency in the geographic modus operandi of serial offenders, as most repeatedly employ the same crime location set (Rossmo, 1995a). This implies that the concept of crime location set could be used as an assessment characteristic for the linking of serial offences[1].

---

[1] ViCLAS, the RCMP computerized linkage analysis system, was designed with certain geographic profiling requirements in mind. It is possible to conduct queries, amongst other search criteria, based on crime location set similarities.

While all crime scene types are important in the construction of a geographic profile, every site type may not possess an equal degree of relevance in all cases. Some locations, particularly in homicides, are not known to investigating police officers. Prior to the apprehension of the offender, these places can only be determined through evidence recovery or witness statements. In a typical unsolved homicide the police know the body dump site (which may or may not be the murder scene) and the place where the victim was last seen. In some circumstances, they may only know one of these locations.

Target Backcloth

Brantingham & Brantingham (1993) suggest that the structure of the target or victim backcloth is important for an understanding of the geometric arrangement of crime sites. The target backcloth is equivalent to the spatial opportunity structure. It is configured by both geographic and temporal distributions of *suitable* — as seen from the offender's perspective — crime targets or victims across the physical landscape. The availability of such targets might vary significantly according to neighbourhood, area or even city, and can also be influenced by time, day of week and season (Brantingham & Brantingham, 1984).

Because victim location and availability play key roles in the determination of where offences occur, non-uniform or 'patchy' target distributions can distort the spatial pattern of crime sites. Victim selections that are non-random, or based on specific and rare traits, will require more searching on the part of the offender than those that are random, non-specific and common (Canter, 1994; Davies & Dale, 1996; Holmes & De Burger, 1988). For example, if an arsonist prefers to select warehouses as targets, their availability and distribution, geographically determined by city zoning bylaws, will have a strong influence on where the crimes occur. If the arsonist has no preferences, then the target backcloth will probably be more uniform as houses and buildings abound, at least in urban areas. The target sites of a predator who seeks out prostitutes will be determined primarily by the locations of *hooker strolls*, while the attack sites of an offender who is less specific could well be found anywhere.

A uniform victim spatial distribution means that the locations of the crimes will be primarily influenced by the offender's activity space; otherwise, crime geography is more closely related to the target backcloth. In the extreme cases of an arsonist for hire or a contract killer, victim location totally determines crime site. The consideration of victim characteristics thus plays an important role in the development of an accurate geographic profile.

The target backcloth is influenced by both the natural and built physical environments as these affect where people live. Housing development is determined by such factors as physical topography, highway networks, national boundaries, city limits, land use and zoning regulations. The Werewolf Rapist, Jose Rodrigues, lived in Bexhill on the south coast of England during his series of 16 sexual assaults. With no potential victims situated in the English Channel to the south, he was forced to confine his attacks to locations north of his residence, resulting in a distorted target pattern. Such problems could be compensated for through the appropriate topological transformation of the physical space within and surrounding the offender's hunting area.

Hunting Typology

> Throughout accounts of serial murders run themes of adventurous risk in the stalking of human prey by stealth or deception, the excitement of the kill ... The egoism of the hunter permits the degradation of potential victims to the level of wild game. The planning, excitement, and thrill of the hunt overrides all other considerations except eluding capture (Green, 1993).

Predatory criminals employ various hunting styles in their efforts to seek out and attack victims. These, in turn, affect the spatial distribution of the offender's crime sites, suggesting that any effort to predict offender residence from crime locations must consider hunting style. It was therefore important to ascertain those methods of hunting that produce target patterns inappropriate for this type of spatial analysis. Previous classifications of serial crime geography have only been descriptive of the final spatial pattern and not of the processes that produced those outcomes. It was therefore necessary to develop a hunting typology relevant to serial offenders. While this scheme was constructed from an exploratory data analysis of serial murderers, it is informed by the geography of crime theory and is applicable, for the purposes of geographic profiling, to certain other types of predatory crime.

While a murder can potentially involve several different types of crime locations, experience has shown that victim encounter and body dump sites are most important in terms of an investigation-oriented geographic analysis. These are the location types most likely to be discovered by the police; attack and murder scenes, if different from encounter and dump sites, are usually known only to the murderer. The hunting typology is therefore concerned with offender behaviour *vis-à-vis* these particular crime locations.

Search and Attack Methods

The serial killer hunting process can be broken down into two components, (a) the search for a suitable victim, and (b) the method of attack. The former influences selection of victim encounter sites, and the latter, body dump sites. The proposed hunting typology results from the categories produced by the combination of these elements.

The following four victim search methods were isolated:

1 *Hunter* — defined as an offender who sets out specifically to search for a victim, basing the search from his/her residence.
2 *Poacher* — defined as an offender who sets out specifically to search for a victim, basing the search from an activity site other than his/her residence, or who commutes or travels to another city during the victim search process.
3 *Troller* — defined as an offender who, while involved in other, nonpredatory, activities, opportunistically encounters a victim.
4 *Trapper* — defined as an offender who assumes a position or occupation, or creates a situation that allows him/her to encounter victims within a location under their control.

The following three victim attack methods were isolated:

1 *Raptor* — defined as an offender who attacks a victim upon encounter.
2 *Stalker* — defined as an offender who first follows a victim upon encounter, and then attacks.
3 *Ambusher* — defined as an offender who attacks a victim once he or she has been enticed to a location, such as a residence or workplace, controlled by the offender[2].

Hunters are those criminals who specifically set out from their residence to look for victims, searching through the areas in their awareness space that they believe contain suitable targets[3]. The crimes of a hunter are generally confined to the offender's city of residence.

---

[2] This typology is remarkably similar to Schaller's (1972) description of certain hunting methods used by lions in the Serengeti, where he observed ambushing, stalking, driving (direct attack) and unexpected (opportunistic) kills.

[3] Westley Allan Dodd, a serial killer executed for the murder of three children in the state of Washington, wrote in his diary, 'Now ready for my second day of the hunt. Will start at about 10 a.m. and take a lunch so I don't have to return home'. He was worried, however, that if he murdered a child in the park through which he was searching, he'd lose his 'hunting ground for up to two to three months' (Westfall, 1992).

Conversely, *poachers* travel outside of their home city, or operate from an activity site other than their residence, in the search for targets. The differentiation between a hunter and a poacher, however, is often a difficult and subjective task.

The terms 'hunter' and 'poacher' are similar to the 'marauder' and 'commuter' designations used by Canter & Larkin (1993) in their study of serial rape in England. *Marauders* are individuals whose residences act as the focus of their crimes. *Commuters*, on the other hand, travel from home into another area to commit their offences. It was hypothesized that marauders would have homes situated within their offence circle, while commuters would have homes located outside. Only 13% of the 45 British serial rapists were found to have their home base situated outside of the offence circle.

The FBI, however, observed that 51% of 76 US serial rapists lived outside of the offence circle (Reboussin, Warren & Hazelwood, 1993; Warren, Reboussin & Hazelwood, 1995). Alston (1994) had similar findings in a study of 30 British Columbia stranger sexual assault series; in 43% of the cases the offence circle did not contain an offender activity node. The inconsistency in these findings may be attributable to differences between European and North American urban structure, neighbourhood density and travel behaviour (Warren, Reboussin & Hazelwood, 1995).

One of the problems with the circle hypothesis is its determination of hunting behaviour solely from crime site point pattern (see Alston, 1994, for a discussion of other associated problems). In cases involving large numbers of offences, the rapist may have commuted to several different areas in various directions, creating an offence circle that contains their residence. And in cases involving small numbers of crimes, a marauder may have found all of his/her victims through travelling by chance in the same direction, resulting in an offence circle that excludes their home base. Offence circles could therefore lead to both commuter and marauder designations, depending upon what point in a serial rapist's career they were generated[4].

This happened in both the Yorkshire Ripper and the Boston Strangler cases (Burn, 1984; Davies & Dale, 1996; Frank, 1966). In other instances, a non-uniform target backcloth may force a commuter pattern regardless of the offender's hunting style. Davies & Dale (1995) warn 'that the commuter and marauder models may just be extremes of

---

[4] The probability that the N crimes of a marauder will appear to be those of a commuter is approximately: $(2^n - 1) / (2^{2n} - 2)$. The odds that such a pattern could happen by chance is not insignificant for low values of n. For example, in a series of 4 crimes the probability is equal to 23%.

a continuum of patterns determined by topography and target availability'. Because of these problems, a more subjective interpretation of offender hunting style is used here to classify serial criminals as either hunters or poachers.

Trollers are those offenders who do not specifically look for victims, but rather encounter them during the course of other, usually routine, activities. Their crimes are often spontaneous, but many serial sex offenders have fantasized and planned their crimes in advance so that they are ready and prepared when an opportunity presents itself ('premeditated opportunism').

Trappers either assume positions or occupations where potential victims come to them, or entice them by means of subterfuge into their homes or other locations under their control. This may be done through entertaining suitors, placing want-ads, or taking in boarders. Black widows, 'angels of death' and custodial killers are all forms of trappers, and most female serial murderers fall into this category (Hickey, 1986; Pearson, 1994; Scott, 1992; Segrave, 1992).

Raptors, upon encountering a victim, attack almost immediately. *Stalkers* follow and watch their targets, moving into the victim's activity space, waiting for an opportune moment to strike. The attack, murder, and body dump sites of stalkers are thus strongly influenced by their victims' activity spaces. *Ambushers* attack those they have brought or drawn into their 'web' — some place where the offender has a great deal of control, most often his/her home or workplace. The victims' bodies are usually hidden somewhere on the offender's property. While victim encounter sites in such cases may provide sufficient spatial information for analysis, many ambushers select marginalized victims whose disappearances are rarely linked, even when missing person reports are made to the police.

Hunting style

Target patterns are determined by offender activity space, hunting method, and victim backcloth. One of the main purposes of the hunting style typology was the identification of those situations where an analysis of the relationship between offender activity space and crime location geography is appropriate. This allows for the elimination of those cases where such an analysis is impossible or redundant. Poachers, for example, who live in one city and commit their crimes in another, may not reside within their hunting area. Stalkers, whose crime locations are driven more by the activity spaces of their victims than by their own, will not usually produce target patterns amenable to this type of spatial investigation.

Table 9.1 shows the matrix produced by a cross-tabulation of the search and attack methods, and the suitability of the resultant cells for a geographic analysis based on encounter and body dump sites. The matrix uses a sliding scale of designations (yes, possible, doubtful, and no) to refer to suitability likelihood. A designation of redundant refers to a situation where such an analysis is possible, but trivial. For example, the offender's address could be accurately determined from an analysis of the body dump site locations of a trapper serial killer (e.g. one who entices victims into his/her home, murders them, and then buries their bodies in the backyard or basement), but such a circumstance negates any need for a spatial analysis. The cases of Belle Gunness, who poisoned her suitors, and Dorothea Puente, who murdered her elderly tenants, are examples of this type of situation.

As there appears to be a correlation between search and attack methods, actual serial criminals tend to fit into some cells more often than others. For example, hunter/raptors and trapper/ambushers are much more common than hunter/stalkers or trapper/raptors. Also, the suitability ratings in Table 9.1 are only suggestive, as individual cases may vary significantly from one another in terms of their spatial details.

Investigative Strategies

Various investigative strategies can be employed in a more effective and efficient manner through a geographic profile, and some examples are discussed below (Rossmo, 1995c, 1996). The choice of a given tactic is dependent upon the specific circumstances in a particular case. As most of our public and private record systems contain address data, it is prob-

Table 9.1. Serial offender hunting typology and geographic analysis feasibility.

	Search method			
Attack Method	Hunter	Poacher	Troller	Trapper
Encounter sites				
Raptor	Yes	Doubtful	Yes	Redundant
Stalker	Yes (if known)	Doubtful	Yes (if known)	Redundant
Ambusher	Yes	Doubtful	Yes	Redundant
Body dump sites				
Raptor	Yes	Doubtful	Yes	Redundant
Stalker	Possibly	No	Possibly	No
Ambusher	Redundant	Redundant	Redundant	Redundant

able that additional investigative techniques will be developed over time. Indeed, several of the approaches presented below were proposed by police detectives themselves.

Suspect Prioritization

Geographic and psychological profiles can help determine which suspects, leads and tips should be prioritized during a major crime investigation. This is particularly important in cases suffering from information overload. More than one murder inquiry identified the correct suspect but failed to realize it at the time.

Patrol Saturation and Static Stakeouts

Areas in the geoprofile most probably associated with the offender can be used as the basis for establishing directed or saturation patrolling efforts and static police stakeouts. This tactic is most viable in those cases where the crimes are occurring during specific time periods. Barrett (1990) describes how Kentucky police, correctly anticipating the movements of a serial killer through the pattern of his crimes, set up road blocks in a park to question late night motorists. This tactic gathered over 2000 names for the purpose of cross-comparison with other investigative information.

Through a geographic analysis of the crime sites in the Atlanta Child Murders, Dettlinger came to the conclusion that the killer was commuting along certain city routes (Dettlinger & Prugh, 1983). But his suggestion that stakeouts be established at the crucial points in this spatial pattern went unheeded by police, and five more bodies would be dumped near these locations before Task Force officers staking out a Chattahoochee River bridge pulled over Wayne Williams.

Neighbourhood Canvasses

A geoprofile can be used for optimizing door-to-door canvasses in urban areas and grid searches in rural areas. Similarly, information requests have been mailed out to target areas established through the prioritization of postal carrier walks. For example, LeBeau (1992) notes the case of a serial rapist in San Diego, who was arrested through canvassing efforts in an area targeted by analysis of the crime locations. The Vampire Killer, serial murderer Richard Trenton Chase, was caught in the same manner after a psychological profile predicted that he would be living near a recovered vehicle stolen from one of his victims (Biondi & Hecox, 1992; Ressler & Shachtman, 1992).

Police Information Systems

Police computerized dispatch and record systems often contain information of potential importance to an investigation. Offender databases, records management systems (RMS), parolee lists, computer aided dispatch (CAD) systems and the like can be strategically searched by address or location with a geoprofile (Brahan, Valcour & Shevel, 1994; Fowler, 1990; Pilant, 1994; Rebscher & Rohrer, 1991; Skogan & Antunes, 1979).

Outside Agency Databases

Parole and probation offices, mental health outpatient clinics, social services offices, and certain commercial establishments are often useful sources of information. Determining which of these are located in the area where the offender most likely lives can assist police investigations.

Postal Code Prioritization

Postal or zip codes can be prioritized with a geoprofile and then used to conduct searches and rankings of address databases. The following case illustrates one example of how this tactic has been used. During the investigation of a sexual murder police learned of a suspicious vehicle seen prowling the area of the attack on the evening of the crime. The only information witnesses could provide concerned the make and colour of the automobile. A geographic profile was prepared, postal codes ranked, and this information then used to optimally search Department of Motor Vehicles computer records.

Even with just a three parameter search — (a) vehicle make, (b) vehicle colour, and (c) registered owner address postal code — this procedure still served as an efficient discriminating method, resulting in only a few dozen records from hundreds of thousands of vehicles. Offender description, and zoning and socio-economic data, further refined the suspect search.

Task Force Computer Systems

A major crime inquiry may lead to the creation of a task force involving dozens of police officers investigating tips and following up leads. The resulting information is often entered and collated on some form of computerized database such as the Home Office Large Major Enquiry System (HOLMES), used by British police forces for managing large volumes of investigative case data (Doney, 1990; US Department of Justice, 1991).

These operations usually suffer from information overload and require some form of data prioritization (Keppel & Birnes, 1995). A geoprofile can determine the street addresses, postal codes and telephone numbers from those areas where the offender most likely resides. This process can also be linked to information available in CD-ROM telephone directory databases listing residential and business names, telephone numbers, addresses, postal/zip codes, business headings and standard industrial classification codes.

Sex Offender Registries

Sex offender registries, such as exist in Washington State (Popkin, 1994; Scheingold, Olson & Pershing, 1992), are a useful information source for geographic profiling in cases of serial sex crimes. By providing a list of addresses of known violent sex criminals, such registries can be used with a geographic profile to help prioritize suspects. The US Violent Crime Control and Law Enforcement Act of 1994:

'... requires states to enact statutes or regulations which require those determined to be sexually violent predators or who are convicted of sexually violent offenses to register with appropriate state law enforcement agencies for ten years after release from prison, or risk the reduction of Federal grant money' (US Department of Justice, 1994).

Peak-of-tension Polygraphy

In suspicious missing persons cases presumed to be homicides, with known suspects, polygraphists have had success using peak-of-tension tests in narrowing the search area for the victim's remains (Cunliffe & Piazza, 1980; Hagmaier, 1990; Lyman, 1993; Raskin, 1989). By exposing the suspect to questions concerning the type of location where the victim's body might have been hidden (e.g. cave, lake, marsh, field, forest, etc.), a deceptive response can help focus the search. The process often involves the use of maps or pictures. The utility of peak-of-tension polygraphy is enhanced when the procedure is directed by a geographic profile.

Bloodings

During certain sexual murder investigations the British police have conducted large-scale DNA testing of all men from the area of the crime (DNA Database, 1995). The first such case was the Narborough Murder Enquiry, when 'all unalibied male residents in the villages between the ages of 17 and 34 years would be asked to submit blood and saliva samples voluntarily in order to 'eliminate them' as suspects in the footpath murders' (Wambaugh, 1989).

Close to 4000 men from the villages of Narborough, Littlethorpe and Enderby were tested during the investigation. Considerable police resources and laboratory costs can therefore be involved in such 'blood-ings'. A geographic profile could efficiently direct the testing process through the targeting and prioritization of residents by address or postal code. The use of such a systematic strategy would result in a more effective and less expensive DNA mass screening sampling procedure.

Trial Court Expert Evidence

In addition to analysing the geographic patterns of unsolved crimes for investigative insights, the spatial relationship between the locations of a crime series and a suspect's or accused offender's activity sites can be assessed in terms of the probability of their congruence (Rossmo, 1994). When combined with other forensic identification findings (e.g. a DNA profile), such information can increase evidential strength and there-fore the probability of guilt. Geographic profiling thus has application in both the investigative and criminal trial stages.

CONCLUSION

> We were just hunting humans. I guess because we thought they were the hardest things to hunt, but humans are the easiest things to hunt Sad to say, but it's true (convicted Canadian murderer; Boyd, 1988).

The ease with which such offenders hunt humans has its roots in the basic nature of our society. We simply do not expect to encounter seem-ingly random violence during the course of our daily lives. Even the offenders themselves may not understand why they do what they do. Albert DeSalvo, the Boston Strangler, could not explain his hunting processes to interviewers.

> 'I was just driving — anywhere — not knowing where I was going. I was coming through back ways, in and out and around. *That's the idea of the whole thing. I just go here and there. I don't know why'* (Frank, 1966).

But while we may not understand them, it is still imperative that we know how to catch them.

Geographic profiling is a strategic information management system used in the investigation of serial violent crime. This methodology was designed to help alleviate the problem of information overload that usu-ally accompanies such cases. By knowing the most probable area of offender residence, police agencies can more effectively utilize their lim-ited resources, and a variety of investigative strategies have now been developed to maximize the utility of this process for unsolved cases.

'Some of our (offender profiling) hypotheses ... seem now to have passed into the general realm of established detective knowledge.... It is this gradual building of elements of certainty by scientific rigour that is the object of the researchers' (Copson, 1993).

But it is also the interaction between academic research and the police field that allows an investigative methodology to grow and develop. The importance of geography for criminal investigation and offender profiling strikes a chord within practitioners, a resonance best explained by an old police truism: 'When all else fails, return to the scene' (Barrett, 1990).

CHAPTER 10

Towards a Practical Application of Offender Profiling: the RNC's Criminal Suspect Prioritization System

John C. House

INTRODUCTION

When the Royal Newfoundland Constabulary (RNC) established its Criminal Behaviour Analysis Unit (CBAU) it was mandated with the task of providing a profiling service that would meet the needs of a relatively small police agency. The RNC's 318 sworn members have law enforcement responsibility for a population base of about 204 000 persons. With one of the lowest crime rates in North America, offender profiling would not have the same operational objectives as is frequently the case in some larger organizations. From a practical point of view, it would be necessary that offender profiling methods contribute to a wide range of crimes to be of any true advantage to the RNC. Investigators with the RNC were more apt to be investigating crimes such as rapes, armed robbery and burglary than they were to be investigating predatory killers.

The current practice of most profiling work is to provide an account that describes the inferred characteristics of an offender. It is up to the investigators to attempt to identify suspects who fit a predicted profile. Very often this can be a daunting task which may be very time-consuming (see Gudjonsson & Copson, Chapter 4, and Jackson, van den Eshof & de Kleuver, Chapter 7 of the present Volume), and there will always be the risk that the offender will be missed by the net that is cast. For profiles to have maximum practical benefit in the investigation of a crime, it would be most productive if they would include a list of potential suspects. Such considerations helped in determining how to proceed with the RNC offender profiling project. This chapter will review how the RNC's Criminal Suspect Prioritization System (CSPS) was developed as a PC-based application to take advantage of the current knowledge in offender profiling and how this system can contribute to active investigations.

PROJECT DEFINITION

The CBAU began its project by establishing whether or not there was any real need for such a profiling system within the RNC. For example, with very few stranger murders, it would not be practical to dedicate a full-time unit to focus exclusively on that type of crime. Such a profiling unit would need to address issues relating to a wider range of crimes. The CSPS was therefore developed to assist in the investigation of crimes that range from burglary and robbery to rape and murder.

The system was based on an accumulation of research from studies reported in the literature in addition to ongoing research at the CBAU. Based on this research, it was hypothesized that procedures could be developed that could analyse data on local offenders which could ultimately provide investigators with a list of potential suspects in a criminal investigation. While most current profiling systems focus on the linking of crimes, the CSPS focuses on correlations of crime behaviour to offender characteristics. In order to provide guidance, a start-to-end model of the project was developed in a manner that in many respects would resemble an hypothesis in a scientific experiment. In that regard the project was research-driven. The project phases are set out as follows:

- Project viability.
- Project research and development.
- Implementation.

An account of each stage will be given.

Project Viability

An extensive review of international research was conducted that examined the subject of criminals and their characteristics. As this progressed it became clear that the details contained in police criminal records were the most important data from which to begin with any meaningful prioritization system. It was apparent that most serious offenders were individuals of previous criminal history, with many studies establishing a strong association between present offending and previous detected criminality (Chappell, 1977; Gebhard et al., 1965; Jenkins, 1988; Leyton, 1995; Scully & Morolla, 1984; Wolfgang, 1958). To be of benefit to the criminal investigator, it is necessary to understand how crime scene behaviour may reveal the nature of such criminal antecedents.

Researchers have consistently reported that most crimes are committed by a minority of offenders (Farrington, 1983; Guttridge et al., 1983; Jansen, 1983; Wolfgang, 1983). These chronic offenders are generally responsible for about half of the total number of crimes, and the likelihood of future offending is reported to increase with the number of prior offences. Some specific studies on recidivism suggest that most offenders will re-offend, often well within a year (Doherty & de Souza, 1995; LeBlanc, Ouimet & Tremblay, 1988). Prolific offenders will offend much more frequently. Other studies report that offenders tend to be relatively young adult and adolescent males (Chard, 1995; Eskridge, 1983; Henn, Herjanic & Vanderpearl, 1976; Hindelang, 1981; Riedel, Zahan & Mock, 1985; Silverman & Kennedy, 1993; Wolfgang, 1958). Depending on the crime, general observations on age range can be inferred. Considered from the perspective of the criminal investigator, these findings can provide powerful analytical potential in terms of suspect reduction on the basis of an age range and likelihood of previous arrest. What is particularly useful is that this data is generally available to the police from their own records.

Further potential for the prioritization of offenders is indicated in the research of the spatial actions of criminals. A considerable body of research in environmental criminology and psychology has suggested that most criminals will commit their crimes within relatively short and predictable distances from their base or residence (Amir, 1971; Brantingham & Brantingham, 1981; Canter & Gregory, 1994; Canter & Larkin, 1993; Davies & Dale, 1995; Farrington & Lambert, 1993; Pope, 1977, 1980; Pyle, 1974; Rossmo, 1995a; see Rossmo, 1997, Chapter 9 of the present Volume). There is a growing body of empirical evidence that suggests that offenders will choose their targets in a deliberate rather than a random fashion. This is not to imply that particular victims are necessarily targeted, but that the location of the crime is not random. This research suggests that people develop mental or cognitive maps that are based on their interactions with and within their environment. In the case of criminals, they develop a knowledge of where suitable targets may be found and the safest and quickest route home so as to avoid apprehension. Some of the studies have suggested that violent offenders were more likely to live closer to the crime scene than were property offenders. Details on an offender's residence is also routinely gathered in police records, which also makes these findings potentially useful.

Project Research and Development

Much behavioural research on crime has focused on clinical issues such as the treatment of offenders. Although useful, the perspective of this work is dramatically different from that of the criminal investigator. The investigator must focus on the crime, as this will be representative of the problem that is presented. With this in mind, the project focused its research on crime scene information and victim/witness statements as a primary source of data from which to develop what will be termed 'investigative classifications'.

This project has been developed through the discipline of investigative psychology, which has evolved with the detective process in mind (Canter, 1989, 1994). The clinical research has revealed that various crimes can be classified and that such classifications can assist in understanding the nature of an offender (Blackburn, 1971; Boudouris, 1974; Cohen, Seghorn & Calmas, 1969; Knight, Rosenberg & Schneider, 1985; McGurk, 1978; Megaree & Bohn, 1979; Prentky, Cohen & Seghorn, 1985; Prentky, Knight & Rosenberg, 1988). Investigative psychology research has brought empirical methods into the realm of the criminal investigation (Canter & Gregory, 1994; Canter & Heritage, 1990; Canter & Larkin, 1993). It is well established that the various criminals who commit crimes will differ in their crime scene behaviour (see Badcock, Chapter 2, and Davies, Chapter 11, of the present Volume). Using rape as an illustration[1], it can be seen that some rapists will reveal themes of aggression while others will not. Some appear to be attempting to develop some sort of distorted relationship, whereas others will reveal a great deal of general criminality. Still others will reveal sadistic tendencies. Some offenders may exhibit two or more of these themes in a single crime. It was necessary to utilize empirical methods to analyse the behaviour in a sample of predatory rape crimes so that the underlying themes could be studied. To undertake this, a suitable sample of detected case files that contained details of the crime and offender was collected.

The following illustrates the process that was followed to analyse the sample of predatory rape cases. From a sample of rape crimes that was

---

[1] Throughout the remainder of this chapter, illustrative references will focus on predatory rape. This will allow for clear and consistent illustration of the procedures used in developing the CSPS system. In practice, the work at the CBAU has been focusing on a wider range of crimes, including burglary, armed robbery and murder.

collected ($N=60$), data were extracted from the victim statements that described the actions of the rapists during their crimes. This phase of the project was to determine whether crimes can be interpreted on the analysis of the criminals' behaviour. The methodology employed to do this is based on an approach called Facet theory.

Facet theory represents a research methodology that integrates content design with data analysis (Borg, 1977; Canter, 1985; Shye, Elizur & Hoffman, 1994). It is a comprehensive approach to the design of observations and analysis of empirical data in behavioural research. It provides practical tools for the entire research endeavour: formal methods for defining concepts for empirical research, techniques for formulating or selecting research variables, and a language for starting hypotheses. It proposes multivariate data-analytic procedures for validating measurements. Facet theory strives to coordinate the research design, observations, data analysis, theory testing and measurements to form an integrated procedure.

Smallest Space Analysis of Rape Sample

A data-analytic computing procedure called smallest space analysis (SSA-I) was used to explore the themes that distinguish all of the rapes from which the sample was drawn. Each rape case was content-analysed to determine the presence or absence of each of 39 pre-determined rape behaviour variables. This work was largely based on studies reported by Canter & Heritage (1990), where the same methodology was employed. The result was to reveal the underlying themes or narratives of the offender as revealed in the rapes in the sample. By taking account of all 60 cases, the SSA-I programme analysed the data and allowed it to be represented in a configuration that is reproduced in Figure 10.1. As Canter (1994) explains, to understand how to interpret the configuration, those actions that appear close to each other in the configuration are those actions that frequently happen in the same crime, for example binding and blindfolding a victim. Those actions that seldom co-occur will be far apart in the configuration. For example, an offender who uses a disguise is not likely to use a confidence approach.

If the actions of rapists were opportunistic and random, with no apparent theme to them, then there would be no discernable structure to the configuration and it would not be possible to interpret it. Research of rape using the facet theory approach has revealed that these configurations do in fact reveal underlying themes (Canter,1994; Canter & Heritage, 1990). The actions that have narrative significance are found together on the plot. At the centre of the configuration are non-discriminating characteristics of rape in general; a surprise attack, the removal of the victim's clothing, and vaginal penetration. Moving away from this central area are the actions that have lowering frequencies, with those at the very edge of the configuration being actions that occur in only a small proportion of rapes.

In interpreting the configuration, consideration must be given to hypotheses proposed in conjunction with the previously published research. It may be that the configuration reaffirms earlier findings, or it may suggest something different. Keeping in mind that this analysis used victim statements as the source of data, the results did support earlier research on the classification of rape. One region (aggression) of the configuration relates to aggressive actions, including physical and verbal violence. Another region (criminality) relates to overtly criminal actions that deal with the extent of organization and criminality in the

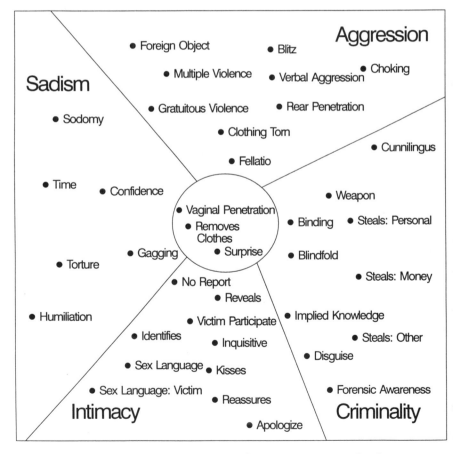

Figure 10.1. Smallest space analysis configuration on a sample of rapes.

offender. Such actions as the wearing of a disguise and using a weapon illustrate this. A third region of the configuration (intimacy) reveals a distorted attempt on the part of the offender to establish a relationship with the victim, a sort of pseudo-intimacy. Compliments of the victim and the need for the victim's 'participation' illustrate this. A fourth region (sadism) deals with actions that are seen as sadistic. Such behaviour that humiliates and tortures a victim would illustrate a sadistic theme in a rapist's behaviour.

CRIMINAL ANTECEDENTS OF RAPISTS

A general analysis of criminal histories was undertaken on the sample of predatory rapists. It should be observed that rather than review the criminal records on the basis of their legal descriptions, an attempt was made to examine the data to reveal the primary criminal theme indicated in the offender's past. This was achieved by four main thematic classifications of crime that were hypothesized as being related to the four rape themes discussed above. These thematic classifications were defined as property, violence, deception and sex. The theme of 'property' is meant to capture those crimes where the crime is directed at property or economic gain. Crimes such as theft, burglary, damage to property and armed robbery could be considered as property crimes. Whether or not armed robbery is a property or violent crime is the subject of debate (Bartol, 1991). Wolfgang & Ferracuti (1967) have argued that robbery develops from a subculture of violence and should be considered as a violent crime. On the other hand, Normandeau (1968) contends that robbers are generally not violent and are associated with a subculture of theft rather than violence. Several studies have found that there was no significant record of violence in the criminal records of robbers (Conklin, 1972; Normandeau, 1968; Spencer, 1966). Research has indicated that robbers who did have violence in their past were more likely to use it in the future, whether in robbery or other crimes (Bartol, 1991). The easiest way to settle the problem raised by this debate is to code robbery as both a property and a violent crime. It is the opinion of Vetter & Silverman (1978) that robbery is more accurately categorized as a violent property crime. In this project, robbery was coded as a property as well as a violent crime. An analysis of the antecedents of local armed robbers revealed that 85% of the sample had a prior arrest for a property crime. Only 47% of the offenders had a prior arrest for a crime of violence.

The theme of 'violence' is meant to capture those crimes where the overt expression of aggression is indicated. This may take the form of direct violence against another person or it may be implied through threats or the use or possession of weapons. Rather than being an economic crime, this theme is more emotional and may help in understanding the personality of the offender. Crimes such as assault, causing a disturbance, armed robbery and other crimes against the person would be characterized as crimes of violence.

The theme of 'deception' is meant to capture those crimes where there is clear intent by the offender to deceive another person. Although there is frequently an economic motivation with this offender, he does reveal a willingness or confidence to deal directly with another person. Crimes such as fraud, impersonation and perjury would fall within this category. The theme of 'sex' is meant to capture those crimes where there is a clearly sexual nature to the crime. Crimes such as sexual assault, indecent acts and indecent exposure would characterize such crimes.

In the overall sample of predatory rapists (N=90), 90% had been arrested previously, with only 43.3% of the cohort being previously arrested for a sex crime. Of the offenders with previous arrests, most were considered to be prolific offenders, with four or more previous separate arrests, and most of them had been previously incarcerated. Examining the criminal histories of these subjects with previous arrests, it was found that 91.4% had been arrested previously for a property crime; 76.5% had been arrested previously for a crime of violence; 24.7% had been arrested previously for a crime of deception, and 48.1% had been previously arrested for a sex crime. Similar findings were seen with a sample of sex killers. Of particular note was that only 24.1% of the 112 sex killers had a previously recorded arrest for a sex crime.

Relating Thematic Classifications and Antecedents

How the investigative classifications of offenders relate to the criminal's antecedents is important to any inferences drawn from these data. Referring again to the rapist sample, each crime was classified on the basis of whether it revealed one or more of the themes of aggression, criminality, sadism, and intimacy. Some offenders revealed more than one theme in their behaviour, while a small number did not reveal any discernable theme. In this analysis, a theme was considered as evident when three or more actions were seen in any one of the four thematic classifications. Of the 60 cases being considered, 10 (16.6%) did not reveal sufficient information from which to classify the behaviour. Those cases were excluded from further consideration. Of the remaining 50 cases, 26 were classified as revealing an aggressive theme; 18 as revealing a criminality theme; 9 as revealing a sadistic theme; and 29 as revealing an intimacy theme. The criminal histories of the offenders who made up the groups were considered separately to determine whether there was any observable variation on the basis of the theme. Table 10.1 illustrates the results. Because of the small size of the sample, these results are best described as exploratory.

As indicated, there does appear to be some variation in the extent and nature of previous criminal behaviour on the basis of the classification. Of particular interest is the observation that the theme of criminality indicates the highest degree of overall deviance in the offenders. A slightly lower percentage is seen with the aggressive and intimacy rapists. The sadistic and intimacy rapists also had a higher incidence of deceptive crimes in their past. Such deceptive crimes as fraud or impersonation clearly would parallel the behaviour of a rapist who uses a ruse to gain the confidence of his victim.

In practice, the development of a profile can be a complicated and detailed activity. In summary, the following observations were made:

- Offenders responsible for serious crimes probably have had previous arrests.
- The underlying theme in an offender's behaviour may be interpreted.
- Most criminals will have a base within close proximity of a crime scene.
- Most offenders tend to be adolescent or young adult males.
- Data on these potential suspects already exist in police records.

The next stage of the project was to convert these findings into something tangible that could actually contribute to the investigative process.

Implementation

The Information Technology Division of the Newfoundland Department of Justice was enlisted to provide programming expertise in developing

Table 10.1. Criminal histories by rape classification/theme (percentage in sample)

Antecedent	Aggression (%)	Criminality (%)	Sadism (%)	Intimacy (%)
Previous arrest	92.3	94.4	77.8	93.1
Previous conviction	92.3	94.4	77.8	86.2
Prolific offender	69.2	77.8	66.7	69
Previous prison	76.9	88.9	77.8	79.3
Property	92.3	94.4	77.8	79.3
Violence	73.1	72.2	55.6	69
Sex	34.6	44.4	44.4	34.5
Deception	26.9	22.2	44.4	51.7

the software component of the system. Prior to this, a review of various problem solving methods was undertaken to determine the best course of action. One approach that seemed to best address the problem at hand is a procedure called a geographic information system (GIS). The function of such a system is to store and manipulate geographically referenced data (Aronoff, 1989; Star & Estes, 1990). The GIS model was that of an information system that takes account of the chain of operations that sees the project from the planning stage through to collection, storage and analysis of the data. The model allows for a project to be customized so as to address its particular goals. The development of the software focused on data entry and query searching. Some of the various research findings revealed powerful investigative potential and the database was built around these findings. This allowed the data collection phase to focus on a relatively small amount of information. The benefit of this was that this phase would be more streamlined and therefore less labour-intensive.

A form was created that was representative of the data entry screen. The data collected included details of the subject's name and date of birth. Also recorded was the subject's most recent known and all previous associated addresses, with the date associated with the contact that generated a record. The offenders' criminal records from local and national data were drawn and analysed. Once all the data was collected and converted, the next step was to enter it into the computer database. Once on line, the database is constantly being revised. Overnight arrests, incarcerations and releases from prison all provide data that must be entered on a daily basis to keep the system current.

Prioritizing Suspects in Practice

From the perspective of an investigator, the most important feature is that the system can and will contribute in a meaningful way to the investigative process. In order for the system to work, several actions must occur, as follows:

- A crime must be reported.
- Investigation fails to identify offender.
- An offender profile is produced through analysis of crime.
- The profile is searched through CSPS.
- A report is forwarded to the investigator.
- Investigator follows up CSPS-generated suspects.

The following is an illustrative case (see Figure 10.2) that will put into context how this may proceed. Although the case relates to a local investigation, it predated the CSPS and was solved independently of this process. Although this summary is very brief, it will provide a useful example of how principles of the system would work in practice.

Illustrative Case Studies

- *Crime 1.* During the early morning hours an elderly woman was awakened by an intruder who was shaking her. The man told her to keep quiet and she would not be hurt. He demanded money from the victim, who told him that she did not have any. The man was armed with a knife and a rifle and carried a small flashlight. He was wearing a balaclava and what seemed to be military attire. While holding the knife to the victim's throat the offender proceeded to rape her. Following the rape the offender warned the victim not to call the police. He was very inquisitive and talkative throughout the assault. He told the victim that he had been waiting for this for a long time.

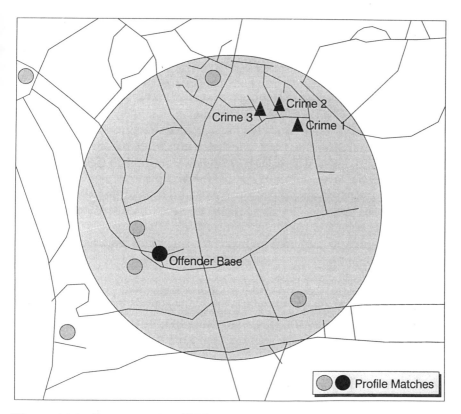

Figure 10.2. Representative CSPS analysis result from serial rape case.

Upon the perpetrator leaving the house the victim heard a shot which was later determined to have hit the side of the house.

- *Crime 2.* Eight months later a 26 year-old woman was attacked shortly after arriving home in the early morning in the company of her boyfriend. While sitting in the kitchen they both became aware of a male intruder who was armed with a rifle. The man was masked and was wearing a military uniform. He ordered the boyfriend to lie under the kitchen table. He then ordered the victim to undress and took her outside the room and raped her at knife point, threatening to shoot her boyfriend if she did not cooperate. During the assault the offender was inquisitive and talkative and told her details about himself. He told her that he had been watching her for some time. After the assault the offender demanded the boyfriend's wallet in an effort to take any money. The offender apologized and warned the victim not to notify the police.
- *Crime 3.* A third assault occurred seven months after the second incident. On this occasion a 17 year-old woman was asleep in her bed when she was awakened by an intruder who was holding a knife to her throat. The intruder had a rifle slung over his shoulder. She looked into the face of a masked man who kept repeating 'Don't scream, or I'll kill you'. The victim screamed and the offender threatened to cut her throat. She resisted and thrust her hands towards the knife in an effort to move the knife away from her throat. This resulted in her face and finger being wounded. The offender apologized for that and pulled her from the bed and escorted her into the back garden. He put her on the ground and ordered her to undress. She said that she couldn't because of her hand injury. The offender, who was wearing military attire, then escorted her back inside and undressed the victim himself. He proceeded to rape the victim. During the assault the offender became very talkative and told her about himself. Following the assault the offender again apologized and, before leaving, warned her not to notify the police.

A number of factors are immediately apparent in these crimes. Of particular significance is that the crimes were in very close proximity to one another. The second crime was approximately 0.08 kilometre from the first scene. The third scene was approximately 0.28 kilometre from the first. Figure 10.2 illustrates the cluster of these crimes.

The offender disclosed that he may have been watching at least one of the victims. This information may be of further benefit in supporting an inference that the offender probably lived in close proximity to the crime scenes. This offender displayed some overtly criminal behaviour, in that he wore a disguise, broke into occupied homes, carried weapons, and attempted to steal money. He also displayed a considerable degree of intimate behaviour in that he was inquisitive, complimentary, and very revealing of personal details (which although somewhat distorted, were largely true). There was no evidence of expressive aggression in this offender with the exception of the third victim's wounding, which probably occurred when the offender lost control of the situation. Once control was regained, there was no further evidence of any aggression. With this information it would be possible to infer an individual of previous criminality who would therefore likely exist in the police files. The clear evidence of his adept burglary skills suggests the possibility of past experience with burglary.

The offender responsible for these crimes was arrested shortly after the third crime. He was 24 years old and had a lengthy history of previous contacts with the criminal justice system. Most of his crimes were theft and burglary crimes in the immediate area of his residence base. This offender lived within about a 0.5 kilometre of the crime scenes.

CONCLUSION

The CSPS was created to make use of minimum data to achieve the best results. Having a firm foundation that was developed on research findings, the strength is its ease of use. Maintenance of the system can be sustained efficiently and quickly. The initial validation trials revealed the strong potential contribution to the full range of crimes. In testing the system with live data it was determined that it did accurately provide very short lists of potential suspects. For example, using information from active armed robbery investigations, it was found that once the offender had been identified, the CSPS had often correctly profiled him and produced his name. The CSPS is now an established system within the Criminal Behaviour Analysis Unit. It provides a powerful analytical tool that can suggest viable lines of inquiry to investigators who require the service. Plans are being worked out for a more comprehensive external examination of the system in the future.

The benefits of the CSPS go beyond those described so far. In terms of training initiatives the approach has become a regular component to the RNC's Criminal Investigative Techniques Course. In this forum the research findings upon which the system is built are passed on to front line police officers, who respond to calls and carry out subsequent investigations. With an understanding of the basic principles of suspect prioritization police officers can coordinate their response to take account of the research findings.

In the final analysis the CSPS will not solve crimes. Police officers will still solve them. The CSPS can contribute to that end by casting a net that makes systematic use of the information that is already in the possession of the police. There will undoubtedly be cases where the offender will be missed by the net that is cast. Sometimes information will not yet have reached the system, and there will be some percentage of offenders that will not fit a profile. Therefore, it is important to recognize that the CSPS is simply a tool, and cannot substitute for good, solid police work.

CHAPTER 11

Specific Profile Analysis: a Data-based Approach to Offender Profiling

Anne Davies

INTRODUCTION

Specific profile analysis (SPA) is defined in police circles as constructing a hypothetical picture of a perpetrator of a crime on the basis of data from the scene of the crime, witness statements and other available information. This is a fairly precise definition of only one aspect of 'offender profiling', which is a generic term. SPA includes a range of methods used to provide specialist help for a detective in various aspects of the investigative process, such as: comparative case analysis (detecting similarities between crimes that point to the same perpetrator or group of perpetrators); preparing for interviewing the suspect; identifying whether a death was likely to be the result of murder, suicide or accident; and identifying false rape allegations.

In a recent study, it was suggested that detectives needed assistance from offender profiling in low-volume crimes, such as stranger rape and sexual murder, where their lack of personal experience with the relevant type of case caused them difficulty in making inferences from the 'domain' layer of offence characteristics (Adhami & Browne, 1996; Oldfield, 1997, Chapter 6 of the present Volume). In a stranger rape this domain layer would include the statements of the victims, the witness to whom the first report was made, the forensic medical examiner, and the forensic scientist. Having made inferences from the information available in the domain layer, the tasks that seemingly need to be done in the course of the enquiry can be identified, and then a strategy can be devised to prioritize these tasks. An ideal strategy, as described by Adhami & Browne, is one that identifies the offender in the least time, with fewest resources (manpower and financial), and that results in a successful prosecution.

Assistance of this type can come from three sources: collating and analysing detective experience of the relevant types of low-volume crime; collating and supplementing relevant research; and through consultation with experts such as clinical psychologists and psychiatrists (Oldfield, 1995). SPA is based on the information gained from relevant published research and has been incorporated by the Metropolitan Police Service (MPS) into an existing repertoire of more traditional crime and crime intelligence analyses. This development has been made possible by employing behavioural scientists who use a data-based approach, not only for SPA, but also for the identification of serial serious crime and for strategic crime pattern analysis (which seeks to identify the nature and scale of crime in a particular area with the aim of informing management decisions). This approach to crime analysis provides support to the police service in a way that could be considered analogous to the service provided by forensic scientists.

The staff of the MPS Crime Analysis Unit are encouraged to undertake research that is both relevant to their work, and makes use of the data collected for intelligence purposes. For instance, a database has been established in order to store the information necessary for the identification of serial sexual offences and for the nomination of possible suspects. It is also used to continue research into the behaviour of stranger rapists in a similar fashion to the project initiated by the Home Office Police Research Group. In this latter project, a database containing information from the offences of 210 stranger rapists was used to test some of the hypotheses that have been generated by offender profilers. The main focus was on the feasibility of predicting aspects of their previous criminal careers (Davies, Wittebrood & Jackson, in press) and on geographical aspects of rapists' behaviour (Davies & Dale, 1996). The results of these two studies have been used as the basis of the present chapter.

THE HYPOTHESES UNDERPINNING THE RESEARCH

There are two hypotheses that were fundamental to the research reported here. The first is that human behaviour is largely the result of previous experience and therefore, aspects of a rapist's behaviour during a sexual assault might be expected to reflect prior criminal experience. Although there is continuing debate on the relative influences of 'nature versus nurture', there is agreement that environmental influences have a significant effect on human behaviour (Bem & Allen, 1974; Plomin & Daniels, 1987).

Insight into some of the events that might contribute to the development of a rapist's offence behaviour has been provided by two research groups. One group described the evolution of the 'modus operandi' (MO) of sexual killers (Douglas & Munn, 1992). MO was defined as the steps taken to protect identity, to ensure success and to facilitate escape, and excluded any overtly sexual behaviour. It was suggested that a killer's MO evolved as he/she gained experience and confidence, learning from mistakes that led to arrest, and from victim's reactions. It was also stated that the time spent in prison had a very significant impact on MO. The second research group studied the behaviour of burglars and found that they consider all those variables which, in their own experience and those of their peers, are perceived to be predictors of success or failure. Moreover, they tend to adopt rules of thumb that are developed and refined by trial and error (Cromwell, Olson & Avary, 1993).

The findings of Cromwell, Olsen & Avary suggest that burglars seem to have some behaviours in common with rapists, particularly those related to targeting. According to this research, there are three main ways of choosing a property to burgle: either just happening to spot a vulnerable target; visiting a potentially suitable property legitimately (and then returning later); or cruising neighbourhoods searching for overt or subtle clues that indicate vulnerability. These methods of selecting properties are remarkably similar to the ways rapists and sexually motivated murderers are thought to select victims — either through premeditated opportunism (McCulloch, Bailey & Robinson, 1995) or by targeting after encountering a potential victim either legitimately or during another type of crime, such as burglary; or by prowling a particular area or hunting in a specific setting (Davies & Dale, 1996; Rossmo, 1995a, 1997, Chapter 9 of the present Volume).

It would seem likely that behaviour patterns learned during either property offences or previous sexual offences, or the enforcement of legal penalties, might well be reflected in an offender's rape 'script'. If different experiences result in 'scripts' comprising clearly different behaviours, then it seems feasible that it would be possible to make inferences about a particular rapist's previous criminal career from his behaviour during a sexual assault. As approximately 84% of the 210 rapists in the sample had a prior criminal record, the potential of this type of research is immediately obvious.

A 'script' is defined by Schank & Abelson (1977) as the way a memory of frequently repeated experiences or 'episodes' is stored cognitively. It is used as a sort of mental shorthand so that every action does not have to be thought out in minute detail and people can function effectively and quickly. Human memory consists of many scripts of different types. There are, for example, scripts that consist of a sequence of possible actions that will lead to a desired goal, for example for getting up in the morning and going to work. There are also others that are a sort of procedure and look very similar to recipes in cookery books. An example of this latter type would be the procedures involved in starting a car. At the beginning, the necessary sequence of using the clutch, accelerator pedal and mirror have to be learned and reinforced by repetition. Eventually, these responses become reinforced through practice and they become incorporated in a 'starting the car script'. A tendency to violence is another example of learned behaviour that is reinforced by experience (Blackburn, 1993). It might be expected that a rapist who resorted to undue violence to control his victim might also be aggressive in other situations and have incurred convictions for other types of violent crime.

The second hypothesis underpinning the present research suggests that peoples' activities are mainly confined to familiar neighbourhoods, which are often, but not always, close to their home base. Each individual has in his/her mind an internal representation of the world that surrounds him/her. This has been referred to as a 'cognitive map' (Brantingham & Brantingham, 1984; Downs & Stea, 1973, 1977). Familiar neighbourhoods are important components of these 'maps' and would typically include localities centred on 'anchor points' such as an individual's present and past homes, places of work, shopping and recreation, together with other frequently visited locations such as the homes of significant family members and friends.

The development of cognitive maps is affected by personal factors, such as age and socio-economic status together with environmental factors such as urban structure. Many criminals are both young and poor and, as might be expected, previous research studies have shown that many crimes occur close to the offenders' homes (Brantingham & Brantingham, 1991). Most research into the distances criminals travel between home and offence site has been carried out using data from property offences, but there is no reason to believe sex offenders would be any different, particularly given that many of them have prior convictions for property offences.

THE OFFENDERS

The information regarding the sample of 210 rapists came principally from the records of the National Identification Bureau. It has already been established that the reliability of police records is poor for some categories of information (see Farrington & Lambert, 1992, 1997, Chapter 8 of the present Volume). Moreover, only recorded convictions could be used to calculate the number of previous offences, although this was not necessarily an accurate reflection of an offender's criminal activities, since many crimes remain unsolved. In addition, it is known that under certain circumstances, convictions under the age of 17 years are removed from offenders' records, and the convictions that are recorded exclude summary offences such as dangerous driving, or driving under the influence of alcohol.

The offenders' ages ranged between 14 and 59 years. The average age was 27 years, and 75% of the sample were under 33 years of age. As shown in Table 11.1, most of the offenders (84%) had a criminal record and these contained a range of crime types, with convictions for property offences, burglary and violence being more common than previous sexual convictions (see Table 11.2). In common with other offenders, rapists generally tend not to be specialists but to have a repertoire of crime types in their police records (Petersilia, 1980).

The rather limited information regarding the personal circumstances of the rapists indicated that about 20% were in accommodation owned

Table 11.1. The types of criminal records possessed by the rapists in the study ($N = 210$)

Recorded convictions	Offenders in each category (%)
None	16
Sexual only	3
Sexual and other	29
Non-sexual crimes only	52
Total	100

Table 11.2. The frequency of the various categories of prior convictions

Category of crime	Offenders with the relevant catergory (%)
Sexual	32
Violent	50
Robbery	23
Burglary	56
Theft	73
Criminal damage	35
Drugs	10
Other	31

by them or their parents; about 50% were in apparently fairly perma-
nent rented accommodation; and 30% were in some way transient, most
being either recorded as being of no fixed abode or being in hostels.
There seemed to be a relationship between type of accommodation and
number of convictions. The offenders in privately owned accommodation had, on average, fewest convictions; those in rented property
tended to have more; and most of the transients had extensive criminal
records, with convictions for at least 10 offences of various types, and
could be considered to be habitual criminals.

Farrington (1993) has said that convicted offenders move home more
often than non-offenders; and it is reasonable to infer that the more
convictions an offender has, the longer the time he is likely to have
spent in prison; and the more socially isolated he is likely to be. Social
isolation amongst the heavily criminalized was also indicated by the
finding that rapists who were unemployed at the time of arrest were
more likely to have a criminal record than were those that were
employed. Furthermore, they were even more likely to have been
awarded a custodial sentence at some time in the past.

THE PREDICTION OF A RAPIST'S CHARACTERISTICS

Each case in the survey included one offender and a female victim. Most
of the information used for the prediction of offenders' characteristics
came from the victims' statements. Such data are likely to be of variable
quality. For example, memory of the events during an assault is reliant
on registering them (acquisition), remembering them (retention), and
recalling what was said and done (retrieval). These stages can be influenced by various factors including personal abilities, past experiences,
mental and physical state and stressors (Gudjonsson, 1992).
Additionally, each victim's recall was guided by a police officer.
Although in recent years the police have been trained in techniques of
cognitive interviewing which is said to enhance recall (Fisher &
Geiselman, 1992), the quality of the statements that the police officers
obtained was very inconsistent. In some cases it was not known whether
a particular behaviour did not happen or whether the relevant questions were never asked, and it became very obvious that it is necessary
to provide interviewers with guidance about the sort of information that
needs to be collected.

As indicated earlier in the chapter, the present research focused on
non-sexual aspects of rape. The behaviours whose presence or absence
during a rape was found to be significant are listed below and their frequencies in the sample are shown in Table 11.3.

Table 11.3. The frequencies of the offence behaviours ($N = 210$)

Offender's behaviour	Frequency in the offences (%)
Fingerprint precautions	15
Semen destruction	5
Sighting precautions	28
Lies to mislead	20
Departure precautions	32
Reference to police	13
Theft from victim	40
Forced entry	25
Weapon	30
Extreme violence	20
Confidence approach	48
Alcohol	35

1. *Precautions taken by the offender to prevent identification or arrest.*
   - Wearing gloves inside premises or causing the victim to notice he was trying not to leave fingerprints (*fingerprint precautions*).
   - Trying either not to leave semen or destroying it (*semen destruction*).
   - Trying to prevent the victim seeing his face by covering all or part of his face, blindfolding her eyes, or otherwise trying to make sure she never saw him (*sighting precautions*).
   - Trying to mislead her about his name, area of residence or race (*lies to mislead*).
   - Taking precautions to ensure that he got away safely afterwards or verbally indicating that the matter concerned him (*departure precautions*).
2. *Behaviours which apparently indicate that the rapist had prior criminal experience.*
   - Making references to the police or any other aspect of the legal process (*reference to the police*);
   - Stealing money or valuables from the victim or indicating verbally that he intended to do so (*theft from victim*);
   - Breaking into the victim's house before sexually assaulting her (*forced entry*).
3. *Behaviours which were used to control the victim.*
   - The display of a weapon of some sort in order to intimidate the victim, usually a knife (*weapon*);
   - Using two or more blows (either slaps, punches or kicks) during the course of the rape (*extreme violence*).
4. *The method of initiating contact with the victim.*

- Talking to the victim in a social manner before sexually assaulting her, rather than 'surprising' her by a sudden attack (*confidence approach* — see Hazelwood & Burgess, 1995, for a comprehensive description).

5. *Use of alcohol.*
   - This variable described the situation where the victim was aware that the offender had drunk alcohol before or during the attack (*alcohol*) (see Brody & Green, 1994).

The offender characteristics used in the analysis are presented in Table 11.4. They include whether an offender had previously been given a custodial sentence; whether he had at least one conviction of any sort; whether he had at least one conviction for one of six categories of offence; and whether he was apparently a *one-off* sexual offender rather than someone who was known to have committed other sexual offences.

The reason for the inclusion of this last characteristic was to identify what behaviours might distinguish an inexperienced rapist from a serial sexual offender. Although only 32% (68/210) of the rapists in the survey had prior convictions for sexual crime, over twice that number (67%, 140/210) were suspected of committing two or more sexual offences, that is, they were serial sexual offenders. This discrepancy could be due in part to the very low conviction rate for sexual offences in British courts. For instance, in 1994, 5039 allegations of rape were recorded by the British police. Only 940 of these cases went for trial at crown court and of these, 425 resulted in conviction (Lees, 1996).

The technique used for analysis of the offence characteristics was logistic regression (see Aitken et al., 1995, 1996; Davies, Wittebrood & Jackson, in press). The method relates the presence or absence of certain offence behaviours to the probability that an offender has a particular characteristic.

Table 11.4. The frequencies of offender characteristics in the sample ($N = 210$)

Description of the offender	%
Offender has been awarded a custodial sentence	61
Offender has at least one conviction	84
Offender has at least one conviction for burglary	56
Offender has at least one conviction for drug-related offences	10
Offender has at least one conviction for robbery	23
Offender has at least one conviction for a sexual offence	32
Offender has at least one conviction for theft	73
Offender has at least one conviction for violence	50
Offender has apparently only ever committed one sexual offence	33

The results of the analysis are summarized below. For the sake of simplicity, the mathematics have been omitted but details of the calculations used to produce the probabilities may be found in the paper by Davies, Wittebrood & Jackson (in press). The first section describes the use of the individual behaviours for prediction and the second describes three combinations of behaviours that gave a significantly better rate of prediction.

The Predictive Powers of Individual Behaviour

As might have been expected, the analysis showed that the behaviour *fingerprint precautions* was an extremely powerful indication that a rapist might have prior convictions of some sort. In particular, the presence of the behaviour indicated that a rapist was approximately four times more likely to be a burglar than was one who took no such precautions. A rapist who took no such precautions was approximately three times more likely to be a *one off* sexual offender than one who did.

Equally predictable was the fact that the best sign of a rapist having a prior conviction for a sexual offence, was *semen destruction*. The presence of this behaviour indicated that a rapist was approximately four times more likely to have prior convictions for sexual offences than one who made no attempt not to leave semen. However, a degree of caution should be used when applying this and other findings in an actual investigation. For instance, it must be borne in mind that just being arrested as a suspect for a sexual offence might teach an offender about the evidential value of semen. In addition, the publicity that DNA profiling has recently attracted will increase general awareness of the topic.

The absence of *sighting precautions* meant that a rapist was approximately three times more likely to be a *one-off* offender than one who took such precautions. In fact, the presence of this behaviour seemed to reflect a preoccupation with personal safety that had to do with general criminal experience of either rape or property crime, rather than being useful for predicting any one characteristic. It tended to co-occur with other offence behaviours such as *fingerprint precautions, departure precautions, theft from victim* and *not* using the *confidence approach*.

The absence of the behaviour *lies to mislead* indicated that a rapist was about twice as likely to have convictions for violence as one who did not lie in this manner. It is not easy to explain this finding. However, other rapists with prior convictions, especially for burglary, were also less likely to exhibit this behaviour. It may be that these men are generally more cautious and therefore less likely to engage in much conversation with their victims. This would suggest that the tendency to lie to the victim in this manner might be a feature of a more talkative rapist.

If a rapist did not take *departure precautions*, then he was nearly three times as likely to be a *one-off* offender and about twice as likely to have prior convictions for drug-related offences than a rapist who was concerned about getting away safely. Another indication of prior drug-related offences was *theft from the victim*. It may be that drug-related convictions are indicators of the continuing use of drugs, which could both affect a rapist's awareness of risk (see Cromwell, Olson & Avary, 1991) and increase his need for money.

If a rapist exhibited the behaviour *reference to the police*, then he was approximately four times more likely to have been in custody, five-and-a-half times more likely to have a conviction and two-and-a-half times more likely to have a conviction for violence than one who did not. It is of note that this conversational theme is related to previous criminality, whereas *lying to mislead* is not. Presumably it signifies a heightened awareness of the police and the possibility of arrest.

The use of the behaviour *theft from victim* indicated that a rapist was approximately four times more likely to have prior convictions for burglary, and also more likely to have prior convictions for property crime in general, or drug-related crime, or to have prior convictions, or to have been awarded a custodial sentence, than one who did not.

If a rapist used the behaviour *forced entry*, he was over five times more likely to have prior convictions for burglary than one who did not. This is in accordance with the hypothesis that rapists' behaviour might reflect experiences of other types of crime. Most people are very territorial, being possessive about their own homes and only entering those of other people when invited, but persistent burglars tend not to have the same inhibitions (Mawston, 1987).

One of the more surprising results of this research was that the use of a weapon to intimidate the victim (*weapon*) indicated that a rapist was less likely to have prior convictions for either burglary or sexual offences, or to have been awarded a custodial sentence, than one who did not use a weapon in this way. This finding is in contrast to the hypothesis of Canter & Heritage (1990), which suggested that controlling the victim with a weapon was one of nine behaviours which indicated the likelihood of an extensive history of non-sexual crimes. There were three behaviour variables that were excluded from this analysis at an early stage because they were apparently not useful for predicting any of the offender characterics under consideration — *threatening the victim with harm if she reported the offence*, and either *tying* or *gagging* her. These were also among the same authors' nine variables, suggesting a serious discrepancy between our findings and their hypothesis. It may be that criminals do tend to carry knives but are often confident enough not to use them. This topic clearly merits further research.

Striking the victim twice or more during a rape, *extreme* violence, indicated that a rapist was over three times more likely to have prior convictions for violent offences than one who did not. The offence behaviour *alcohol* was included in the analysis because of the known association between alcohol and violence. However, the results proved to be more understandable in relation to the effect of alcohol on the reduction of fear and inhibition (see Cromwell, Olson & Avary, 1991). The rapist who had used alcohol prior to or during a rape was approximately two-and-a-half times more likely to be a one-off sexual offender, that is, less likely to be a serial rapist.

The rapist who used the *confidence approach* was also approximately two-and-a-half times more likely to be a *one-off* sexual offender, suggesting that serial rapists are more likely to use the surprise approach. In fact, despite the seemingly rather unsatisfactory nature of a characteristic defined as 'an apparent *one-off* sexual offender', the results of the analysis gave some very clear indications that this type of offender may be indicated by a lack of *fingerprint, sighting* or *departure precautions*, and the use of the *confidence approach* and *alcohol*.

Combinations of Behaviours

Having used logistic regression to determine the predictive power of each behaviour individually, it was then used to assess the behaviours in combination with one another. There were three combinations of behaviours whose presence or absence in an offence could be used to calculate probabilities of certain offender characteristics more successfully than a priori guesses. The relevant characteristics were: having prior convictions for burglary; having prior convictions for violence; and being a *one-off* offender.

The behaviours which are useful for predicting the characteristics 'prior conviction for burglary' are *fingerprint precautions, theft from a victim, forced entry, weapon* and *alcohol*. If all the behaviours except threatening the victim with a weapon are present in a rape, then the probability that the offender has prior convictions for burglary is between 93 and 100%. On the other hand, if only threatening the victim with a weapon was present, then the probability would lie between 8% and 31%.

The significant behaviour for predicting the characteristic 'prior convictions for violence' are *extreme violence, reference to police*, and *lies to mislead*. The rapist is most likely to have the characteristic if the first two behaviours are present in the offence and the last is absent.

The significant behaviours for predicting the characteristic '*one-off* sexual offender' are *fingerprint precautions, departure precautions, forced entry, confidence approach* and *alcohol*. The rapist is most likely to have this characteristic if *fingerprint* and *departure precautions* are absent, *alcohol* is present and either *forced entry* occurred or the *confidence approach*. Clearly the last two characteristics could not be present in the same offence, as *forced entry* can only be a surprise. These findings suggest that there may be two subsets of apparent *one-off* sexual offenders in the database.

THE GEOGRAPHY OF RAPE

The study of the geography of rape was carried out using the data available from approximately 300 crimes of a sub-set of 79 of the rapists in the Police Research Group database. This study provided a general overview of the geographic aspects of the offences. In each instance where the offender's address at the time of the assault was known, the distance between the offender's home base and the site where he approached his victim was measured. Straight line measurements ('crow flight') were used. These do not accurately reflect how individuals move through the environment. However, the author did not have access to a computerized geographic information system at the time of the analysis so more realistic estimates of the minimal distances using street networks could not be made.

As can be calculated from Table 11.5, most rape victims (90%) were approached within 10 miles of the offender's home base; over half within two miles; just under a third within one mile and about a fifth within half a mile. The frequency of offences declined rapidly with distance from base. This effect is termed 'distance decay'. It has been observed in other types of crime and is, in fact, a feature of normal human behaviour (Brantingham & Brantingham, 1984; Rossmo, 1993b). Generally, people travel no further than is necessary to achieve their objectives. They are subject to time constraints imposed by obligatory activities such as work and sleep, and discretionary activities such as socializing (LeBeau, 1990). Movement between the places where the various activities occur also requires time. In fact, as Hagerstrand (1973) observed, available time places more limitations on human activity than do spatial considerations.

It was demonstrated that the distance between base and approach site tended to correlate with the age of the offender ($\chi^2 = 67$, df $= 1, p = 0.00$), with the younger men tending to offend nearer home. The small number of cases where rapists had approached their victims more than 10 miles from base were examined in detail. It may be significant that all involved serial rapists. There were several reasons for these longer distances, and sometimes it was obvious that two or more of these reasons could apply in

Table 11.5. The distance from the offenders' bases to the locations where the victims were approached, expressed in numbers and percentages for: (a) a set of data containing one rape from each of 71 offenders with a known base (either the only one for which a victim's statement was available or the first in the series); and (b) a set of data containing all 299 sexual offences in the sample where the offender had a known base

Distance from base (miles)	Number of offences (one case per offender) (%)		Number of offences (all cases in the sample) (%)	
0 – 0.5	17	(23.9)	52	(17.4)
0.51 – 1.0	8	(11.3)	35	(11.7)
1.1 – 2.0	15	(21.1)	67	(22.4)
2.1 – 3.0	7	(9.9)	25	(8.4)
3.1 – 4.0	3	(4.2)	26	(8.7)
4.1 – 5.0	3	(4.2)	21	(7.0)
5.1 – 10	9	(12.7)	39	(12.9)
over 10	9	(12.7)	34	(11.4)
Total	71	(100)	299	(100)

any one case. Longer distances were recorded in the following circumstances. Specific points are then discussed in more detail.

1   An offender having dispersed anchor points such as work-places, previous area of residence, and the homes of friends and relatives (the victims were usually either approached in the vicinity of an anchor point, or less often on a route between base and a second anchor point).

2   Carrying out a rape whilst on holiday.

3   Having a transient type of life-style.

4   Having a requirement for a specific type of victim or a particular location where suitable victims might be relatively numerous.

5   Targeting suitable properties for either 'up-market' burglary or armed robbery.

6   Spending large amounts of time prowling or 'hunting' for victims, and having access either to a vehicle, or a good transport network (e.g. the underground and railways in London).

7   Changing a 'hunting area' (geographical displacement) because of awareness of police activity either experienced directly or perceived through the media.

Examples of specific victim or location requirements which sometimes necessitated travel were (a) the choice of prostitutes from a red light district, or (b) the targeting of females on 'routes' along which they were journeying to and from home, and at 'nodes' of more intense activity such as train stations or entrances to blocks of flats. Night-time assaults on routes or near nodes tended to be focused on women leaving areas of entertainment, whereas those females who were attacked during the day were likely to be commuting between either work, school, shopping or other social activities. Of course, the distance travelled by the offender is likely to depend on his proximity to the aforementioned sites. A city-dweller may live quite near, but a country-dweller or someone from a small town is more likely to have to travel. Indications of travel are obviously having a car, or dispersed assault sites in a known series.

There were several instances of excessive travel where the rapists could also be considered as 'professional' burglars, that is, they broke into upmarket property and stole money and worthwhile items. There was also one armed robber who carried out a series of raids on off-licences (liquor stores). The premises he chose were between seven and 24 miles from his home base, and the distance travelled was in part determined by the sites of suitable shops which were open late in the evening when the neighbourhood was quiet. It has been shown that the average length of robbery trips is a function of the value of the property obtained (Capone & Nicholas, 1975) and this could also apply to other property crimes such as burglary. Although LeBeau (1987) found that the shortest journeys to rape were made by offenders who broke into the victims' homes, it would seem that if a rapist was also a fairly sophisticated burglar, he might be expected to travel as far as was necessary to reach districts termed by Wikstrom (1991) as 'high social rank', targeting affluent property rather than a particular type of victim.

A characteristic of some active thieves was the long time interval that occurred between sexual offences. During a period of four years, one regular night prowler, who stole from cars and unoccupied premises, also sexually assaulted five victims whom he apparently happened across. Had it not been for an index recording the DNA results from unsolved stranger rapes, it is unlikely that the series would ever have been recognized. Perkins, Hilton & Lucas (1990) observed that the more convictions a man has for burglary, the longer the time-span between the rapes is likely to be. This is presumably because for some offenders, their main criminal activity is repeated theft and the sexual offences are to some degree opportunistic, perhaps being an 'added bonus', as described by Scully & Marolla (1985). However, this is not always true, as was demonstrated by one active burglar whose rapes formed part of this study. He 'hunted' for his rape victims by waiting outside train stations. Thus, he used a different method of target location for the two types of offence rather than coming across potential rape victims during his burglaries.

There are several offence characteristics that might indicate a professional burglar or robber who is prepared to travel, namely: the type of property in which the victim is attacked; the socio-economic status of the neighbourhood; the type of goods stolen; and the degree of organization or planning that is apparent, including the precautions taken to prevent identification and arrest.

There were three prolific 'prowling' rapists, all of whom had travelled over 10 miles on at least one occasion. Two were Londoners who spent large amounts of time roaming, and who sometimes used public transport to access approach locations. For a period of at least four years, the third was known to have gone out frequently at nights in his car, committing minor property thefts. His wife said that his staying out 'happened in waves'. He would come home on time for weeks and would then suddenly stay out all week. His sexual offences occurred over two years. He travelled between 10 and 42 miles to offend and broke into sheltered accommodation in order to attack the elderly. Most of his crimes were within the same area. As he had lived and worked in several small towns in that particular part of the south-east of England, the area included all the localities with which he was familiar. His wife's comments on his absences from home were echoed by the wife of another rapist who was known to have attacked three prostitutes. She said, 'For years he has gone driving by himself in the evening. Sometimes he would be away for hours. He said he just drove around and around, not particularly going anywhere'.

There are other cases in the database where offenders were known to spend long periods of time prowling, including one who kept a diary of his movements. It is likely that this behaviour is related to extensive fantasizing. Gresswell (1994) said of multiple murderers 'that many hours are spent in fantasy, 'try-outs', acquiring weapons, selecting victims . . . offending and following their cases in the media'. This is also undoubtedly true to some degree for all serial sexual offenders.

It may also be relevant that Dietz, Hazelwood & Warren (1990) noted that excessive driving was a characteristic of 12 of the 30 sexual sadists in their study. Enjoying driving for its own sake would militate against the general tendency of offenders to travel minimal distances. Certainly another two of the long-distance travellers whose cases were in the sample satisfied the criteria for sexual sadists, and both have murdered. They were relatively sophisticated and drove expensive cars. One lived in Bristol, a city in the south-west of England, but regularly commuted the 100 miles or so to the West Midlands where he had been brought up and where members of his family still lived. He was also familiar with London. He raped a woman at a location 60 miles from Bristol, en route to London. The other, who had a flat in South London but often slept in his car, abducted one victim from a motorway 95 miles from London and then drove her to London to rape her in a location near to where his father lived.

The final reason for carrying out offences some distance from base is spatial displacement (see Rossmo, 1997, Chapter 9 of the present Volume). There were three series in which this appeared to have happened. In one, having realized that the police suspected him of rape, the offender significantly increased the length of the journey to areas where he prowled, escaping arrest for some considerable time (spatial displacement). In the second, intense media publicity seemingly caused the offender to lie low for several months and then change area for his last attack (temporal and spatial displacement). Displacement also occurred in a third series because, according to the offender's testimony when interviewed, he said that he thought that he saw a policeman with a 'walkie-talkie' in the bushes of the cemetery where he was loitering. This caused him to move to a different area of London and to change his method of approach (spatial and behavioural displacement). He started to follow women home rather than attacking them in open spaces. He then began travelling even further from base and carried out his last three offences in a different county.

SUMMARY

This chapter had two main aims. One was to explain the nature of specific profile analysis, illustrating how it is based on published research. The second was to describe some of the relevant research in more detail. The focus of the research was on the criminal antecedents of stranger rapists and geographical aspects of their crimes. The research indicates that analyses of police data have great potential, particularly if the quality of the data were to be improved. There are various ways in which this could be achieved which would, in turn, facilitate both further research and police intelligence. For instance, an 'aide memoire' could be developed to ensure that the information necessary for inferring offender characteristics is obtained from victims of stranger rape.

Consideration could also be given both to developing geographic information systems within the police service and to storing and standardizing the addresses of locations of significance to offenders, such as present and previous homes, locations of work and offence sites, and the addresses of significant people. If a sexual offence occurs and the offender's behaviour indicates the presence of a criminal record, then suspects may be elicited by identifying criminals with the right sort of criminal history and with anchor points in the neighbourhood of the offence. One of the advantages of this type of research is that it can be carried out in-house by suitably qualified personnel. As the data are improved, more research could be undertaken so as to provide an up-to-date resource for investigators and to create an evolving a basis for specific profile analysis.

CHAPTER 12

Critical Issues in Offender Profiling

Debra A. Bekerian & Janet L. Jackson

The preceding chapters illustrate that offender profiling uses principles and methodologies derived from a number of different disciplines. Clinical psychology, forensic psychiatry, environmental psychology, social psychology and cognitive psychology have each contributed to the development of profiling procedures. The overall consensus is that profiling may have an important future part to play in criminal investigations, and that profiling has already demonstrated its usefulness in aiding the apprehension of criminal offenders. In this final chapter, we consider what challenges are likely to confront researchers in the future.

A LACK OF UNIFICATION

All profiling techniques focus on behaviour; and, there is a good deal of diversity in the techniques that are employed. Variation in an area of research is important for scientific progress. However, too much diversity can result in the field becoming fragmented theoretically, and therefore less accessible to application. There are at least three ways in which fragmentation might occur in the area of offender profiling: differences in frameworks, individual differences between profiles, and differences in culture.

Difference in Frameworks

A major debate between profilers regards the appropriate methodological framework for analysing behaviour (see discussions in Gudjonsson & Copson, Chapter 4; Jackson, van den Eshof & de Kleuver, Chapter 7; Farrington & Lambert, Chapter 8; and Davies, Chapter 11 of the present Volume). One framework incorporates concepts and techniques that are familiar to experimental psychology: for example, hypothesis testing; statistical analyses of findings (see Davies, Chapter 11). Some researchers refer to this as the scientific approach (e.g. Canter, 1994). This approach is reflected in Farrington & Lambert's analyses of burglaries and violent crimes (see Chapter 8), House's cross-cultural data regarding behavioural characteristics of rape (see Chapter 10), and Davies' database for rape (see Chapter 11). Other examples are Rossmo's discussion of mental maps (see Chapter 9) and Canter's (1994) discussion of life-narratives; they are concepts taken from basic theories of cognition and memory (e.g. Schank, 1982; Conway & Bekerian, 1987). Some have argued that a scientific approach is the only acceptable way to proceed with profiling (Canter, 1994).

The alterative framework relies on concepts found in clinical psychology and forensic psychiatry (see Badcock, Chapter 2; Boon, Chapter 3). The profiler adapts clinical methodologies, arguably as highly formalized and rigorous as experimental paradigms, and makes inferences about the offender's unconscious psychological processes. Conclusions about the relationship of personality and behaviour are drawn from multiple observations of single cases, rather than from population statistics that generalize across multiple cases. Importantly, single case studies are highly valued in other areas of psychology and have contributed greatly to theoretical development in these fields (see Shallice, 1992).

Both have distinct advantages and disadvantages. Scientific methods provide important information regarding the reliability and robustness of behavioural relationships, thereby ensuring that spurious conclusions are less likely. However, such methods average across individual cases, which can obscure highly essential information regarding crime features of the individual case (e.g. Bekerian & Dennett, 1995). Single case studies, while focusing on important individual characteristics, are less likely to identify invariances in relationships between variables, and may therefore have less predictive power when applied to the general population.

If debates over theoretical frameworks are conducted dispassionately, and with a healthy degree of open-mindedness, both science and the applied situation should benefit. Unfortunately, similar debates in other forensic domains have developed into irreconcilable differences or a disastrous 'war of the experts' (see Bekerian & Goodrich, 1995). Were this to happen in the area of profiling, it would prove beneficial neither to theory nor to the criminal investigator.

As a consequence, it is likely that some consideration should be given to 'hybrid' profiling techniques, where the procedures incorporate features of both frameworks. For example, multiple profilers might be employed, each adopting a different framework and, therefore, each providing different types of information. When different approaches are adopted, the quality and quantity of information is likely to be superior. Problems with this suggestion are, first, that it is costly and second, that it might lead to the situation where two profilers, adopting different frameworks, produce two disparate profiles. Of course, this latter situation can occur even when profilers share frameworks. Like all people, profilers are idiosyncratic.

Differences between Individual Profilers

No two profilers will necessary produce the same profile (see Stevens, Chapter 5). As noted in Jackson et al. (Chapter 7), differences between investigators emerge at all levels, e.g. information detection, organization of information, etc. Thus, one could conclude that the act of profiling is personal. It is important to clarify why this is the case, as this obviously has implications for the application of the procedures to real investigations.

A profiler has expert knowledge about domains of interrelated topics, e.g. police procedures, characteristics of different offences. The repertoire of expert knowledge will take a variety of forms (see Gill, 1995, for a discussion of expert knowledge). One will be referred to as formal knowledge. Formal knowledge is 'knowledge about' or 'knowledge that' and can be expressed explicitly, for example, in rules (see Jackson et al., Chapter 7). It would be expected that non-experts lack this knowledge (again see Jackson et al., for a discussion). Importantly, since formal knowledge can be made explicit, it can be learned by the novice. Thus, much of what is taught in training courses on offender profiling is formal knowledge.

An expert's formal knowledge will be determined in part by the particular framework that has been chosen. For example, a profiler using a more scientific framework might have expert knowledge about correlational analyses; whilst a profiler adopting a more clinical framework might have knowledge about clinical symptoms associated with different psychological disorders. Profilers adopting the same framework would be expected to share more formal knowledge than profilers adopting different frameworks.

In contrast, tacit knowledge is 'knowing how' or 'knowing of'. It includes skills (physical and mental), 'intuition', the processes of insight, and it is acquired through experience. Canter (1994) provides excellent examples of tacit knowledge in the context of expert profilers when he describes an expert's ability to perceive patterns, or an expert's sensitivity to detail. Tacit knowledge is generally regarded as being outside awareness, e.g. one cannot say how one perceives, one just does.

Not surprisingly, such knowledge is difficult to teach through traditional teaching methods, although certain formats, like metaphors or stories, can be effective communication devices (see Gill, 1995).

Because tacit knowledge develops through experience, it will vary with the personal experience of the profiler. This includes direct experience within a particular domain (e.g. compiling a profile) and also more general life experiences (e.g. previous background in policing vs. background in psychology). To the extent that profilers share similar experiences, they are likely to share some tacit knowledge.

The discussion of formal and tacit knowledge is brief and overly simplified. However, it serves to provide some background for understanding why two profilers can produce different profiles. As suggested above, it is likely that two profilers sharing the same training background will share formal knowledge. This would lead one to expect that the procedures used and the profiles compiled would show significant similarities. However, a profiler who has had experience in policing is likely to conduct his/her analyses in a way that is different from a profiler who has experience as an experimental psychologist. Thus, differences in both formal and tacit knowledge will influence the extent to which two profilers draw the same conclusion about the likely offender.

There is probably as much variability in the way that profilers compile a profile as there is in the way that offenders carry out criminal acts. Questions about differences between profilers will only be answered when the process of profiling is better understood. This will require an examination of the types of knowledge on which profilers rely. Such research will also be particularly critical when considering standards of assessment of expertise in profiling. This will be briefly considered below.

Defining and Assessing the Expert

Investigators may have difficulty in selecting a profiler (see Jackson & Bekerian, Chapter 1; Gudjonsson & Copson, Chapter. 4). Who constitutes an expert? What determines an expert's competence? What type of expert is best suited to the case in question? Concerns over these questions have led some investigators to treat profilers with suspicion (see Gudjonsson & Copson, Chapter 4). It is clear that some standards for assessment are necessary. Of course, this applies generally to the topic of expert evidence in any forensic investigation, rather than offender profiling *per se*. Importantly, guidelines for expert evidence are currently being considered by professional bodies (e.g. British Psychological Society's Working Party on Expert Evidence). However, the means by which such assessments might be accomplished in the context of offender profiling are not obvious at this time. Procedures underlying profiling are not well identified, nor understood; there is also a great individual variability in the way people compile profiles. Establishing adequate assessment procedures will be a highly complex and difficult task. It is one that researchers in offender profiling will need to consider seriously.

Differences in Culture

Profiling methods were first developed in the USA (see Jackson & Bekerian, Chapter 1). These methods have been taught to professionals in other countries (see Jackson et al., Chapter 7; Rossmo, Chapter 9; House, Chapter 10; Davies, Chapter 11). In order for this to be a sensible way to proceed, it must be assumed that profiling procedures developed in one culture can transfer to another. If it were the case that offender characteristics were 'culture'-specific, this would cast doubt on the utility of any cross-cultural training and, indeed, on profiling techniques. Canter (1994) provides an example when he points out that certain features of criminal behaviour that are critical in some countries are sensibly ignored in other countries, e.g. location of crimes in England vs. the USA, where location information is rarely used by the FBI.

There has been extensive academic discussion on the cultural determinants of criminal behaviour (see House, Chapter 10). However, few data exist that directly address the impact that culture has on the success of profiling. House (see Chapter 10) provides some important preliminary analyses in his comparison of Canadian and British rapists. The evidence suggests that similar features can be used to describe data from both these samples. However, as House acknowledges, the comparison of Canada and Britain may not constitute sufficient differences in cultural standards so as to provide firm answers.

Many researchers have made strong arguments for more systematic research into the area of cross-cultural differences. Most agree that profiling must be tailored to the needs of the specific police force, which will reflect not only regional but also cultural variables (see Jackson et al., Chapter 7; House, Chapter 10; Davies, Chapter 11). Profiling procedures will need to be sensitive to the cultural constraints on crime, offender behaviour and its investigation.

THE DEVELOPMENT OF THEORY

Profiling, in whatever form it takes, will be successfully applied only when there is a direct interaction between basic theoretical hypotheses and the applied domain. Thus, it is not sufficient for the applied researcher to demonstrate a relationship between, say, marital status and offence type. The researcher must also demonstrate that he/she has a theoretical explanation for the relationship. Without sound theoretical explanations, any conclusions might be spurious, and the subsequent advice that is given might simply be wrong.

Establishing a symbiotic relationship between theory and application is difficult, albeit feasible. This is perhaps the most pressing problem that will confront the area of research known as offender profiling. For example, Farrington & Lambert (Chapter 8) have already noted how the absence of comprehensive theories of personality restricts any firm conclusions regarding the empirical evidence.

However, it is doubtful that any one theory should be used to guide future research in profiling. For example, Boon (Chapter 3) demonstrates that the theoretical framework selected for profiling will be determined by the behavioural characteristics, rather than any inherent superiority of one framework over another. Of course, different researchers may find it difficult to coordinate their efforts if they are being motivated by different theoretical constructs. Because of this and the complexity of the applied situation, multi-faceted theories may be useful in providing hybrid theoretical frameworks (e.g. Teasdale, in press). Such theories reflect concepts from more than one domain of study (e.g. clinical and experimental psychology). Consequently, they are broader in their scope and can address a greater variety of variables.

INFORMATION GATHERING

A profile is only as good as the information that has been collected about the crime (see Stevens, Chapter 5). Profiling requires the careful detection and documentation of all information relevant to the crime, e.g. forensic evidence, autopsy reports, offender details (see Farrington & Lambert, Chapter 8; Davies, Chapter 11). If policing procedures do not conform to these standards, profiling will be severely impaired if not impossible to conduct. For example, Farrington & Lambert (Chapter 8) emphasize that tendencies to use unrecorded warnings are likely to reduce significantly the efficiency of any profiling system.

Accounts given by witnesses, victims and perpetrators can be useful sources of information. All will be required to provide an account of what happened on specific occasions or events. Because the quality of this information is so important to profiling systems, it becomes important to anticipate specific memory problems that might be encountered. Here, the psychological literature is replete with advice.

Emotional Arousal and Memory

In most cases of serious crimes, victims are likely to be under some state of emotional arousal. The relationship between emotion and memory has been the focus of extensive empirical study (see Powell & Dalgleish, in press). Empirical evidence suggests that immediately after an emotionally arousing event, people are likely to provide incomplete narrative accounts, due to the restrictive effects that emotions can have on memory processes. As levels of arousal dissipate, the person can provide more complete accounts (see Bekerian & Goodrich, 1997, for a discussion). Such evidence implies that interviews should take place some time after the event when the victim is less emotionally aroused, although accounts that are given after delays of more than 48 hours may suffer from processes of forgetting (see Fisher & Geiselman, 1993).

Some researchers advise investigators that changes in a witness's/victim's account are normal and not cause for concern (see Reyna & Titcomb, 1996). Preliminary data on victims' memory for real trauma supports this view. Victims' memory for the event can change, with significant new information regarding central and peripheral details being reported months after the crime had been committed (see Bekerian & Goodrich, 1997). This strongly implies that victims/witnesses participate in multiple interviews, with some delays between interviews. Even after claims by the victim that memory has been depleted, new information may still be forthcoming depending on the skills of the interviewer.

Interview Techniques

All information about an offence, such as conversations, moods, duration of events, is important for profiling systems (see Boon, Chapter 3; Farrington & Lambert, Chapter 8; House, Chapter 10; Davies, Chapter 11). A variety of factors will contribute to the accuracy of the information reported in an account (see Wells, 1993, for a discussion of estimator and system variables). Some reflect factors outside the control of the investigator, e.g. viewing conditions of the witness/victim, individual differences in witnesses and victim. Other factors are under the investigator's control; interviewing techniques fall into this category. It is essential that techniques used for interviewing are based on the psychological literature. Fortunately, this is one area where application has excelled and there are many comprehensive interview packages that the criminal investigator can adopt and modify (see the Cognitive Interview technique, Fisher & Geiselman, 1993). Most police forces are well aware of the importance of interview techniques, and of the availability of expertise. However, ideal interview techniques are often difficult to put into practice. For example, Farrington & Lambert (Chapter 8) note that in many cases, details of victim characteristics were not routinely noted, thereby preventing examination of what might be important variables.

Certain techniques developed by applied psychologists, like the Cognitive Interview (CI) technique, are useful tools for the investigator (e.g. Fisher & Geiselman, 1993). In the case of CI, the techniques incorporate powerful mnemonics known to enhance the recall of accurate information. However, there are dangers with such techniques (see Bekerian & Dennett, 1993). For example, CI can render confabulated accounts indistinguishable from accurate ones (Steller & Boychuk, 1995). Fact can become very difficult to distinguish from fantasy.

Interviewers need to be sensitive to the fact that some information may be difficult for the person to remember easily; and, because of this, the information may be more vulnerable to the misleading effects of an interviewer's questioning. For example, lower-level details (e.g. colour of clothing) can be more susceptible to forgetting processes, such as decay or interference. Such details may be more difficult to remember over time than who the perpetrator was, or where the event took place. Similarly, reported speech (e.g. the content of conversations) is also variably accurate. Gist can be retained for a considerable time but surface form (i.e. the exact words) can be difficult to remember. Retrospective reports of emotions that are attributed to the offender, e.g. he was angry, are also potentially variable, as they can be influenced by the emotional states of the victim, and any emotional reappraisal that has occurred regarding the event. In some instances, such information may be reconstructed (see below). Estimations of durations of events, e.g. it took about 20 minutes, are likely to be influenced by a variety of factors, particularly level of emotional arousal at the time of the event.

Reasons for Remembering

Information given by witnesses/victims and the perpetrator about the crime(s) is not useful if the person is deliberately lying. We do not consider here whether it is a reasonable assumption that a killer or rapist is not, at the same time, a liar; nor whether all witnesses and victims should be assumed to be naive reporters of fact. Instead, we illustrate how the motivation or reason for remembering has been discussed in the context of memory research.

Neisser (1987), in his discussion of autobiographical memory, suggests that there are at least two reasons why people tell others about a past event. One, they want to recapture what actually happened in the past. The act of remembering will be dominated by the *ideal of verity*:

report that which is true. Under these conditions, Neisser argues that memory will be largely free of errors. Two, they want to achieve some objective in the present. The person uses the past, describes it in a particular way in order to achieve some currently important goal. This second reason is dominated by what Neisser calls the *ideal of utility*: use the past to accomplish something in the present. Under the ideal of utility, memory is likely to be reconstructive and to include errors. Somewhat worryingly, the person may actually believe that what he/she is reporting is true, and be unaware of his/her motives (see Neisser's discussion, 1981, of John Dean's memory).

Neisser has argued that the type of retrieval conditions imposed on the person will determine which ideal is dominating. Retrieval conditions in the context of criminal investigations refer to the interviewing techniques that are employed. If the conditions are open, or unrestricted, the person will be dominated by the ideal of verity and produce an accurate account. If the conditions are constrained, where the person is required to produce specific types of information, then the ideal of utility will dominate and the person will introduce errors into their account to comply with the demands. This is pertinent to forensic investigations, as most evidential interviews will be directed by 'points to prove' (see Bekerian & Dennett, 1995). For example, a witness eager to please the interviewer may be providing information of which he/she is uncertain, merely to comply with the demands of the interviewer's questions. For these reasons, it is essential that the witness/victim is first allowed a free narrative phase, which does not constrain memory.

In the case of the offender, it is not clear which ideal will be dominating. Both Badcock (Chapter 2) and Boon (Chapter 3) describe the different reactions offenders have about 'confessing' to their crimes. Nonetheless, at least some serial criminals who have been successful are likely to have hidden agendas when discussing details of their crimes with investigators, e.g. overly inflated egos, delusions of grandeur (see Badcock, Chapter 2). Consequently, there is good reason to argue that some offenders will provide accounts which are highly reconstructive and prone to errors. Were such erroneous information to be incorporated into profiling systems, this could prove potentially damaging.

LEARNING TO COMMIT CRIME

A profile attempts to discriminate those features and actions of crimes that 'uniquely' identify one perpetrator from another. Obviously, discriminative features must be regular in their occurrence in order to serve any function. Behaviour must be stable in order to detect any repeated patterns over time (see Oldfield, Chapter 6).

Theories of memory have long suggested that people form 'schemas' or 'scripts' of regularly occurring events in their daily lives (see Bartlett, 1932; Canter, Mischel & Schwartz, 1982; Eldridge, Barnard & Bekerian, 1994; Schank, 1982); and such concepts are commonly employed when explaining an offender's behaviour (see Rossmo, Chapter 9; Davies, Chapter 11). Schemas identify critical, regular and frequently occurring features of a class of events. They provide information about likely reactions and actions, participants and sequences. Schemas enable the person to interpret and comprehend new situations, e.g. problem solve, and provide the basis for remembering specific experiences.

It is assumed that an offender has a schema for committing a particular type of crime, much in the same way that he/she has a schema for going to a restaurant. They can describe the invariant, general procedures and steps he/she takes in committing a crime, just as he/she can tell you what generally happens at restaurants. To the extent that the offender's schema is well developed and stable, a profiler will be able to isolate discriminating, stable characteristics of the offender.

Of course, offenders, like all organisms, learn (see Canter, 1994). A process of trial and error occurs. The offender learns which aspects of his/her behaviour need to be changed, and how the schema can be modified to produce more effective results. As the offender becomes more knowledgeable and experienced in crime, his/her behaviour will change, with the schema developing in accordance. Unfortunately, there is no agreed explanation of how offenders learn, nor how long they take to develop stable, schematic knowledge.

A schema for a crime will be complex, depending on the number of different components that it contains. This leaves open the possibility that specific components of the schema will stabilize at different rates. For example, lower level skills may stabilize faster than ones requiring more specialized knowledge. Equally, skills that are already learned and easily transferred to new situations may become more automated and invariant than skills which are unique to a particular type of criminal offence. Any learning would, of course, depend on the ability and intelligence of the individual offender, and the sources available to the offender.

Rossmo (Chapter 9) illustrates how different components of a schema could develop at different rates, when he discusses various location types that may be associated with a single crime. He notes that the location types have different meanings to the offender, and consequently, different 'choice properties'. There is no reason to suppose that choices in location types will become stabilized at the same rate, or at the same time.

Any instability in behaviour is likely to constrain the use of profiling techniques. Perhaps profiling may be most effective in investigations where it is believed that the offender has reached some 'plateau' or asymptote in his/her learning. Identifying when this 'learning plateau' may occur in the career of a serial offender is not likely to be easy.

CONCLUDING COMMENT

Offender profiling operates in the sensitive area of criminal investigations. Criminal investigations, by their very nature, involve acts that are deemed socially unacceptable by the public at large. The apprehension of criminals, and techniques that are used to assist in this process, are topics that will therefore be given greater public attention (e.g. media coverage). This means that profiling techniques are more likely in the first instance to attract critical comment than are other areas of applied psychology. For these reasons, it is likely that profilers will need to be more cautious about the conclusions they draw, and the manner in which they promote their own particular technique over that of their colleagues.

The topic of offender profiling has promoted multidisciplinary discussion. The interaction between different professionals broadens awareness. Researchers in the area of profiling can be a source of useful information to the forensic investigator in at least three ways. One, they can become directly involved in phases of the investigation. Two, they can be informally involved, providing an alternative perspective and enhancing creative problem solving. Third, they can be involved in training, where the investigator is made aware of relevant psychological and psychiatric concepts and research. The outcome is that professionals from diverse areas are enlivened by the knowledge and expertise of colleagues outside their own field.

One final point should be raised. It has already been noted in earlier chapters that forensic awareness gives major advantages to the offender (see Rossmo, House, Davies, Farrington & Lambert, all in this Volume). Such forensic awareness can come from a variety of sources, e.g. association with successful offenders, or previous criminal history. An equally fertile source of information for the offender is academic papers, such as this Volume. Such publications are not designed to contribute to the knowledge base of an offender (e.g. Boon, Chapter 3). Unfortunately, the fact of the matter is that they can, and do. Offenders can become more forensically aware through reading discourses on theory and research.

Of course, it is essential that such discourses are encouraged. Every effort must be made to disseminate research findings in the area of profiling. Nonetheless, one question that faces all professionals is how to balance the need for open communication and debate, with the possible consequence of educating the offender.

References

Adhami, E. & Browne, D. (1996). *Major crime enquiries: improving expert support for detectives* (Paper 9). London: Police Research Group Special Interest Series, Home Office.

Adler, A. (1925). *The practice and theory of individual psychology.* London: Kegan Paul.

Aitken, C., Connolly, T., Gammerman, A., Zhang, G. & Oldfield, D. (1995). *Predicting an offender's characteristics: an evaluation of statistical modelling* (Paper 4). London: Police Research Group Special Interest Series, Home Office.

Aitken, C., Connolly, T., Gammerman, A., Zhang, G., Bailey, D., Gordon, R. & Oldfield, D. (1996). Statistical modelling in specific case analysis. *Science and Justice, 36*, 245–255.

Alston, J. D. (1994). The serial rapist's spatial pattern of target selection. Unpublished Master's thesis, Simon Fraser University, Burnaby, BC.

Amir, M. (1971). *Patterns in forcible rape.* Chicago: University of Chicago Press.

Aronoff, A. (1989). *Geographic information systems: a management perspective.* Ottawa: WDL Publications.

Bartlett, F. (1932). *Remembering.* Cambridge: Cambridge University Press.

Bandura, A. (1962). Learning through imitation. In M. R. Jones (Ed.), *Nebraska symposium on motivation.* Lincoln, NE: University of Nebraska Press.

Bandura, A. (1976). *Social learning theory.* Morriston, NJ: General Learning Press.

Bandura, A. (1978). The self system in reciprocal determinism. *American Psychologist, 33*, 344–358.

Bandura, A. (1989). Human agency in social cognitive theory. *American Psychologist, 44*, 1175–1184.

Barrett, G. M. (1990). Serial murder: a study in psychological analysis, prediction, and profiling. Unpublished Master's thesis, University of Louisville, Louisville, KY.

Bartol, C. (1991). *Criminal behavior: a psychosocial approach* (3rd edn). Toronto: Prentice-Hall.

Bekerian, D.A. & Dennett, J.L. (1993). The cognitive interview technique: Reviving the issues. *Applied Cognitive Psychology, 7*, 275–297.

Bekerian, D.A. & Dennett, J.L. (1996). *The child's account: evidential interview with children*. Cambridgeshire County Council: Cambridge.

Bekerian, D.A. and Goodrich, S.J. (1997). Recovered memories of child sexual abuse. In G. Berrios & J.R. Hedges (Eds), *Memory disorders in psychiatric practice*. Cambridge, MA: Cambridge University Press.

Bekerian, D.A. & Goodrich, S.J. (1995). Telling the truth in the recovered memory debate. *Consciousness and Cognition*, **7**, 24–31.

Bem, D. Y. & Allen, A. (1974). On predicting some of the people some of the time. *Psychological Review*, **816**, 506–520.

Biondi, R. & Hecox, W. (1992). *The Dracula killer*. New York: Simon & Schuster.

Blackburn, R. (1971). Personality types among abnormal homicides. *British Journal of Criminology*, **11**, 14–31.

Blackburn, R. (1993). *The psychology of criminal conduct*. Chichester: Wiley.

Boon, J. & Davies, G. (1993). Criminal profiling. *Policing*, **9**, 218–227.

Boon, J. C. W. (1995). Offender profiling: Distinguishing the media prurience from the real-life science. *Inter Alia*, **1**, 31–35.

Boon, J. C. W. (in press). *The role of theory and data in the science of psychology: epistemological issues in psychological profiling*. Frankfurt: Interpol.

Borg, I. (1977). Some basic concepts of facet theory. In J. Lingoes (Ed.), *Geometric representations of relational data*. Ann Arbor: Mathesis.

Bourdouris, J. (1974). A classification of homicides. *Criminology*, **11**, 525–540.

Boyd, N. (1988). *The last dance: murder in Canada*. Scarborough, ON: Prentice-Hall.

Brahan, J. W., Valcour, L. & Shevel, R. (1994). *The investigator's notebook: Applications and innovations in expert systems*. Cambridge: Cambridge University Press.

Brantingham, P. J. & Brantingham, P. L. (1981). *Environmental criminology*. Beverley Hills, CA: Sage.

Brantingham, P. J., & Brantingham, P. L. (1981). Notes on the geometry on crime. In P. J. Brantingham & P. L. Brantingham (Eds), *Environmental criminology*. Beverly Hills, CA: Sage.

Brantingham, P. J. & Brantingham, P. L. (1984). *Patterns in crime*. New York: Macmillan.

Brantingham, P. J. & Brantingham, P. L. (1991). The dimensions of crime. In P. J. Brantingham & P. L. Brantingham (Eds), *Environmental criminology*. Prospect Heights, IL: Waveland.

Brantingham, P. J. & Brantingham, P. L. (1993). Environment, routine and situation: Toward a pattern theory of crime. In R. V. Clarke & M. Felson (Eds), *Routine activity and rational choice*. New Brunswick, NJ: Transaction.

Briar, S. & Piliavin, I. (1965). Delinquency, situational inducements, and commitment to conformity. *Social Problems*, **10**, 35–45.

Britton, P. (1992). Home Office/ACPO review of offender profiling (Unpublished).

Britton, P. (1997). *The jigsaw man*. London: Bantam Press.

Brody, A. L. & Green, R. (1994). Washington State's unscientific approach to the problem of repeat sex offenders. *Bulletin of the American Academy of Psychiatry and Law*, **22**, 343–356.

Brussel, J.A. (1968). *Casebook of a crime psychiatrist*. New York: Simon and Schuster.

Burn, G. (1984). *Somebody's husband, somebody's son.* New York: Penguin.

Burnside, S. & Cairns, A. (1995). *Deadly innocence.* New York: Warner Books.

Campbell, C. (1976). Portrait of a mass killer. *Psychology Today,* **9,** 110–119.

Canter, D. (Ed.) (1985). *Facet theory: approaches to social research.* New York: Springer-Verlag.

Canter, D. (1989). Offender profiles. *The Psychologist,* **2,** 12–16.

Canter, D. (1994). *Criminal shadows: inside the mind of the serial killer.* London: Harper Collins.

Canter, D. & Gregory, A. (1994). Identifying the residential location of rapists. *Journal of the Forensic Science Society,* **34,** 169–175.

Canter, D. & Heritage, R. (1990). A multivariate model of sexual offence behaviour: Developments in offender profiling. *Journal of Forensic Psychiatry,* **1,** 185–212.

Canter, D. & Larkin, P. (1993). The environmental range of serial rapists. *Journal of Environmental Psychology,* **13,** 63–69.

Canter, N., Mischel, W. & Schwartz, J. (1982). A prototype analyses of psychological situations. *Cognitive Psychology,* **14,** 45–77.

Capone, D., & Nichols, W. J. (1975). Crime and distance: an analysis of offender behavior in space. *Proceedings of the Association of American Geographers,* **7,** 45–49.

Castell, J. H. F. (1966). *The court work of educational psychologists.* Leicester: British Psychological Society.

Chappell, D. (1977). *Forcible rape: a national survey of the response by police* (Law Enforcement Assistance Administration). Washington, DC: US Government Printing Office.

Chard, J. (1995). *Breaking and entering in Canada* (Juristat 15: 13). Ottawa: Canadian Centre for Justice Statistics.

Chiswick, D. (1990). Fitness to stand trial and plead, mutism and deafness. In R. Bluglass & P. Bowden (Eds), *Principles and practice of forensic psychiatry.* London: Churchill Livingstone.

Clare, I. C. H. (1993). Issues in the assessment and treatment of male sex offenders with mild learning disabilities. *Sexual and Marital Therapy,* **8,** 167–180.

Cohen, J. (1960). A coefficient of agreement for nominal scales. *Educational and Psychological Measurement,* **20,** 37–46.

Cohen, M., Seghorn, T. & Calmas, W. (1969). Sociometric study of sex offenders. *Journal of Abnormal Psychology,* **74,** 249–255.

Cohen, L. & Felson, M. (1979). Social change and crime rate trends: a routine activity approach. *American Sociological Review,* **44,** 588–608.

Conklin, J. (1972). *Robbery and the criminal justice system.* Philadelphia, PA: Lippincott.

Connolly, K. & McKellar, P. (1963). Forensic psychology. *Bulletin of the British Psychological Society,* **16,** 16–24.

Conway, M. & Bekerian, D.A. (1987). Organization in autobiographical memory. *Memory and Cognition,* **15,** 119–132.

Copson, G. (1993). Offender profiling. Presentation to the Association of Chief Police Officers Crime Sub-committee on Offender Profiling, London.

Copson, G. (1995). *Coals to Newcastle? Part 1: A study of offender profiling* (Paper 7). London: Police Research Group Special Interest Series, Home Office.

Copson, G. & Holloway, K. (in preparation). *Coals to Newcastle? Part 2: An analysis of offender profiling advice.* London: Police Research Group Special Interest Series, Home Office.

Copson, G., Badcock, R., Boon, J. & Britton, P. (in press). Articulating a systematic approach to clinical crime profiling. *Criminal Behaviour and Mental Health.*

Cromwell, P., Olson, J. N. & Avary, D. A. W. (1991). *Breaking and entering: An ethnographic analysis of burglary.* London: Sage Publications, Ltd.

Cromwell, P., Olson, J. N., & Avary, D. A. W. (1993). Modelling decisions by residential burglars. *Studies on Crime and Crime Prevention,* 2, 113–121.

Cunliffe, F. & Piazza, P. B. (1980). *Criminalistics and scientific investigation.* Englewood Cliffs, NJ: Prentice-Hall.

Cunningham, C. (1964). Forensic psychology. *Bulletin of the British Psychological Society,* 17, 7–12.

Davies, A. & Dale, A. (1995). *Locating the stranger rapist* (Paper 3). London: Police Research Group Special Interest Series, Home Office.

Davies, A. & Dale, A. (1996). Locating the rapist. *Medicine, Science and the Law,* 18, 163–178.

Davies, A., Wittebrood, K. & Jackson, J. L. (in press). *Predicting the criminal antecedents of a stranger rapist.* London: Police Research Group Special Interest Series, Home Office.

Dettlinger, C. & Prugh, J. (1983). *The list.* Atlanta, GA: Philmay Enterprises.

Dietz, P. E. (1985). Sex offender profiling by the FBI: a preliminary conceptual model. In M. H. Ben-Aron, S. J. Hucker & C. D. Webster (Eds), *Criminal criminology: The assessment and treatment of criminal behaviour.* Pittsburgh, PA: American Academy of Psychiatry and Law.

Dietz, P. E., Hazelwood, R. R. & Warren, J. (1990). The sexually sadistic criminal and his offences. *Bulletin of the American Academy of Psychiatry and Law,* 18, 163–178.

DNA Database (1995). How the DNA database & caseworking units will function! (1995, February). *DNA Database,* 2 (February).

Doherty, G. & de Souza. (1995). *Recidivism in youth courts 1993–94* (Juristat 15: 16). Ottawa: Canadian Centre for Justice Statistics.

Doney, R. H. (1990). The aftermath of the Yorkshire ripper: the response of the United Kingdom police service. In S. A. Egger (Ed.), *Serial murder: an elusive phenomenon.* New York: Praeger.

Douglas, J. (1981). Evaluation of the psychological profiling program: Institutional Research and Development Unit, FBI Academy: unpublished Source.

Douglas, J. E. & Munn, C. (1992). Violent crime scene analysis: modus operandi, signature and staging. *FBI Law Enforcement Bulletin,* 62, 1–100.

Douglas, J. & Olshaker, M. (1995). *Mindhunter.* New York: Scribner.

Douglas, J.E., Ressler, R.K., Burgess, A.W. & Hartman, C.R. (1986). Criminal profiling from crime scene analysis. *Behavioral Sciences and the Law,* 4, 401–421.

Downs, R. M. & Stea, D. (1973). Cognitive maps and spatial behaviour. In R. M. Downs & D. Stea (Eds), *Image and environment: cognitive mapping and spatial behavior*. Chicago: Alsine.

Downs, R. M. & Stea, D. (1977). *Maps in mind: reflections on cognitive mapping*. New York: Harper and Row.

Egger, S. A. (1984). A working definition of serial murder and the reduction of linkage blindness. *Journal of Police Science and Administration, 12*, 348–357.

Egger, S. A. (Ed.) (1990). *Serial murder: an elusive phenomenon*. New York: Praeger.

Eldridge, M., Barnard, P. & Bekerian, D. (1994). Autobiographical memory and daily schemas at work. *Memory, 2*, 51–74.

Eskridge, C. (1983). Prediction of burglary: a research note. *Journal of Criminal Justice, 11*, 67–75.

Farrington, D. (1983). Offending from 10 to 25 years of age. In K. V. Dusen & S. Mednick (Eds), *Prospective studies in crime and delinquency*. Hingham, MA: Kluwer Nijhoff.

Farrington, D. P. & Dowds, E. A. (1985). Disentangling criminal behaviour and police reaction. In D. P. Farrington & J. Gunn (Eds), *Reactions to crime*. Chichester: Wiley.

Farrington, D. P. (1986). Les signeaux précoces de l'agir délinquent fréquent. *Criminologie, 19*, 9–32.

Farrington, D. (1987). Epidemiology. In H. C. Quay (Ed.), *Handbook of juvenile delinquency*. New York: Wiley.

Farrington, D. P. (1992). Trends in English juvenile delinquency and their explanation. *International Journal of Comparative and Applied Criminal Justice, 16*, 151–163.

Farrington, D. P. & Lambert, S. (1992). *The feasibility of a statistical approach to offender profiling: burglary and violence in Nottinghamshire*. London: Home Office.

Farrington, D. P. & Burrows, J. N. (1993). Did shoplifting really decrease? *British Journal of Criminology, 33*, 57–69.

Farrington, D. & Lambert, S. (1993). Predicting violence and burglary offenders from witness and offence data. Paper presented at the First NISCALE Workshop on Criminality and Law Enforcement, The Hague, The Netherlands.

Farrington, D. P. (1993). Have any individual, family or neighbourhood influences on offending been demonstrated conclusively? In D. P. Farrington, R. J. Sampson & P. H. Wikstrom (Eds), *Integrating individual and ecological aspects of crime*. Stockholm: National Council for Crime Prevention.

Farrington, D. P., & Lambert, S. (1994). Differences between burglars and violent offenders. *Psychology, Crime and Law, 1*, 107–116.

Farrington, D. P. & Lambert, S. (in press). Predicting offender profiles from offence and victim characteristics. In P.H. Wikstrom, L. W. Sherman & W. G. Skogan (Eds), *Problem-solving policing as crime prevention*. Bolder, Co: Westview.

Feshbach, S., Weiner, B. & Bohart, A. (1996). *Personality*. Lexington, MA: D.C. Heath.

Fisher, R. P. & Geiselman, R. E. (1992). *Memory-enhancing techniques for investigative interviewing: the cognitive interview*. Springfield, IL: Charles C. Thomas.

Fleiss, J. L. (1981). *Statistical methods for rates and proportions* (2nd edn). New York: Wiley.

Fowler, K. (1990). The serial killer. *RCMP* (Royal Canadian Mounted Police) *Gazette*, **52**, 1–11.

Frank, G. (1966). *The Boston strangler*. New York: Penguin.

Friedman, R. D. (1994). The death and transfiguration of Frye. *Jurimetrics Journal*, **Winter**, 133–148.

Geberth, V.J. (1981). Psychological profiling. *Law and Order*, **29**, 46–49.

Gebhard, P., Gagnon, J., Pomeroy, W. & Christenson, C. (1965). *Sex offenders*. New York: Harper and Row.

Geiselman, R.E. & Fisher, R. (1997). Ten years of Cognitive Interviewing. In D. Payne & F. Conrad (Eds), *Intersections in basic and applied memory research*. Mahwah, NJ: Erlbaum.

Gill, S. (1995). The role of formal and tacit knowledge in the design process. Doctoral dissertation, University of Cambridge.

Glueck, S. & Gleuck, E. (1930). *Five hundred criminal careers*. New York: Knopf.

Goldblatt, P. (1992). *An assessment of the effectiveness of offender profiles in a police investigation*. Guildford: University of Surrey.

Green, E. (1993). *The intent to kill: making sense of murder*. Baltimore, MA: Clevedon.

Grenier, C. E. & Roundtree, G. A. (1987). Predicting recidivism among adjudicated delinquents: a model to identify high risk offenders. *Journal of Offender Counselling, Services and Rehabilitation*, **12**, 101–112.

Gresswell, S. M. (1994). Multiple murder in England and Wales 1982–1991: an analysis. Unpublished PhD Thesis, University of Birmingham.

Grisso, T. (1986). *Evaluating competencies, forensic assessments and instruments*. New York: Plenum.

Groth, A. N., Burgess, A. W. & Holmstrom, L. L. (1977). Rape: power, anger and sexuality. *American Journal of Psychiatry*, **134**, 1239–1243.

Grubin, D., & Gunn, J. (1990). *The imprisoned rapist*. London: Department of Forensic Psychiatry.

Grubin, D., Kelly, P. & Ayis, S. (1997). *Linking serious sexual assaults*. Police Research Group Technical Paper. London: Home Office Police Policy Directorate.

Grubin, D. (1995). Offender profiling. *Journal of Forensic Psychiatry*, **6**, 259–263.

Gudjonsson, G. H., & Sartory, G. (1983). Blood–injury phobia: a 'reasonable excuse' for failing to give a specimen in a case of suspected drunken driving. *Journal of the Forensic Science Society*, **23**, 197–201.

Gudjonsson, G. H. (1984). The role of the 'forensic psychologist' in England and Iceland. *Nordisk Psykologi*, **36**, 256–263.

Gudjonsson, G. H. (1985). Psychological evidence in court: results from the BPS survey. *Bulletin of the British Psychological Society*, **38**, 327–330.

Gudjonsson, G. H. (1987). The significance of depression in the mechanism of 'compulsive' shoplifting. *Medicine, Science and the Law*, **27**, 171–176.

Gudjonsson, G. H. (1992). *The psychology of interrogation, confessions and testimony*. Chichester: Wiley.

Gudjonsson, G. H. (1993). The implications of poor psychological evidence in court. *Expert Evidence*, **3**, 120–124.

Gudjonsson, G. H. (1994a). Psychological evidence in court. In S. J. E. Linsay & G. E. Powell (Eds), *Handbook of clinical adult psychology* (2nd edn), London: Routledge.

Gudjonsson, G. H. (1994b). Confessions made to the expert witness: some professional issues. *Journal of Forensic Psychiatry*, **5**, 213–217.

Gudjonsson, G. H. (1996a). Psychological evidence in court. Results from the 1995 survey. *The Psychologist*, **5**, 213–217.

Gudjonsson, G. H. (1996b). Forensic psychology in England: one practitioner's experience and viewpoint. *Journal of Criminological and Legal Psychology*, **1**, 131–142.

Guttridge, P., Gabrielli, W. Jr., Mednick, S. & van Dusen, K. (1983). Criminal violence in a birth cohort. In K. V. Dusen & S. Mednick (Eds), *Prospective studies of crime and delinquency*. Hingham, MA: Kluwer Nijhoff.

Hagerstrand, T. (1973). The domain of human geography. In R. J. Chorley (Ed.), *Directions in geography*. London: Methuen.

Hagmaier, B. (1990). Ted Bundy, a case study. Lecture presented at the FBI National Academy retraining session. Bellingham, WA, September.

Hassin, Y. (1986). Two models for predicting recidivism: clinical versus statistical – another view. *British Journal of Criminology*, **26**, 270–286.

Haward, L. R. C. (1961). Forensic psychology. Some problems and proposals. *Bulletin of the British Psychological Society*, **14**, 1–5.

Haward, L. R. C. (1981). *Forensic psychology*. London: Batsford.

Hazelwood, R. R. & Burgess, A. W. (1987). An introduction to the serial rapist. *FBI Law Enforcement Bulletin*, **56**, 16–24.

Hazelwood, R. R. & Warren, J. I. (1989). The serial rapist: his characteristics and victims. *FBI Law Enforcement Bulletin*, **58**, 10–18.

Hazelwood, R. R. (1995). Analyzing the rape and profiling the offender. In R. R. Hazelwood & A. W. Burgess (Eds), *Practical aspects of rape investigation* (2nd edn). Boca Raton, FL: CRC Press.

Hazelwood, R.R. & Burgess, A.W. (Eds) (1995), *Practical aspects of rape investigation* (2nd edn). Boca Raton, FL: CRC Press.

Henn, F., Herjanic, M. & Vanderpearl, R. (1976). Forensic psychiatry: profiles of two types of sex offenders. *American Journal of Psychiatry*, **133**, 694–696.

Heritage, R. (1992). Facets of sexual assault: five steps in investigation classifications. Unpublished Master's thesis, University of Surrey, Guildford.

Hickey, E. W. (1986). The female serial murderer 1800–1986. *Journal of Police and Criminal Psychology*, **2**, 72–81.

Hindelang, M. (1981). Variations in sex–race–age specific incidence rates of offending. *American Sociological Review*, **46**, 461–474.

Holmes, R. M. & De Burger, J. E. (1988). *Serial murder*. Newbury Park, CA: Sage.

Holmes, R. M. & Rossmo, D. K. (1996). Geography, profiling, and predatory criminals. In R. M. Holmes & S. T. Holmes (Eds), *Profiling violent crimes: an investigative tool* (2nd ed.). Thousand Oaks, CA: Sage.

Home Office (1985). *Police and Criminal Evidence Act, 1984.* London: HMSO.

Home Office (1991). *Police and Criminal Evidence Act 1984 (s.66). Codes of Practice* (revised edn). London: HMSO.

Home Office (1993). *Criminal Statistics, England and Wales, 1991.* London: HMSO.

Jackson, J. L., van Koppen, P. J. & Herbrink, J. C. M. (1993). *Does the service meet the needs?* (93–05). Leiden: NSCR (Nederlands Studiecentrum Criminaliteit en Rechshandhaving).

Jackson, J. L., Herbrink, J. C. M. & van Koppen, P. J. (in press). An empirical approach to profiling. In S. Redondon, V. Garrido, J. Perez & R. Barbaret (Eds), *Advances in psychology and law: international contributions*. Berlin: De Gruyter.

James, E. (1991). *Catching serial killers.* Lansing, MI: International Forensic Services.

Jansen, C. (1983). Delinquency among metropolitan boys: a progress report. In V. D. K. Mednick & S. Mednick (Eds), *Prospective studies of crime and delinquency*. Hingham, MA: Kluwer Nijhoff.

Jenkins, P. (1988). Serial murder in England 1940–1985. *Journal of Criminal Justice,* **16**, 1–15.

Johnson, G. (1994). ViCLAS: violent crime linkage analysis system. *RCMP Gazette,* **56**, 9–13.

Kennedy, D. (1991). *William Heirens: his day in court.* Chicago: Bonus Books.

Keppel, R. D. & Birnes, W. J. (1995). *The riverman: Ted Bundy and I hunt for the Green River Killer.* New York: Simon and Schuster.

Kind, S. S. (1987). *The scientific investigation of crime.* Harrogate: Forensic Science Services.

Knight, R., Rosenberg, R. & Schneider, B. (1985). Classification of sexual offenders: Perspectives, methods and validation. In A. Burgess (Ed.), *Rape and sexual assault: A research handbook*. New York: Garland.

Knight, R. A. & Prentky, R. A. (1987). The developmental antecedents and adult adaptations of rapist subtypes. *Criminal Justice and Behavior,* **14**, 403–426.

Lanning, K. V. (1995). Child molestation: law enforcement typology. In R. R. Hazelwood & A. W. Burgess (Eds), *Practical aspects of rape investigation*. Boca Raton, FL: CRC Press.

LeBeau, J. L. (1987). The methods and measures of centrography and the spatial dynamics of rape. *Journal of Quantitative Criminology,* **3**, 125–141.

LeBeau, J. L. (1992). Four case studies illustrating the spatial–temporal analysis of serial rapists. *Police Studies,* **15**, 124–145.

LeBlanc, M., Ouimet, M. & Tremblay, R. (1988). An integrative control theory of delinquent behaviour: a validation 1976–1985. *Psychiatry,* **51**, 164–176.

Lees, S. (1996). *Carnal knowledge.* London: Hamish Hamilton.

Leyton, E. (1995). *Men of blood: murder in modern England.* London: Constable.

Loeber, R. & Stouthamer-Loeber, M. (1986). La prédiction de la délinquance. *Criminologie*, **19**, 49–78.

Lord Taylor of Gosforth. (1994). The Lund Lecture. *Medicine, Science and the Law*, **35**, 3–8.

Lyman, M. D. (1993). *Criminal investigations: the art and the science*. Englewood Cliffs, NJ: Regents/Prentice Hall.

MacKay, R. E. (1994). Violent crime analysis. *RCMP Gazette*, **56**, 11–14.

Mawston, A. R. (1987). *Transient criminality: a model of street-induced crime*. New York: Praeger.

McCann, J. T. (1992). Criminal personality profiling in the investigation of violent crime: recent advances and future directions. *Behavioral Sciences and the Law*, **10**, 475–481.

McCulloch, M., Bailey, J. & Robinson, C. (1995). Mentally disordered attackers and killers: Towards a taxonomy. *Journal of Forensic Psychiatry*, **6**, 41–61.

McGurk, B. (1978). Personality types among abnormal homicides. *British Journal of Criminology*, **18**, 146–161.

Megaree, E. & Bohn, M. J. (1979). *Classifying criminal offenders: a new system based on the MMPI*. Beverly Hills, CA: Sage.

Montgomery, J. E. (1993). Organizational survival: continuity or crisis? In M. Layton (Ed.), *Policing in the global community: the challenge of leadership*. Burnaby, BC: Simon Fraser University.

Neisser, U. (1981). John Dean's memory: a case study. *Cognition*, **9**, 1–22.

Newton, M. B. J. & Swoope, E. A. (1987). Geoforensic analysis of localized serial murder: the Hillside stranglers located. Unpublished manuscript.

Nicholson, M. (1979). *The Yorkshire ripper*. London: W.H. Allen.

Nijboer, J. A. (1975). *Voorspellen van recidive*. Assen: Van Gorcum en Comp. B.V.

Normandeau, A. (1968). Patterns in robbery. *Criminologica*, **1**, 2–13.

Oldfield, R. (1995). PRG Offender profiling research programme: investigative support for low volume crime. *Focus*, **6**, 34–37.

Oleson, J. (1996). Psychological profiling: does it actually work? *Forensic Update*, **46**, 11–14.

O'Reilly-Fleming, T. (1992). Serial murder investigation: prospects for police networking. *Journal of Contemporary Criminal Justice*, **8**, 227–234.

Pearson, P. (1994, June). Murder on her mind. *Saturday Night*, 46–53, 64–68.

Perkins, D., Hilton, M. & Lucas, M. (1990). A study of serial sexual offenders in special hospital and prison settings. Unpublished Home Office Report, London.

Pervin, L. A. (1989). *Personality: theory and research*. New York: Wiley.

Petersilia, J. (1980). Criminal career research: a review of recent evidence. In N. Morris & M. Tonry (Eds), *Crime and justice* (Vol. 2). Chicago, IL: University of Chicago Press.

Pilant, L. (1994, January). Information management. *The Police Chief*, 30–38, 42–47.

Pinizzotto, A. J. (1984). Forensic psychology: criminal personality profiling. *Journal of Police Science and Administration*, **14** (3), 32–40.

Plomin, R. & Daniels, D. (1987). Why are children in the same family so different from one another? *Behaviour and Brain Sciences*, **10**, 1–60.

Pope, C. (1977). *Crime-specific analysis: An empirical examination of burglary offender characteristics* (Law Enforcement Assistance Administration). Washington, DC: US Government Printing Office.

Pope, C. (1980). Patterns in burglary: an empirical examination of offense and offender characteristics. *Journal of Criminal Justice, 8*, 39–51.

Popkin, J. (1994, September 19). Natural born predators. *US News and World Report*, 64–68, 73.

Powell, M. & Dalgleish, T. (in press). *Handbook of cognition and emotion.* Chichester: Wiley.

Prentky, R., Cohen, M. & Seghorn, T. (1985). Development of a rational taxonomy for the classification of rapists: the Massachusetts treatment center system. *Bulletin of the American Academy of Psychiatry and Law, 13*, 39–70.

Prentky, R., Knight, R. & Rosenberg, R. (1988). Validation analyses on a taxonomic system for rapists: disconfirmation and reconceptualization. In R. Prentky & V. Quincy (Eds), *Human sexual aggression: current perspectives.* New York: New York Academy of Science.

Pron, N. (1995). *Lethal marriage.* Toronto: Seal Books.

Pyle, G. (1974). *The spatial dynamics of crime* (Research Paper No. 159). Chicago: Department of Geography, University of Chicago.

Raskin, D. C. (Ed.)(1989). *Psychological methods in criminal investigation and evidence.* New York: Springer.

Reber, A. S. (1985). *The Penguin dictionary of psychology.* Harmondsworth: Penguin.

Reboussin, R., Warren, J. & Hazelwood, R. R. (1993). Mapless mapping and the windshield wiper effect in the spatial distribution of serial rapes. In C. R. Block & R. L. Block (Eds), *Questions and answers in lethal and non-lethal violence: proceedings of the Second Annual Workshop of the Homicide Research Working Group (NIJ Publication No. NCJ-147480).* Washington, DC: US Government Printing Office.

Rebscher, E., & Rohrer, F. (1991). Police information retrieval systems and the role of electronic data processsing. In E. Kube & H. U. Strazer (Eds), *Police research in the Federal Republic of Germany: 15 years' research within the Bundeskriminalamt.* Berlin: Springer-Verlag.

Reiss, A. J. & Farrington, D. P. (1991). Advancing knowledge about co-offending: results from a prospective longitudinal survey of London males. *Journal of Criminal Law and Criminology, 82*, 360–395.

Ressler, R. K., Burgess, A. W. & Douglas, J. E. (1988). *Sexual homicide: patterns and motives.* New York: Lexington Books.

Ressler, R. K., Douglas, J.E., Burgess, A. W. & Burgess, A.G. (1992). *Crime classification manual.* New York: Simon and Schuster.

Ressler, R. K. & Shachtman, T. (1992). *Whoever fights monsters.* New York: St. Martin's Press.

Reyna, V. & Titcomb, A. (1997). Constraints on the suggestiblity of eyewitness testimony: a fuzzy-trace theory analysis. In D. Payne & F. Conrad (Eds), *Intersections in basic and applied memory research.* Mahwah, NJ: Erlbaum.

Riedel, M., Zahan, M. & Mock, L. (1985). *The nature and patterns of American homicide.* Washington, DC: US Government Printing Office.

Robertson, B. & Vignaux, G. A. (1995). *Interpreting evidence. Evaluating evidence in the courtroom.* Chichester: Wiley.

Rogers, C. R. (1961). *On becoming a person.* Boston, MA: Houghton Mifflin.

Rogers, C. R. (1963). Actualizing tendency in relation to 'motives' and to consciousness. In M. R. Jones (Ed.), *Nebraska symposium on motivation.* Lincoln, NE: University of Nebraska Press.

Rogers, C. R. (1980). *A way of being.* Boston, MA: Houghton Mifflin.

Rossmo, D. K. (1993). Geographic profiling: locating serial killers. In D. Zahm & P. F. Cromwell (Eds), *Proceedings of the International Seminar on environmental criminology and crime analysis.* Coral Gables, FL: Florida Criminal Justice Executive Institute.

Rossmo, D. K. (1994, Fall). STAC tools: the crime site probability program. *STAC News,* 9, 14.

Rossmo, D. K. (1995a). Geographic profiling: target patterns of serial murderers. Unpublished Doctoral Dissertation, Simon Fraser University, Burnaby, BC.

Rossmo, D. K. (1995b). Multivariate spatial profiles as a tool in crime investigation. In C. R. Block, M. Dabdoub & S. Fregly (Eds), *Crime analysis through computer mapping.* Washington, DC: Police Executive Research Forum.

Rossmo, D. K. (1995c). Place, space, and police investigations: hunting serial violent criminals. In J. E. Eck & D. A. Weisburd (Eds), *Crime and place: crime prevention studies* (Vol. 4). Monsey, NY: Criminal Justice Press.

Rossmo, D. K. (1996). Targeting victims: serial killers and the urban environment. In T. O'Reilly-Fleming (Ed.), *Serial and mass murder: theory, research and policy.* Toronto: Canadian Scholars Press.

Rumbelow, D. (1988). *Jack the Ripper: The complete casebook.* Chicago: Contemporary Books.

Schaller, G. B. (1972). *The Serengeti lion: a study of predator–prey relations.* Chicago: University of Chicago Press.

Schank, R. (1982). *Dynamic memory: a theory of learning in computers and humans.* Cambridge: Cambridge University Press.

Schank, R. & Abelson, R. (1977). *Scripts, plans, goals and understanding: An inquiry into human knowledge structures.* Hillsdale, NJ: Erlbaum.

Scheingold, S. A., Olson, T. & Pershing, J. (1992, November). Republican criminology and victim advocacy: Washington State's sexual predator legislation. Paper presented at the meeting of the American Society of Criminology, New Orleans, LA .

Schultz, D. & Schultz, S. E. (1994). *Theories of personality.* Pacific Grove: Brooks/Cole.

Scott, H. (1992). The female serial killer: a well-kept secret of the gentler sex. Unpublished Masters Thesis, University of Guelph, Guelph, ON.

Scully, D. & Marolla, J. (1984). Convicted rapists' vocabulary of motive: excuse and justifications. *Social Problems,* 31, 530–544.

Scully, D. & Marolla, J. (1985). Riding the bull at Gillies: convicted rapists describe the rewards of rape. *Social Problems,* 32, 251–263.

Segrave, K. (1992). *Women serial and mass murderers: a worldwide reference, 1580–1990.* Jefferson, NC: McFarland.

Shallice, T. (1988). *From neuropsychology to mental structures*. New York: Cambridge University Press.

Shye, S., Elizur, D. & Hoffman, M. (1994). *Introduction to facet theory*. London: Sage.

Silverman, R. & Kennedy, L. (1993). *Deadly deeds: murder in Canada*. Scarborough: Nelson.

Skogan, W. G. & Atunes, G. E. (1979). Information, apprehension, and deterrence: exploring the limits of police productivity. *Journal of Criminal Justice, 7*, 217–241.

Smith, D. R. & Smith, W.R. (1984). Patterns of delinquent careers: An assessment of three perspectives. *Social Science Research, 13*, 129–158.

Spencer, C. (1966). *A typology of violent offenders*. Administrative Abstract No. 23. Sacremento, CA: California Department of Corrections.

Stander, J., Farrington, D. P., Hill, G. & Altham, P. M. E. (1989). Markov chain analysis and specialization in criminal careers. *British Journal of Criminology, 29*, 317–335.

Star, J. & Estes, J. (1990). *Geographic information systems: An introduction*. Toronto: Prentice-Hall.

Steller, M. & Wellershaus, P. (1992). Information enhancement and credibilty assessment of children's statements: The impact of the cognitive interview technique on criteria-based content analysis. Paper presented at the Third European Conference of Law and Psychology, Oxford, September.

Teasdale, J. (in press). Multifaceted theories of cognition and emotion. In M. Powell & T. Dalgleish (Eds), *Handbook of cognition and emotion*. Chichester: Wiley.

The Law Society (1996). *Access to justice: Lord Woolfe Inquiry Issue Papers. Responses by the Law Society Civil Litigation and Courts and Legal Services Committees, May 1996. Volume 1: Fast track, housing, multi-party actions, expert evidence, cost*. London: The Law Society.

Thompson, M. (1996). Zeroing in on the serial killer. *RCMP Gazette, 58*, 14–15.

US Department of Justice (1991). *Serial murder investigation system conference (Federal Bureau of Investigation)*. Washington, DC: US Government Printing Office.

US Department of Justice (1994, October 3). *Violent crime control and law enforcement act of 1994*. (Fact sheet No. NCJ-FS000067). Washington, DC: US Government Printing Office.

Van de Bunt, H. G. (1988). Criminele carrières en selectieve onschadelijkmaking. *Justitiële Verkenningen, 4*, 78–99.

Van den Eshof, P. & Van der Heijden, A.W.M. (1990). Tienduizend overvallen. Beschrijving van de overvallen sinds 1980. *Tijdschrift voor Criminologie, 32* (2).

Van den Eshof, P., De Kleuver, E.E. & Ho Tham, V. (in press). General profile analysis of sexual assault and rape cases. In P. Friday, G.F. Kirchoff & F.W. Winkel (Eds), *Victimology, victimization and victim assistance: psychological and Legal Aspects*. Mönchengladbach: World Society of Victimology.

Van den Eshof, P., Jackson, J.L. & Nierop, N. (1997). Profielanalyse in de recherchepraktijk. In P.J.van Koppen & D.J. Hessing (Eds), *Het hart van de zaak: Psychologie voor juristen*. Deventer: Gouda Quint.

Van der Heijden, A. W. M., van den Eshof, P. & Schrama, C. D. S. (1990). *Rules based on the practical experience of vice squad detectives in The Netherlands*. The Hague, The Netherlands.

VanLehn, K. (1989). Problem solving and cognitive skill acquisition. In M. I. Posner (Ed.), *Foundations of cognitive science*. Boston, MA: MIT Press.

Vetter, H. & Silverman, I. (1978). *The nature of crime*. Philadelphia, PA: W.B. Saunders.

Wambaugh, J. (1989). *The blooding*. New York: Bantam.

Warren, J. I., Reboussin, R.R., Hazelwood, R.R. & Wright, J.A. (1991). Prediction of rapist type and violence from verbal, physical and sexual scales. *Journal of Interpersonal Violence, 6*, 55–67.

Warren, J., Reboussin, R. & Hazelwood, R. R. (1995). *The geographic and temporal sequencing of serial rape (Federal Bureau of Investigation*. Washington, DC: US Government Printing Office.

Wells, G. (1978). Applied eyewitness testimony: system varibles and estimator variables. *Journal of Personality and Social Psychology, 36*, 1546 – 1557.

West, D. J. & Farrington, D. P. (1973). *Who becomes delinquent?* London: Heinemann.

Westfall, B. (1992). Wesley Allan Dodd. *Police, 16*, 58–60, 84.

Wikstrom, P.H. (1991). *Urban crime, criminals and victims*. New York: Springer-Verlag.

Wolfgang, M. (1958). *Patterns in criminal homicide*. Philadelphia, PA: University of Pennsylvania Press.

Wolfgang, M. & Ferracuti, F. (1967). *The subculture of violence*. London: Tavistock.

Wolfgang, M. (1983). Delinquency in two birth cohorts. In K. V. Dusen & S. Mednick (Eds), *Prospective studies in crime and delinquency*. Hingham, MA: Kluwer Nijhoff.

Wormith, J. S. & Goldstone, C.S. (1984). The clinical and statistical prediction of recidivism. *Criminal Justice and Behaviour, 11*, 3–34.

Index

Related titles of interest...

Therapeutic Communities for Offenders

Edited by **Eric Cullen, Lawrence Jones** and **Roland Woodward**
Foreword by **John Gunn**
Summarising examples of 'best practice' that therapeutic communities can offer
to offenders in the UK, Europe and the USA, the emphasis is on jargon-free,
practical guides and descriptions of requisite skills, procedures and organisations
to allow readers to understand how to build and sustain therapy in prisons.
Wiley Series in Offender Rehabilitation
0-471-96545-6 296pp March 1997 Hardback
0-471-96980-X 296pp March 1997 Paperback

Addicted to Crime?

Edited by **John E. Hodge, Mary Mcmurran** and **Clive R. Hollin**
Criminal behaviour that is highly repetitive appears to bring "internal rewards"
for some offenders. Using previous research, conceptual development, empirical
work, and individual casework, expert researchers and practitioners attempt to
explore the potential link between addiction and crime.
Wiley Series in Offender Rehabilitation
0-471-95079-3 254pp April 1997 Hardback
0-471-95777-1 254pp April 1997 Paperback

Handbook of Psychology in Legal Contexts

Edited by **Ray Bull** and **David Carson**
An authoritative summary of key legal procedures and issues together with
practical reviews of psychological concepts, research and practice that bear on
these topics. The conjunction of psychology and legal material, and the focus on
the UK/European context and practice, will make this book invaluable.
0-471-94182-4 694 pp May 1995 Hardback

What Works: Reducing Re-offending

Guidelines from Research and Practice

Edited by **James Mcguire**
This book assembles and consolidates evidence which demonstrates the
possibilities for reducing re-offending, and indicates the implications for both
practice and research. The specific programmes described here include
interventions related to violence, car crime, and sexual offences, and a key
emphasis of the book is the relationship between research and practice.
Wiley Series in Offender Rehabilitation
0-471-95053-X 264 pp July 1995 Hardback
0-471-95686-4 264 pp July 1995 Paperback

Visit the Wiley Home Page http://www.wiley.co.uk